CONSPIRATOR

Also by Anthony Read (with David Fisher)

COLONEL Z
THE DEADLY EMBRACE
KRISTALLNACHT
OPERATION LUCY

CONSPIRATOR

The Untold Story of
Churchill, Roosevelt and
Tyler Kent, Spy

Ray Bearse
and
Anthony Read

MACMILLAN
LONDON

First published in the United States of America 1991 by
Bantam Doubleday Dell Publishing Group Inc., New York

First published in the United Kingdom 1991 by
MACMILLAN LONDON LIMITED
Cavaye Place London SW10 9PG
and Basingstoke

Associated companies in Auckland, Delhi, Dublin, Gaborone,
Hamburg, Harare, Hong Kong, Johannesburg, Kuala Lumpur,
Lagos, Manzini, Melbourne, Mexico City, Nairobi, New York,
Singapore and Tokyo

ISBN 0-333-56707-2

A CIP catalogue record for this book is available
from the British Library

Printed by Billing & Sons Limited, Worcester

For Virginia and Rosemary
with love and gratitude

Contents

Prologue

ON MAY 20, 1940, Hitler's rampaging tanks reached the French coast of the English Channel near Abbeville. In a mere ten days since the "phony war" had erupted into the real thing, the all-conquering Wehrmacht had overrun Holland and Luxembourg, crushed most of Belgium, and had now, in Winston Churchill's words, "swept like a sharp scythe" behind the Allied armies. Along with the French First Army, the entire British Expeditionary Force, a quarter of a million men with virtually all of Britain's modern weapons and equipment, was caught in a vast trap.

Cut off from supplies of food, fuel, and ammunition, with powerful German forces closing in on three sides and the French armies in the south already on the point of surrender, the British Army could be saved from annihilation only by a miracle. It was clearly just a matter of time—and a very little time at that—before the Nazi swastika was flying over the whole of Western Europe. Britain would be protected only by twenty miles of sea and the inexperienced young fliers of the RAF as she stood alone against "a monstrous tyranny, never surpassed in the dark, lamentable catalogue of human crime."

In the early hours of that day, Winston Churchill, prime minister of the United Kingdom for only ten days, handed a piece of paper to his private secretary, John Colville. "Here's a telegram for those bloody Yankees," he said. "Send it off tonight." Colville duly had it delivered to the American embassy, in Grosvenor Square, for transmission to Washington.

The telegram was one of a series of highly secret personal messages that had been flashing across the Atlantic between

Churchill and President Franklin D. Roosevelt since the outbreak of the Second World War in September 1939. Five days before, on May 15, 1940, the prime minister had sent a plea for all possible American help short of the actual engagement of America's then thinly armed forces. "[T]he scene," he cabled, "has darkened swiftly . . . If necessary, we shall continue the war alone and we are not afraid of that. But I trust you realize, Mr. President, that the voice and force of the United States may count for nothing if they are withheld too long. You may have a completely subjugated Nazified Europe established with astonishing swiftness, and the weight may be more than we can bear."

Britain's immediate needs, Churchill said, were for the loan of forty or fifty old American destroyers, several hundred of the latest types of fighter aircraft, antiaircraft guns and ammunition, and a guarantee that American steel would be supplied even when Britain ran out of dollars. In addition, he sought American support in preventing German airborne landings in Ireland and in "keeping that Japanese dog quiet in the Pacific."

Roosevelt had replied that he would do what he could, but that he was hampered by the need for congressional approval in sending the ships. He said nothing about another request by Churchill—that the United States should declare itself nonbelligerent rather than neutral. American public opinion in 1940 might have supported the loan of war materials, but it would certainly not have accepted any more direct involvement.

Churchill's response, in his telegram of Monday, May 20, repeated the seriousness of the situation. "I understand your difficulties but I am very sorry about the destroyers," he said. "If they were here in six weeks they would play an invaluable part . . . Our most vital need is therefore the delivery at the earliest possible date of the largest possible number of Curtis's P-40 fighters." Excusing himself for "putting this nightmare bluntly," Churchill stressed that "in no conceivable circumstances will we consent to surrender. If members of this administration were finished and others came in to parlay amid the ruins, you must not be blind to the fact that the sole remaining bargaining counter with Germany would be the fleet, and if this country was left by the United States to its fate no one would have the right to blame those responsible if they made the best terms they could for the surviving inhabitants."

It was a bleak message at a bleak moment in history.

At 11:20 that same morning of May 20, Captain Maxwell Knight, head of Section B5(b) of MI5, the British Security Service, arrived at the black front door of 47 Gloucester Place, a six-story town house in the affluent central London district of Marylebone. He was accompanied by Detective Inspector Pearson and Detective Constables Scott and Buswell of Scotland Yard's Special Branch, and Franklin C. Gowen, second secretary at the American embassy. Pearson rang the bell and asked the maid for Mr. Tyler Kent, a code clerk in the American embassy, who was a tenant of the building.

The maid said they would have to speak to the landlady, Mrs. Edith Welby, and went back down the stairs to the basement. One of the detectives, Constable Scott, followed her while the other men climbed to the second story, where they found Mrs. Welby. When they showed her a warrant, she pointed down the hall to a door, indicating that it led to Kent's flat. Detective Inspector Pearson, after trying the door and finding it locked from the inside, rapped on it. A man's voice called out, "Don't come in!" Pearson rapped again, and again the voice called, "Don't come in!" Pearson put his shoulder to the door, smashing both a panel and the lock—damage that would cost Kent £5 for repairs. Gowen, Knight, and Buswell poured into the room behind Pearson. They were faced by an indignant young man of twenty-nine, standing beside his bed in pajamas.

"Tyler Kent," Max Knight announced as the young man started to protest. "You know Secretary Gowen. We're from Scotland Yard. We have a warrant to search your premises. You are hereby warned that you do not have to say anything, but that anything you do say will be taken down and may be used in evidence. Do you have here in this house or elsewhere in your possession any documents that are the property of the United States government, and more specifically that of the American embassy in London?"

"I have nothing belonging to the American government," Kent replied. "I don't know what you mean."

Detective Constable Buswell made for a closed door leading to another room.

"You can't go in there! There's a lady!" Kent yelled.

Opening the door, Buswell discovered an attractive red-headed woman. Irene Danischewsky, thirty-year-old wife of Alexander Danischewsky, owner of an import company that did business with the Soviet Union, was known by the police to have been Kent's mistress since January of that year. Gowen's report states that, like Kent, she was in pajamas, though in an interview in 1982 she denied that, saying she had not been in bed with Kent but was fully dressed and preparing to go to Kew Gardens for a day's outing.

Gowen recorded that Kent was not particularly upset by the sudden appearance of the police: "He gave me the impression that he was not overly concerned as to what his fate might be; perhaps he was only showing off or has powerful friends who are involved in his activities." Irene Danischewsky also took the raid very calmly, almost as though she had been expecting it. Gowen suspected from the way she behaved and looked at the police officers that she may even have been planted on Kent by Scotland Yard; he was unaware of the involvement of MI5 or of the true identity of Max Knight. "The police told me that she knew nothing about the matter," he wrote with some skepticism, "but these comments are offered for what they may be worth."

Gowen's suspicions may well have been justified, because Danischewsky was especially vulnerable to being blackmailed into cooperation by MI5. As though to confirm this, Knight allowed her to dress and go home to her own flat, at 5C Queensborough Terrace, off the Bayswater Road opposite Hyde Park. He told Gowen that "the police had nothing to fear about her because it was a case of real infatuation with Kent, and the police already knew that she was frightened lest her liaison with Kent became known to her husband." He added that her telephone was tapped and she was under constant observation.

While Kent was dressing, Knight asked him whether he knew certain people in London. In most cases, Kent said he did but could not say whether they were loyal to Great Britain or to their particular country. After a while Kent, turning to Gowen, asked, "Do you think I should answer these questions?"

"By all means," the embassy second secretary replied. "Answer everything."

The detectives, meanwhile, were searching the flat. In an unlocked cupboard they found stacks of documents piled on shelves, in a large brown leather suitcase, and in cardboard boxes. There were almost two thousand documents in all, plus glass photographic negatives, copies of Churchill's telegrams dated January 29 and February 28. There were also two sets of keys to the embassy's code and index file rooms, and an expensive record book, measuring twelve inches by nine and about one and a half inches thick, bound in fine red leather with the word LEDGER impressed on its spine in gold, and pages edged with heavy gold leaf. The covers were patterned on the inside with a gold motif and were fastened with a built-in brass lock. In Kent's jacket pocket they found a penciled copy of the "telegram for those bloody Yankees" sent that same morning from Churchill to Roosevelt.

Obviously, Kent's protestation that he had no embassy property was an outright lie. What was more, MI5 already knew, through early successes in the Ultra decrypt program, that the contents of some of the documents in Kent's possession had been passed to the Nazi government in Berlin.

The raid on Kent's flat was the final move in an operation that had been proceeding for several months, and that involved all the elements found in the best spy novels of the time: beautiful women agents working under cover, secret societies meeting behind locked doors, dirty deeds committed by some in the White Russian émigré community, Gestapo agents being tracked through the streets of blacked-out London, an Italian duke collecting secrets in high society circles, blackmail carried out by the Soviet NKVD.

With the arrest of Tyler Kent and his principal accomplice, a White Russian woman named Anna Wolkoff, the stage was set for the first major espionage trial of the Second World War. It was ironic that the accused was not a German or Japanese, or even an Italian, but a citizen of the United States of America, the nation that was to become Britain's closest ally.

The Tyler Kent case was unique in the Anglo-American alliance. It was also unique in a century and a half of American diplomacy; indeed, Kent's perfidy was unequaled in the history of the American people. Had Benedict Arnold succeeded in turning over the fortress of West Point to the British during the War of Independence, the loss might not have been significant. But by plundering the most secret communications between the two highest elected leaders of the English-speaking world and illegally passing those secrets to outsiders, Kent was endangering the very existence of a friendly power that was then truly fighting for its life. Had Britain fallen, the United States would have been left to fight the inevitable war against Nazi Germany across three thousand miles of ocean instead of across the North Sea and the English Channel, making victory uncertain if not impossible. As Assistant Secretary of State Breckinridge Long told Kent's mother, "Nothing like this has ever happened in American history."

But was Kent a spy? And if so, for whom was he spying? Why, at the end of the war, did MI5 and later the CIA classify him as a Soviet rather than as a German agent? Was he a traitor to his country, if not technically a spy, or was he, as he always claimed, a true patriot with his country's best interests at heart? The answers are not simple; very little of Kent's life was. They can be found only by asking another question: Who was Tyler Kent?

ONE

High Hopes

TYLER GATEWOOD KENT was born on March 24, 1911, in the mission hospital at Newchwang, Manchuria, where his father, Captain William Patton Kent, was the United States consul. At birth he weighed eight and a half pounds, had brown hair and blue eyes. His father, a fifty-four-year-old attorney, had married his second wife, Ann Herndon Patrick, a native of Staunton, Virginia, on August 25, 1906. She was exactly half his age. Their first child, Ann Patrick Kent, was born on March 26, 1908, in Waynesboro, Virginia, but they moved to Manchuria two years later, arriving in Newchwang on August 21, 1910.

The Kents had been a distinguished Virginia family since the eighteenth century, when Jacob, an Englishman who arrived in New York City in 1750, settled in the Shenandoah Valley. Ten years later, on April 5, 1760, he signed a marriage agreement with Mary Crockett, a member of the family that produced

Davy Crockett, hero of the Alamo. Through his paternal grand-mother, Tyler Kent was also related to the Pattons, another notable Virginia clan, of which the Second World War hero General George Smith Patton, Jr., was a member.

William Patton Kent, Tyler's father, was a graduate of the College of William and Mary, and held the bachelor of laws degree from the University of Virginia. He practiced law for ten years, and then worked as a newspaper editor and stock raiser, taking time out in 1898 to become a captain in the 2nd Virginia Infantry in the Spanish-American War. In 1906, he joined the United States Consular Service and was appointed consul general in Guatemala.

Despite the illustrious pedigree, the Kents had no family fortune. Like so many others who remained loyal to Virginia, they and the Patricks both suffered substantial property and financial losses during the "War for Southern Independence," as Tyler always insisted on describing the Civil War. Neverthe-less, although they could not be described as rich, they were not paupers, and their offspring enjoyed a privileged upbring-ing.

Young Tyler's early life was spent mainly on the move with the Consular Service: in 1914, Captain Kent was posted to Leipzig, Germany, in 1917 to Berne, Switzerland, in 1920 to Belfast, Northern Ireland, and in 1923 to Hamilton, Bermuda. The boy did not set foot in America until 1919, when at the age of eight he attended school in Staunton, Virginia, for one year. He then spent two years at a preparatory school in Dublin known as Campbell College, before returning to the United States on his father's retirement, when he entered the presti-gious Kent School in Connecticut.

Kent School, housed in attractive, white-painted Colonial buildings, is in the village of Kent in the pleasant Housatonic River valley of western Connecticut. Founded in 1906, it is one of those famed New England high-church Episcopalian institu-tions modeled on English public schools like Eton, Harrow, and Winchester, and designed for the East Coast social elite. In 1924, its fourteen teachers, known as masters, in the English tradition, taught Latin, Greek, French, German, mathematics, history, English, chemistry, biology, and music. In sports, the school had teams in football, baseball, hockey, tennis, and crew.

Tyler Kent entered the second form as one of thirty-nine students, mostly from New England. Nearly half of the graduating class normally entered Yale—the Kent Club of Yale actively recruited among the student body—and most of the others chose Princeton, Harvard, Williams, or Amherst. Of the graduating class of 1925, only two students did not go to Ivy League colleges.

But Tyler's travels were not yet over. In 1926 he moved on to St. Albans, another high-church Episcopalian establishment, in Washington, D.C. In contrast to Kent School, the architecture of St. Albans was cold Gothic stone, but in other respects—size, courses, sports, and ethos—it was much the same as Kent and similar schools like Groton, St. Paul's, St. Mark's, Phillips Andover, Phillips Exeter, Gunnery, and Hotchkiss. Most of the students were the sons of diplomats, upper-echelon journalists, politicians, mid- to upper-level civil servants, and politically appointed bureaucrats, a perfect match for Tyler Kent.

At St. Albans, Kent displayed his athletic prowess by winning his A in soccer and football. He also won the school's top prize for languages; outside the classroom he sang in the Glee Club and was an editor of *The Albanian.* Raymond Carter, a classmate both at St. Albans and later at Princeton—in 1987 he was president of the class of 1933—remembers Kent as "a whiz in mathematics, a brilliant linguist, and a loner." John Davis, a St. Albans staff member for nearly forty years, recalls that when Kent graduated, his mother told Master Stephen Augustus Hurlbut, "All he will become he owes to you," an unconsciously prophetic statement, for Hurlbut was renowned as an admirer of all things German.

Like most Albanians, Kent opted on graduation for Princeton, which carried out an active recruiting program at the school. He entered in the fall of 1929, a handsome young man despite a slightly weak chin, five feet nine inches tall, with wavy brown hair, and a smart wardrobe by Brooks Brothers. Throughout his entire life, he was well dressed, wearing nothing but the best tailor-made clothes. His major was languages, in which he displayed an impressive ability. A former classmate recalls that he learned Icelandic during one summer just to

show that he could do it. As at St. Albans, he made his mark on
the soccer field and was a member of the Glee Club. And he
was elected a class officer.

But the effects of constantly moving about the world during
his formative years were evident: in spite of his academic bril-
liance, athletic excellence, and personal charm, he was still a
loner, choosing to live by himself at 74 University Place instead
of in a fraternity house or shared accommodation. Indeed, the
collective memory of his classmates—recalled for this book at a
luncheon on September 16, 1989, before Princeton played
Dartmouth's eleven at Hanover—was simply "brilliant linguist
and a loner." But he is not forgotten: members noted that
whenever the class of 1933 holds a full-scale reunion, "Tyler is
always a subject of lively interest."

Kent's restlessness soon showed itself again, however. He
left Princeton halfway through his sophomore year to study
Russian at the Sorbonne, and followed this with a summer at
the University of Madrid, studying Spanish. In the fall of 1933,
in an abrupt change of course, he entered George Washington
University as a special student majoring in history and economics. This was clearly part of his preparation for a career with the
United States Foreign Service—a natural ambition for Kent,
with his aptitude for languages and his father's background in
the Consular Service, which had been consolidated with the
Diplomatic Service into the Foreign Service by the Rogers Act
of 1924.

In those distant days, the world's foreign services were all
much smaller and tighter than they have since become; openings were limited. But in early December 1933, Kent heard that
an opportunity was about to present itself: Ambassador William C. Bullitt was looking for clerks with a knowledge of Russian for the brand-new embassy he was about to open in Moscow, bringing to an end sixteen years of nonrecognition of the
Soviet regime by the United States.

William Christian Bullitt, a Philadelphia Main Line aristocrat
born in 1891 into yet another distinguished Virginia family,
was a fitting choice as the first ambassador from the United
States to the USSR. Slightly built, of medium height, with a
round face and bald head, he was a brilliant conversationalist

and, according to Charles Bohlen, a member of Bullitt's mission and later himself an ambassador in Moscow, "he had an effervescent personality, which he could turn on and off at will. His brilliant smile and his eloquence, coupled with his wide knowledge, usually succeeded in charming even the most dubious." Although his background was decidedly patrician, Bullitt was a democrat with both a small and a large D; he abhorred snobbery and, when necessary, had a vitriolic tongue.

Coupled with a continuing ingenuousness, Bullitt's main character flaws were always impatience and impetuosity. As a young Yale graduate, he had become bored with his studies at Harvard Law School and taken off across the Atlantic. With his retentive memory and a hard core of intellectual toughness, he became a first-rate roving reporter for the *Philadelphia Ledger* in the capitals of Europe. When Henry Ford, at his own expense, sent the Ford Peace Ship to Europe early in the First World War, Bullitt was assigned to cover the mission. His reports on the antics and high jinks of the oddly assorted passengers turned him into one of the nation's best-known journalists. As it became clear that America would enter the war, he joined the Department of State as chief of the desk covering Germany, Austria-Hungary, and Belgium.

Bullitt's analyses of the Central Powers' press were much admired by President Wilson's friend and adviser, Colonel Edward M. House, who saw to it that the young Philadelphian was included in the American delegation to the Paris Peace Conference in 1919. There, he put his journalistic experience to good use as director of current intelligence summaries, but this task was soon overridden by a more specific assignment: making contact with the new Bolshevik regime in Russia.

Bullitt had been sympathetic to the Bolsheviks from the start; as early as February 1918, he had written to House, "Trotsky is the kind of man we need to have in power in Russia." He had urged the recognition of the new government, and suggested that the United States send an envoy to Moscow "to see what the Bolsheviki are about." A year later, in February 1919, it was agreed that Bullitt should be that envoy. It was also agreed, according to Bullitt, that he should sound out the Bolshevik leaders about possible peace terms to help bring to an end the civil war then ravaging the old Russian Empire. Several foreign armies were involved against the reds: British, American, French, Japanese, Chinese, and Czech prominent among them, to say nothing of the Finns, Balts, Georgians, Ukrainians, and other national groups seeking their freedom.

Bullitt arrived in Petrograd on March 8, when he began preliminary talks with Foreign Commissar Georgi Chicherin, a courtly gentleman, "very much the aristocrat," who could play perfect Beethoven on the piano, and his equally charming deputy, Maxim Litvinov. Two days later he went to Moscow for a further three days of talks with them, at the end of which he had a long session with Lenin himself. To Bullitt's delight, Lenin told him he was prepared to accept the unofficial peace terms the American had brought from Paris. These had been prepared by Bullitt himself and Philip Kerr—later the eleventh Marquess of Lothian and British ambassador to the United States in 1939–1940—who was then secretary to Prime Minister David Lloyd George. Supposedly Bullitt had the tacit approval of Wilson and Lloyd George.

The terms that Lenin was prepared to accept involved his signing away all Soviet claims to the Murmansk-Archangel region, the Baltic states, the western part of Byelorussia, half the Ukraine, the Crimea, the northern Caucasus, Transcaucasia, the whole of the Urals, and all Siberia. Effectively, this would have reduced Soviet Russia to little more than the old Grand Duchy of Muscovy. In return, Lenin demanded that the Allies stop providing all the other combatants, including the White armies, with military equipment, and eventually withdraw their own armies from Russia. The other points in the Anglo-American proposals included free right of entry to Russia for Allied subjects, with the right to go freely about their business, provided they did not interfere in politics; an amnesty for all political prisoners on both sides; and full restoration of trade relations.

Bullitt, understandably elated, hurried back to Paris in late March with the draft agreement. The immediate reaction from Colonel House and the American delegation was enthusiastic. But there was controversy over Bullitt's role. Officially, it seems, he had been authorized only to undertake a fact-finding mission, and by starting peace negotiations—with or without the tacit approval of president and prime minister—he had considerably stretched his brief. If it had been accepted, the plan Bullitt brought back, apparently with Lenin's blessing, could have changed the face of the world and the course of history. But it was not to be. Realpolitik quickly replaced enthusiastic idealism.

Fired in part by White Russian propaganda, and in part by a genuine fear of the growing threat of worldwide revolution, the British and Americans were becoming increasingly anti-Bolshevik; the French, who had not been told in advance of Bullitt's secret mission, were irate; powerful elements within the Department of State were fiercely anti-Soviet; and in the American delegation, Bullitt's opponents, led by Colonel House's son-in-law and aide, intrigued against him, claiming he had been completely taken in by the devious Bolsheviks.

Lloyd George had seemed to be in favor of the proposals, but he too suddenly developed second thoughts; these followed editorials in the British press fiercely condemning any suggestion of recognizing the Bolshevik government. Harried by opponents from all sides, led by Winston Churchill, the architect of armed intervention in Russia, the British premier denied Bullitt's report both in private and publicly on the floor of the House of Commons. President Wilson canceled a meeting with Bullitt, pleading a headache. He not only ignored the report, he also suppressed it.

Disillusioned and disappointed by the attitude toward Russia and with the impossible terms being imposed on Germany at the Peace Conference, Bullitt resigned from the State Department. He concluded his letter of resignation to Wilson on May 17, 1919: "I am sorry that you did not fight our fight to the finish and that you had so little faith in the millions of men, like myself, in every nation who had faith in you."

On September 12, 1919, Bullitt appeared, at his own request, before the Senate Committee on Foreign Relations, headed by Wilson's archenemy, Henry Cabot Lodge. There, he calmly made public the whole business of the secret negotiations with the Bolsheviks, including the proposals drawn up by Philip Kerr with Lloyd George's approval, which the British prime minister had denied in Parliament. His British friends never forgave him. And in spite of his pleas, the American government decided not to recognize the Bolshevik regime.

For fourteen years, Bullitt watched and waited, keeping in close touch with events in the Soviet Union. His connections even extended to marrying Louise Bryant Reed, widow of the communist journalist John Reed, author of *Ten Days That Shook the World*. He continued to believe that if the Peace Conference had agreed to negotiate with Lenin on the basis of his plan, relations with the west would have been more friendly, even though there might have been little effect on the Soviet Union's internal affairs. Most experts tend to disagree. George F. Kennan, for example, looking back after forty years, described Bullitt as "inexperienced and greatly excited."

On Saturday March 4, 1933, a big man in a dark blue U.S. Navy cape, his battered fedora perched on top of his head, hunched his massive shoulders forward and told the people of the United States that "the only thing we have to fear is fear itself—nameless, unreasoning, unjustified terror which paralyzes needed efforts to convert retreat into advance." The newly inaugurated president, Franklin Delano Roosevelt, injected hope into the hearts of millions of Americans with his philosophy that "the country needs bold, persistent experimentation. Take a method and try it; if it fails, admit it, and try another. But above all, try something."

With more than fifteen million unemployed in the United States, Roosevelt's main efforts at the beginning of his presidency were inevitably directed toward problems at home—during his first hundred days in office he dealt with no fewer than seventeen major domestic issues. But foreign policy could not be ignored, and he brought the same bold, fresh approach to this aspect of government, too.

The question of relations with the Soviet Union was high on his agenda: two weeks after the 1932 Democratic National Convention selected him as candidate, he had invited to his New York governor's mansion in Albany the man considered by many Americans to be the number one authority on Soviet affairs, Walter Duranty. Duranty, an Englishman with a wooden leg who had that year been awarded a Pulitzer Prize, had served the *New York Times* as its Moscow correspondent since 1920. He was an unashamed admirer of Stalin and gave Roosevelt favorable reports about life in the USSR. Immediately after his stunning electoral victory in November, FDR sent an unofficial envoy to Moscow—his old friend Bill Bullitt, whom he had known since his days as assistant secretary of the Navy during the First World War.

Although the State Department's Division of Eastern European Affairs, which covered Russia along with the Baltic states, Finland, and Poland, was chary of recognizing the Soviet government after sixteen years of suspicion and estrangement, there were many other groups strongly in favor of doing so. Those exerting most pressure included American businessmen like Averell Harriman, who held stocks in companies whose assets had been seized following the November 1917 revolution, some trade unions, and members of the New Deal. They were supported by a prorecognition group in the State Department and White House, which saw any sign of a toughening stance toward the Soviets as dangerous.

The Soviets themselves were eager for recognition for several reasons, in addition to the simple matter of improving their international standing, a standing that had been damaged during 1933 after a show trial of six British engineers in Moscow, on patently trumped-up charges of espionage. They needed United States credits to purchase urgently needed manufactured goods, and hoped, too, that recognition would help deter the Japanese, who had recently occupied Manchuria, from invading Siberia. On a more sinister note, there was the question of intelligence gathering and espionage: the Soviets had maintained a trading organization, Amtorg, in the United States since the early 1920s. It provided cover for "illegal" agents; recognition would mean that "legals," agents under diplomatic cover, could operate in Washington.

It was clear from an early date that Roosevelt was determined to put an end to the years of estrangement between his country and the Soviet Union. This probably explains Tyler Kent's sudden decision to quit Princeton and study Russian in Paris, a strong center for the language at that time because of its large White Russian population. Kent's astute move paid off. On October 20, 1933, Roosevelt invited Maxim Litvinov, who had succeeded Chicherin as foreign commissar, to Washington to discuss recognition with Secretary of State Cordell Hull. After the acceptance of five major conditions laid down by the president, covering the repayment of war debts, the protection and freedom of American nationals living in the Soviet Union, the banning of Comintern—Communist International—activities designed to overthrow the U.S. government, and the creation of a credit agreement, the document of recognition was signed on November 17, 1933. Four days later, William C. Bullitt was named the first American ambassador to the USSR.

True to his impetuous nature, Bullitt decided to leave immediately for Moscow, taking with him twenty-nine-year-old George Frost Kennan, a Soviet expert from the State Department who had impressed him with his knowledge of the country and his ability to speak Russian. He presented his credentials to President Mikhail Kalinin on December 11, 1933, then proceeded to persuade Stalin to agree to the erection of a chancery building in the Lenin Hills on the outskirts of Moscow, and to grant a number of concessions, not the least of which was permission to bring in his personal airplane and pilot. Leaving Kennan behind to start the arrangements for the new embassy, Bullitt returned to the United States to select his staff.

Kennan was joined shortly afterward by his Norwegian-born wife, Annelise, and together they spent the winter in the National Hotel just off Red Square, where Lenin had lived during and immediately after the revolution. His staff consisted of a male stenographer and Charles Wheeler Thayer, a Philadelphia socialite and West Point graduate, class of 1933, who had opted against an Army career and become a free-lance writer. He was living just down the hall from Kennan, who employed him as embassy messenger at forty dollars a month, since he had somehow acquired an ancient Harley-Davidson motorcycle, complete with sidecar.

Thayer, round-faced and blue-eyed, was a fun-loving prankster with a well-developed sense of the ridiculous. Totally unawed by authority, he soon proved his ability to cut through Soviet red tape to secure things needed for the ambassador's residence and the chancery. Taken on as a clerk when the embassy began to function properly, he enlivened many a diplomatic function. On one occasion he borrowed three seals from the Moscow state zoo to provide cocktail hour entertainment. All went well until they caught the aroma of fish being prepared, whereupon they slithered down the stairs to the kitchens and devoured every piece of fish within smelling distance. And when they were being returned in disgrace to the zoo, at least one managed to escape from the station wagon and had to be chased through the streets by Charlie and the trainer.

In 1937, Thayer joined the Foreign Service proper, and was appointed a third secretary. He finally fell foul of Senator Joseph McCarthy, and left the service in 1953.

Back in Washington, Bullitt set about equipping his new embassy with the same enthusiasm he had used to charm Stalin. Amazed by the promises he had obtained from the Soviet dictator, various departments granted him a series of first-ever concessions. The Army agreed to provide a plane, pilot, crew, fuel, oil, and spare parts. The Navy agreed to provide the embassy residence with a full silver service, normally available only for battleships flying a vice admiral's stars. The Army and Navy between them provided medical equipment, bedding, and medicines usually found in military hospitals. The section of the State Department charged with providing minimal furniture for embassies found itself supplying everything Bullitt requested, and agreeing to expedite shipment to Moscow. The Passport Division agreed to an unheard-of precedent by providing embassy clerks with diplomatic passports, a concession that Tyler Kent was to find particularly useful.

While all this was going on, Bullitt began picking his staff with great care, determined that his new mission should be a complete success. Each member was selected either from personal acquaintance or on the recommendation of people he knew and trusted. Some measure of the quality of those he obtained may be gauged from the fact that no fewer than five of his Foreign Service officers later became heads of mission themselves, two of them in Moscow.

As counselor, the senior Foreign Service officer in the embassy, Bullitt chose John C. Wiley, who had been in the service since 1915, a tall, impressive man with a deep voice and a good sense of humor. According to Charles Bohlen, "Wiley's steadiness was a good offset to Bullitt's exuberance and tendency to go to extremes." Born in Bordeaux, where his father, a former congressman, was U.S. consul, Wiley was educated abroad by private tutors and in the United States in private schools; he attended Union College and graduated from Georgetown Law School. Although he spoke no Russian, he was fluent in Spanish, German, and French, and had seen service in South America, Warsaw, and Berlin. He was later to become ambassador to several countries, including Portugal, Iran, Colombia, and Panama.

The first secretary and chief political officer was Loy W. Henderson, a friend of Tyler Kent's father from the time when they had both served in Ireland. A specialist in Soviet economic matters, though he spoke only a little Russian, Henderson was a thorough gentleman and a dedicated diplomat. He later served as chargé d'affaires in Moscow during the time between the departure of Bullitt and the arrival of his successor, Joseph E. Davies. During Davies's disastrous tenure, Henderson was responsible for steering the embassy through the rocky shoals of Stalin's great purges. He later became ambassador to Iraq, Iran, and India.

Regarded by many as the most brilliant member of an outstanding staff was George F. Kennan, who even as a young man managed to look distinguished. Tall, thin, and slightly balding, Kennan had a fine mind and was an excellent political analyst and reporter. As a brilliant policy planner in the State Department, he became famous for his authorship of the "containment" policy during the later Stalin years, but in time he regretted this and promoted unilateral disarmament. He served as ambassador to the USSR in 1952–1953 and to Yugoslavia during the Kennedy years.

The other future ambassador to the Soviet Union—he succeeded Kennan in 1953—was Charles (Chip) Bohlen, who worked alongside Kennan in the political department of the embassy under Henderson. Bohlen, a Harvard graduate who had won early distinction when he was expelled from St. Paul's School for using an inflated condom as a soccer ball, was the son of a noted family that occasionally found itself short of money. He entered the Foreign Service in 1929 and served two years in Prague before studying Russian in Paris. An extraordinarily likable man, Bohlen married the sister of Charles Thayer in 1935. Following his four-year term as ambassador in Moscow, he was appointed first as ambassador to the Philippines and then to France, before ending his career back at the State Department in Washington as under secretary for political affairs.

The third Russian-language officer in the embassy was Bertel T. Kuniholm; Kennan, Bohlen, and he made up no less than half of the Russian-speaking officers in the State Department at that time. Kuniholm, "a man of great ambition," graduated from the U.S. Military Academy and served several years in the Army before resigning to enter the Foreign Service in 1928. He reported on economic affairs. He would later report on Soviet activities from Iran before retiring in the mid-1950s.

In the consulate was Elbridge Durbrow, a thirty-one-year-old native Californian, who had joined the Foreign Service four years after his 1926 graduation from Yale. Durbrow, a man of great energy and good humor, went on to become chief of the Division of Eastern European Affairs in the State Department in 1944, and for several years headed the Foreign Service personnel division. He served as ambassador to Vietnam before the war there, and later was deputy U.S. representative to NATO.

One other member of the embassy in 1934 who went on to a distinguished career was Lieutenant Thomas D. White, assistant military attaché for air and the pilot of Bullitt's plane; he became chief of staff of the Air Force after the Second World War.

Among such an outstanding company, the clerks must have seemed insignificant. But they were selected by Bullitt with reasonable care. Kent was chosen because of his knowledge of Russian, but his references were impressive for one applying for a relatively lowly post. They included the powerful Democratic Senator Harry F. Byrd of Virginia, brother of the polar explorer Admiral Richard E. Byrd, millionaire publisher of the *Winchester Virginian,* and owner of vast tracts of orchards; Gordon C. Sykes, assistant to the dean of Princeton University; John B. Cochran, president of the Franklin National Bank in Washington; and Charles Warden, a noted Washington businessman. A 1941 FBI report on Kent commented that "these letters were very profuse in their praise of the ability and background of Kent."

On February 12, 1934, Kent duly received a letter from the State Department:

The Department takes pleasure in offering you the position of clerk in Moscow . . . with compensation per annum of $2500. If quarters are not available in the Government building . . . you will be entitled to . . . an allowance for rent, heat, light and fuel . . . [T]he position is on the condition that you are single, it not being found practical to appoint married persons to clerical positions in the Foreign Service.

You will be allowed transportation expenses in proceeding to your post from your home in the United States . . . [T]he Department will make no reimbursement for expenses incurred in the transportation of effects other than those carried as personal luggage.

Appointees are expected to remain in the Service for at least two years . . . their expenses in returning to the United States are not payable unless they have served for that period . . . [T]he benefits of civil service retirement system have been extended to include members of the Foreign Service who are American citizens.

You should immediately make application for a "special" passport . . . an application is enclosed. The Department desires a written acceptance or non-acceptance of this offer.

(signed) WILBUR CARR, Assistant Secretary

Kent immediately wired his acceptance, and that same day the State Department wrote back:

You are hereby appointed to the position. You will proceed at once via Berlin, Germany . . . On the date of your departure you should take an oath as American clerk in the Foreign Service . . . A form is enclosed.

Two days later, Kent took the oath and boarded the S.S. *Washington* shortly before it sailed from New York at 10:00 A.M. On the main deck he noticed more than a dozen young men wearing black suits, black hats, black ties, and white shirts, all busily throwing up over the rail, even though the ship was still tied up at the dock. Having just signed up himself for a minimum of two years in Moscow, he was amused to learn that they were Mormons, also heading for Europe for two years' missionary service.

Bullitt's party on the *Washington* numbered twenty-five men and one woman, the wife of Captain David R. Nimmer, commander of a detachment of six Marines who would form the embassy guard. The Foreign Service officers were Henderson, Wiley, Kuniholm, and A. Dana Hodgson, a visa officer who was headed for Riga. Bohlen was to join them in Paris; Durbrow and his consul, Angus Ward, would report direct to Moscow from their current stations. Besides Kent, there were eight clerks, including Henry W. Antheil, Jr., brother of the pianist and composer George Antheil, who was to be chief code clerk and become one of Kent's best friends in Moscow. Antheil was to play a vital part in Kent's future perfidy and may well have been an even worse traitor, before meeting a violent and unexpected end.

Two essential members of the party were a Navy chief pharmacist's mate, a medic who would serve as the mission's doctor for more than a year, and a Navy electrician's mate second class, who would be responsible for maintaining electrical equipment and, more important, checking for bugs in the embassy. Three more clerks and four air crew mechanics were to follow later.

But perhaps the most unusual member was Father Leopold Braun, a Catholic priest selected by the church, at Roosevelt's request, to be the unofficial spiritual adviser to the mission. FDR's reasons for the request were more political than religious: he hoped it would quiet any Catholic protests over his recognition of the godless Russians.

Soon after sailing from New York, Bullitt called a meeting of all State Department personnel and told them he did not approve of the usual hierarchy and that all department staff would be treated the same, professionally and socially. It was a brave attempt at introducing democracy and even egalitarianism, which no doubt the idealistic ambassador thought suitable for Moscow. But it was doomed to failure, simply because of human nature. From the beginning, the Foreign Service officers socialized only among themselves, and with those of equal rank and status in the rest of the diplomatic community in Moscow. With the single exception of Charlie Thayer, clerks and the other lower orders had no place in this community; they were the noncoms and enlisted men of the service.

This division must have been an important element in shaping Tyler Kent's attitudes and actions, both in Moscow and in London. With his social and academic background, Kent certainly regarded himself as at least the equal of any of the Foreign Service officers in the mission. Humility never figured large in his personality, and being treated as an inferior, a mere clerk, must have rankled; it would have been entirely in character for him to have obtained satisfaction in outwitting both the officers and the system. His intellectual arrogance, in evidence until the end of his life, would have thrived on the possession of secret knowledge and therefore of secret power.

All that, of course, was still to come. In the meantime, the voyage on the *Washington* was to expose another personality flaw that would play an important part in his downfall: an irrepressible passion for womanizing and sexual adventuring.

Among the other passengers on the ship was George H. Earle, a feisty Philadelphian and friend of Bullitt and Roosevelt, who in 1935 was to become Pennsylvania's first Democratic governor of the twentieth century. He was accompanied by his very attractive secretary. One afternoon, when she slipped into her shoes beside the pool, she discovered a note from Kent proposing an evening rendezvous. For once, the Kent charm failed. She told Earle, who complained to Henderson, who duly rapped Kent over the knuckles for treading on forbidden territory. No doubt the reprimand was stored in Kent's memory as a score to be settled sometime. It certainly did nothing to curb his sexual activities.

Bullitt disembarked at Le Havre and proceeded to Moscow via Paris, Berlin, and Warsaw in order to make brief visits to the American embassies in those cities. He took with him Wiley, Kuniholm, Captain Nimmer, and Lieutenant White, plus a clerk to act as his secretary. The rest of the party, under the command of Henderson, stayed on the ship until it reached Hamburg, from where they traveled to Moscow by train via Berlin. Henderson's major concern was protecting the security of the many trunks and footlockers containing confidential documents and secret code books.

They arrived in Berlin on February 24 and departed on the twenty-eighth. During those four days, keeping the Marines and sailors in line posed no problem, but the clerks were something of a headache, as they all tended to wander off on sightseeing junkets—all, that is, apart from Kent, who had visited Berlin before and knew exactly where to go for amusement. They all survived unharmed, to continue their journey through Poland, reaching the Soviet frontier at Negoreloye, where they changed to a broad-gauge Russian railroad train. At last, they had their first sight, and smell, of the Soviet Union. Travelers in the 1930s noted that they could tell when they were there even if they were blindfolded, by the smell that permeated rail coaches and depots. The scent of Makhorka, the cheap Russian tobacco, mixed with paraffin, strong soap, urine, strong cheese, sweaty bodies, and fish, combined in the unique and unmistakable aroma of Russia.

Henderson's contingent was greeted at the rail station in Moscow by George Kennan, Charlie Thayer, a State Department buildings man named Davies, Spencer Williams, head of the Russian-American Chamber of Commerce, and lower echelon members of the Commissariat of Foreign Affairs. They were convoyed through the city to the Savoy Hotel, an aging and run-down establishment where two floors had been reserved for the residence and offices of the mission. Temporary offices were also established in the ambassador's residence, where the confidential codes were locked in a safe imported from the United States and guarded round the clock by Marines in plain clothes.

During his visit the previous December, Bullitt had arranged to have as his residence a grand mansion standing in its own grounds close to the center of Moscow on Spasopeskovskaya Ploschad, Square of the Sacred Sands. Spaso House had been built shortly before the First World War by a wealthy sugar merchant who was slain by his deranged son. It was a classical building faced with stucco, with a columned, semicircular balcony at the front, and a main hall eighty feet long and twenty-eight feet high, with marble columns all around and an enormous chandelier hanging from the ceiling. A gallery running around the great hall's second story had entrances to ten rooms—the ambassador and his family had their living quarters here—and there were five more bedrooms on another part of this floor.

Beyond the great hall was a small state dining room, where intimate dinners for up to twenty people were held. Grand dinners, dances, and other entertainments were held in a larger dining room adjacent to the first, or in the great hall itself. The basement, a warren of small rooms and mysterious passages, housed kitchens, storerooms, servants' quarters, and furnaces.

For many months, Spaso House was handicapped by a shortage of telephones. The one phone frequently rang at night and when answered produced nothing but heavy breathing. There was no Moscow phone directory, which was perhaps hardly surprising, since very few Muscovites other than government functionaries had telephones. Another irritant was the lack of matches: the only ones available were produced in the state factory and were of such poor quality that barely one in nine ever lit.

Bullitt and his party, now swelled to fifteen or twenty members, arrived in Moscow on March 8. As he stepped from the train, the ambassador was delighted to find a large band playing, apparently to welcome him. His pleasure was short-lived, however, for he soon realized the band was positioned opposite the third-class cars to serenade the arrival of a delegation of communist women coming to celebrate Red International Women's Day. Bullitt had to be content with a low-key greeting from the Soviet chief of protocol and George Andreychin, a handsome young man whom he had known in the United States, described by Roosevelt as Bullitt's "little playmate."

The coolness of Bullitt's reception proved to be a portent of the weeks that followed, as the Americans struggled to organize and equip the residence and the as yet nonexistent chancery. The Foreign Commissariat, Narkomindel, was responsible for supplying Soviet personnel for service as messengers, drivers, clerks, translators, and professional assistants such as economists and regional specialists. A separate division, known as Burobin, headed by the future Soviet ambassador to the United States, Constantine Umanski, was charged with meeting and fulfilling requests from diplomatic missions for furniture and other necessities. Both proved to be singularly uncooperative.

After three months, Bullitt noted his frustrations in a personal letter to Assistant Secretary of State Judge R. Walton Moore, but although the seeds of disillusionment were already planted, he was not yet prepared to admit that the Russians, or the communist system, were to blame. Instead, he sought to find other scapegoats:

We are staggering along here not only meeting with disappointments in major matters but having to endure a thousand petty vexations . . . life is not pleasant. My own house, for example, still resembling the Grand Central Station more than a private residence. We still have not yet been able to install the furniture from the Department and when I receive a visitor, however distinguished, I have to do so in the central hall with streams of visitors and chancery employees marching through. Moreover, I have not yet been able to have anyone in for a meal. I understand that my fellow diplomatists are beginning to comment adversely on this fact . . . I had word from the Kremlin to the effect that Stalin had chided some of his intimate associates for not seeing more of me and that they replied that I had not yet invited them to call . . .

The Burobin has been just as unpleasant as it possibly could be . . . the impression of my staff is that the unpleasantness has been dictated by the Foreign Office due to the influence of Mr. Umanski, the wretched little kike who accompanied Litvinov as press representative [to the negotiations in Washington in November 1933] . . . The Foreign Office, as you know, has been purged recently of all its non-Jewish members, and it is perhaps only natural that we should find the members of that race more difficult to deal with than the Russians themselves.

While his staff continued their uphill fight against Soviet bureaucracy, Bullitt was able to find relief from his frustrations by flying about the country in his plane. Whatever his disappointments, his wide-eyed enthusiasm remained undiminished:

My first long flight . . . was highly successful. I visited Kharkov, Yalta, Odessa and Kiev . . . Heard later from a number of sources that the trip had made not only a profound impression throughout the Ukraine but also in the Kremlin. I made speeches in Russian at each stop! Please do not imagine that I have learned Russian. I have merely learned sufficient phrases to make diplomatic addresses. There seems to be only 300 words required! Lieutenant White is not only an admirable aviator but is also a delightful traveling companion. All the ladies automatically fall in love with him. And the men are not far behind in their appreciation of his qualities.

After three months of impatient waiting, the embassy offices and staff quarters were moved from the ramshackle old Savoy Hotel to the new Mokhovaya building, located just off Red Square and across the street from the Kremlin. Originally designed to house the Soviet state tourist bureau, Intourist, with upper floors given over to studios for state-supported painters and sculptors, the building was leased to the American government, on a temporary basis, until the new chancery could be built on the riverside site that Stalin had promised Bullitt in the beautiful Lenin Hills. But Stalin had changed his mind, it seemed: all discussions about the new site quickly became bogged down in Soviet obstructions. The temporary lease on the Mokhovaya building lasted twenty years, until the embassy promised for 1935 was finally erected in 1953–1954—in the city center.

Location in the new building, which was to be Tyler Kent's base until 1939 and his home for most of that time, meant that everyone was working under one roof at last. The ground floor housed the consular offices, headed by the colorful Angus Ward, and the offices of the service attachés. The second floor was occupied by the code and file rooms and the accounting offices. The offices of the ambassador and his Foreign Service officers were on the third floor, and the fourth contained the library, translators, and the all-important commissary, where mission employees secured canned foods and staples like sugar, flour, coffee, tea, tobacco, and liquor, all of which were in short supply in Moscow.

The upper floors contained between twenty-five and thirty apartments for the use of embassy staff. For a while, three were occupied by Soviet officials, but, one after another, they were arrested and exiled or executed, and their flats were taken over by mission members. The smallest or basic flats—usually occupied by clerks and service personnel—were studio units with small kitchenettes. Senior Foreign Service officers had living room, dining room, kitchen, two bedrooms, and bath. Each flat had at least one Soviet servant; most of the servants lived in the chancery basement, which they decorated with huge revolutionary posters, and all were required to report regularly to the secret police, the NKVD.

Throughout Kent's Moscow years, there were on average thirty Americans working in the building. There was also about the same number of Soviet employees, whose annual salaries ranged from $400 for messengers to $900 for translators and more for professionals. These employees were issued special identity cards to get them past the Soviet policemen permanently stationed outside the embassy, whose primary function was to prevent Soviet nationals from entering the building, except in special circumstances.

One of the irksome drawbacks of a clerk's lowly position in the embassy pecking order was that he could be ousted from his flat on the arrival of a senior officer. Kent spent a whole year in the Hotel Moscow when his flat was pre-empted by a newly arrived vice consul. For most men, being moved to a hotel meant losing the camaraderie of the Mokhovaya flats, being deprived of the chance of dropping in on your neighbor for a predinner drink and chat. Kent, ever the loner, did not miss such neighborly exchanges, though he must have felt his lack of status keenly. Indeed, there were even certain advantages for a man of his nature in being separated from his fellows.

Living in hotels did not preclude visitors of the opposite sex. Charles Bohlen recalls seeing an attractive, heavily made-up woman asking the desk clerk at the Savoy Hotel for a Marine sergeant, Odien. When the clerk asked why she wanted to see him, she replied smoothly, "I'm his Russian language teacher," and was promptly admitted. In such a climate, it is hardly surprising that Tyler Kent very quickly formed highly agreeable—and highly dangerous—friendships outside the embassy.

TWO

Moscow: Lost Illusions

MOSCOW IN THE THIRTIES was drab and dreary. The predominant colors were gray, gray, and yet more gray, enlivened only by the spasmodic green of grass and trees and the occasional splash of scarlet provided by the red flag. The buildings, few of which had been repaired or renovated since the revolution, were gray. The people seemed to wear only gray clothes, mostly old and patched. Even their faces were gray in their solemn seriousness—and with good reason, for all the necessities of life were in short supply and luxuries were totally nonexistent. Arriving in such a city after the glitter of New York, Paris, and Berlin must have been a great culture shock, and the prospect of a stay of six years quite daunting.

The stress involved in living in Moscow is reflected in the fact that embassy staff there have always been subject to a wider range of illnesses than in other embassies. Bullitt, like FDR, suffered from sinusitis, for which there was no known cure at that time. The ambassador asked the U.S. Public Health Service to provide a physician for the embassy; the pharmacist's mate could not deal adequately with all the work. They assigned a Dr. Rumreich, but he seems to have been delayed, and Bullitt wrote anxiously to Judge Moore:

I am really eager to have Rumreich come as soon as possible . . . [T]he absence of an American doctor here, plus the inefficiency of Russian doctors and the difficulty of obtaining their services plus their fear of contact with foreigners, results in a complete disregard of minor ailments. Many members of the staff are suffering from this or that indisposition in regard to which they would normally consult physicians but in Moscow do not because they have no confidence in the Russian physicians and because the effort necessary to obtain medical advice is too great. So far as I am concerned and everyone else the sooner Rumreich arrives the better.

Another factor that undoubtedly contributed to the prevalence of illness was the difficulty in maintaining an adequate and healthful diet. In winter, the only fresh vegetables available were potatoes, beets, and sometimes cabbages. Fresh meat was in desperately short supply—the beautiful cuts of meat to be seen in some shop windows were actually rubber models—though it was sometimes possible to obtain a limited amount through Torgsins, special stores that could be used only by those with the passes issued to diplomats and selected Soviet citizens.

Although the prohibition on Russians' mixing with foreigners was not yet in force in 1934 and 1935, there were still grave obstacles in the way of young men, like Tyler Kent, who hoped to become involved in normal social life among Muscovites. The language, of course, was a barrier for most of them. But even when this could be overcome, there were few opportunities to meet and mix with ordinary citizens. There was a paucity of bars and cafés where people could meet and talk, where opinions could be exchanged—and plots hatched. Too many revolutions had been born in such surroundings. Anyone wanting to relax over a drink or a coffee had to use hotel bars, from which most Muscovites were excluded, and which they could not have afforded in any case.

Bullitt, in his enthusiasm for all things Russian, tried to create opportunities for closer contact between his staff and the Russian people, believing this would be a help in developing understanding. Writers, composers, artists, attended embassy entertainments; young Komsomol members took part in weekly baseball games organized by the staff on the ambassador's orders; at one time, Charlie Thayer even tried to introduce polo to the Red Army.

To the delight of the young male members of staff, Bullitt invited the corps de ballet of the Bolshoi to visit the embassy. But the delight turned to disappointment when they arrived. "To our dismay," Charles Bohlen later recalled, "a dreary, scrubby-looking group of young ladies appeared. They were abominably dressed, their faces plain, without make-up; their hair indifferently combed. Nevertheless, the evening was gay and we made a number of pleasant acquaintances." For some time afterward, there were usually two or three dancers or actresses running around the embassy, arriving for lunch or dinner and staying to drink and talk till dawn. A few formed temporary liaisons; one girl developed an abiding but unrequited passion for Bullitt.

Kent, always urbane and well dressed, collected or was collected by a starlet whose nude photograph was later found in his effects. But most of the socializing at this level was reserved for the Foreign Service officers, as was the general social life among the diplomatic corps. The younger American diplomats, led by Bohlen and Thayer, rented a dacha, a country cottage, about twenty kilometers to the west of Moscow on the road to Stalin's country home. It was a two-story log building, painted light yellow, with four bedrooms, a large living room, dining room, kitchen, and verandahs on both levels offering beautiful views of the surrounding countryside. There was a two-horse stable, a tennis court, and a nearby stream for swimming. Modest hills provided sufficient slope for cross-country skiing in winter.

For the diplomats, the dacha provided a haven from the dreary streets of Moscow, where even the ballet, opera, and theater palled. Bohlen, who served several tours of duty in Moscow, recalled that because of the Bolshoi's limited repertoire, he saw *Swan Lake* at least fifty times and knew every step.

Based in the American dacha, the younger members of the diplomatic corps made up an informal club, which they dubbed their "mutual admiration society." The inner circle of this group consisted of second and third secretaries from the American, British, French, Italian, and German embassies, who each contributed national delicacies for the communal larder: peanut butter sandwiches and hot dogs from America, Scotch from Britain, wine, beer, and sausages from Germany, more wine from Italy, and so on. Members of other embassies and legations came from time to time as guests. It all helped to counter the sense of isolation.

But for the clerks, there was no such relief: they were driven in on their own company. Inevitably, in such circumstances, they were sitting targets for the Soviet intelligence services. Each evening, when the embassy completed its day's routine, several attractive women waited across the street for emerging males. Claiming they spoke no English, though in fact they were all selected for their proficiency in the language, the girls led their clients to the bars of the National and Metropol hotels.

Unable to talk to the girls, the embassy clerks or servicemen naturally chatted to one another. Since they were cut off from home and the usual subjects of barroom conversation like sports, they often talked about their work, frequently dropping pieces of information that were readily seized on by the girls and reported back to their masters. Two typical bits of information that were known to have been passed in this way were that Charles Bohlen had just brought new confidential codes to Moscow, and that a diplomatic messenger—in reality an FBI agent investigating the leakage of information—was about to leave for Persia to buy Russian currency on the black exchange.

After a few rounds of drinks and a satisfactory amount of loose talk, couples adjourned to the men's Mokhovaya apartments or hotel rooms. The FBI agent's report on the situation in 1940 recorded: "These women have, up until a short time ago at least, had free access to the Embassy building and there was hardly a night when several of them were not there."

These comings and goings were all carefully monitored by the NKVD, which maintained a permanent watch outside the embassy. When one of the regular girls picked up an embassy employee, the watchers made no attempt to follow them. But if any other girls tried to muscle in, they were followed until they left the company of the men they had picked up, then arrested and taken in for questioning. Though they were sometimes referred to as prostitutes, it is not known whether the NKVD girls received cash from the men or were satisfied with information as payment for their services.

In this atmosphere of heavy drinking and easy womanizing, Kent was soon in trouble. Even when surrounded by other men enjoying similar pleasures, he was seen to be running wild, neglecting his work and behaving scandalously. In an interview for this book, Kent dismissed the trouble with typical nonchalance: there was insufficient translation work to keep him occupied, he claimed, and he was bored with mere clerical duties. He would have preferred, he said revealingly, to have been a Foreign Service officer.

However, the trouble was serious enough to have got him nearly thrown out after only a few weeks. He was hauled up before the ambassador himself to be disciplined. But Bullitt, ever the man of the world and well aware of human frailties, contented himself with a stiff dressing-down. Two and a half months after the mission arrived in Moscow, the ambassador wrote to Judge Moore in Washington:

I am delighted to let you know that young Kent seems to have turned over a new leaf and that his work is giving satisfaction. The talk I had with the youngster evidently did him good and I am exceedingly glad that I did not acquiesce in the universal recommendation of the officers of the Embassy and the Consulate that he should be fired at once.

But others were not so easily convinced that Kent had "turned over a new leaf." Later in 1934, the counselor, John Wiley, also wrote about him to Judge Moore:

I am writing to you in connection with Mr. Tyler G. Kent, a Clerk of this Embassy, as I recall that you were personally interested in him when he applied for a position here. (Mr. Kent is the son of Consul William Patton Kent, a retired Foreign Service Officer.) He has undoubtedly very good qualities, but after observing him over a period of some months, I reluctantly feel that it would be advisable, in his own interest, to transfer him to some other post; preferably to a

Consulate in a city with the usual amenities of life where he would be under strict discipline but with fewer temptations.

Moscow has great disadvantages as a Foreign Service post. These disadvantages are particularly unfortunate in the case of young unmarried members of the staff. Wholesome diversions are very few and the bar of the Metropol is not far or difficult of access.

I have written to you personally in the matter of Mr. Kent so that you could take such action as you think best: and without anything going on his record.

No immediate action was taken, and either Kent must have altered his way of life or Wiley had a change of heart, because he cabled Judge Moore on January 3, 1935:

PERSONAL FOR JUDGE MOORE
Please disregard my letter regarding Kent for the present. Am writing Ambassador Bullitt fully. Greetings.

Wiley's letter to Bullitt, being a personal one, is in the possession of Bullitt's heirs, who shortly after his death, in 1967, removed his papers from Yale's Sterling Library. They are not available to the public or to researchers. However, on April 25, 1935, Bullitt wrote again to Moore, noting:

You will be glad to hear that although Kent is still keeping his nose firmly pointed to the North Star, his work has improved greatly.

From their different attitudes, it would seem that the sophisticated Bullitt was primarily concerned with Kent's assignment efficiency, the prim and proper middle-class Wiley with wenching and drinking. It was, and still is, totally unrealistic to expect healthy young men to abstain from normal pleasures even in a hostile environment. It was also unrealistic to assign these young men—Kent was just short of his twenty-third birthday when he arrived in Moscow, and his friend Henry Antheil was even younger—for a period of six years.

Foreign Service officers in Moscow frequently complained to Washington, but the bureaucrats in the foreign personnel section, few of whom had ever served on foreign stations, did nothing to alleviate the situation, either in terms of the length of tours or the shortage of feminine company. During the entire five and a half years of Kent's stay in Moscow, there was apparently only one American woman on the clerical staff: she worked in the military attaché's office, and she was married (though that state was never much of a deterrent to Kent's sexual adventures). Denied social contact with the females of the foreign colony, clerks and enlisted military personnel were left with only one option—the women provided by the NKVD, which also provided for the wants of American homosexuals in order to entrap them with the threat of blackmail.

If Tyler Kent seemed to have calmed down by early 1935, there may well have been a simple, if not a good, reason: around that time he was introduced to the woman who would remain his principal paramour for the rest of his Moscow years. Blond, voluptuous, with classic Slavic cheekbones and slightly slanting green eyes, Tatiana (Tanya) Alexandrovnaya Ilovaiskaya was the very image of the beautiful woman agent, the femme fatale of spy fiction. She was a part-time translator for the International News Service and a full-time operative of the NKVD. In the latter role, she may have worked occasionally as an interpreter for the American embassy.

It was mainly due to Tanya that Kent, in marked contrast to most bachelors who served in Moscow, had a good time there. Once he met her, he had no need to play the field for female company or sex; he became a regular visitor to her comfortably furnished apartment at 53 Priatnitskaya, which she shared with another NKVD agent, named Valentina, or entertained her in his own Mokhovaya flat or a hotel room. They frequently spent weekends together at a dacha rented for Tanya by Kent at a cost of four thousand rubles, along with Valentina and her regular boyfriend, Sylvester A. Huntowski, a Navy Department employee. (Later, Huntowski rented a dacha for Valentina, too.) Often, Kent would invite other embassy personnel to join them at the dacha, and on these occasions Tanya and Valentina would provide other Russian girls, supposedly unable to speak English but fluent in the language of love.

Tanya made no attempt to conceal from Kent her connection with the secret police. Indeed, it would have been difficult for her to do so, since in addition to the flat and other obvious privileges she had an NKVD driver's license and traveled extensively throughout Europe, presumably on assignment, something that was impossible for the ordinary Soviet citizen.

No doubt the knowledge added spice to the relationship for Kent, enabling him to feel secretly superior to his fellows in the embassy. It would have been completely in character for him to have despised the Foreign Service officers and to have gained great satisfaction from deceiving both them and the NKVD. In the interview shortly before his death, he claimed, "We used to lie abed mornings and laughingly discuss what she would tell her bosses that day."

There can be little doubt that despite this apparently light-hearted approach to feeding the NKVD, Kent must also have passed substantial quantities of genuine information from the embassy. The NKVD were not fools, and Kent was not their only source of supply. If his material had not checked out, it would have become obvious that he was trying to outsmart them. It is also possible that Kent had another motive, in addition to sex and his secret satisfaction: money.

Throughout his life, Kent was fond of high living and high spending. His family was not wealthy, he had no private income, and his salary as a clerk was extremely modest. Nevertheless, he managed to display a certain affluence; according to a 1951 FBI report on his Moscow and London years, he "lived in a style far above his known income." He was, for instance, one of only two or three members of the embassy staff to own an automobile in Moscow. This was a most desirable asset, for public transportation in the city was severely limited: taxis were rarities, with horse-drawn droshkies more common; buses were unreliable and overcrowded; and the subway system, which would be one of the best in the world when it was completed, was then in the early stages of construction. Other embassies provided staff transport, but Americans had to hitch rides with friends in the foreign colony, hire a rare taxi, or walk.

The secret police were always attentive toward the diplomatic community: all ambassadors in Moscow were the subject of twenty-four-hour surveillance by teams of nine agents working in three eight-hour shifts of three men at a time. When anyone complained, the answer was that the watchers were merely "curious Soviet citizens." There was little attempt on the part of the diplomats to elude the watchers, and even less attempt by the NKVD to disguise the surveillance. When Loy Henderson was chargé d'affaires, every morning he would give his Soviet chauffeur his itinerary for the day, including the number of his seat for the opera, theater, or ballet if he was attending a performance that evening. The driver would then openly hand the itinerary over to the watchers. On one memorable occasion while on vacation on the Black Sea, Bullitt, a powerful swimmer, had to rescue his tail from drowning, as the man was no match for the ambassador in the water.

At the beginning of Bullitt's mission, the NKVD—or GPU, as it was until it changed its name in July 1934—seemed prepared to give the Americans special status, particularly in regard to their relations with Soviet citizens. "The GPU at that time apparently did nothing to prevent this free, or comparatively free association," wrote Walter Thurston, chargé d'affaires in 1942, in a report to Secretary of State Cordell Hull, outlining the attitude of the secret police toward foreign officials.

However, major political disagreements gave rise to minor irritations and gradually Russians were discouraged from frequenting the company of Americans. Private citizens began to find it inconvenient to see them and by the middle of 1935 the Embassy found itself as isolated as any other in Moscow. It can hardly be doubted that this state of affairs was the direct result of a change in GPU policy. It was further aggravated by the purge of 1936–39 when relations with foreigners came to be regarded as the first step toward exile or death.

Vice Consul Donald Nichols, who took over as Tanya Ilovaiskaya's lover when Kent left Moscow in 1939, had previously had another Russian girlfriend who was not working for the NKVD. Before long she suddenly disappeared; she was exiled to Siberia for associating with him. There was never any question, though, of Tanya's being exiled or executed. Her friendship with Kent continued to flourish, even though relations between the embassy and the Soviets declined. And decline they did, with surprising speed.

The "major political disagreements" centered on the continuing requests from the United States that the Soviet Union fulfill the contractual obligations agreed to in the recognition pact of November 1933. At the end of his mission's first complete year in Moscow, Bullitt noted that the Soviets had not honored a single promise. There had been no compensation payments for American-owned property seized after the November 1917 revolution; Foreign Commissar Litvinov had continually and aggressively misinterpreted the credits clause in the agreement, demanding straight loans from the United States; protection promised U.S. citizens visiting or living in the Soviet Union had not been forthcoming, nor had the promised freedom of religion.

Although his early optimism was waning fast, Bullitt still hoped that the notoriously slow-moving Russians would eventually fulfill these promises. But on the remaining issue, the one deemed most important by the United States, he could retain no illusions. The Russians deliberately and blatantly ignored their promise that the Comintern's policy of overthrowing all capitalist governments would not be exercised in the United States; rather, they invited America's two leading Communist Party members, Earl Browder and William Z. Foster, to be featured guests and leading speakers at the Seventh All-World Congress of the Communist International held in Moscow between July 20 and August 15, 1934.

The Moscow mission, the Department of State, and the American public were all loud in their condemnation of the Soviets' overtly provocative act. Bullitt and his officers seriously discussed recommending withdrawal of recognition, but eventually settled for measures that were only slightly less drastic. Coming from the man who had spent so many years energetically campaigning for friendship with the Soviet Union, Bullitt's signal to Hull represented a remarkable change after barely six months in Moscow:

I believe that we should employ this occasion to make clear to the American people the aims of the Soviet Government which lie behind the mask "united front against Fascism and war" . . .

[W]e should revoke the exequaturs of all Soviet Consuls in New York and San Francisco, leaving only the consular section in the Soviet Embassy in Washington.

I believe that we should restrict to a minimum the granting of visas to Soviet citizens.

I venture to suggest that henceforth the law excluding Communists from the United States should be applied rigidly and that you should instruct all American missions to refuse visas to Soviet citizens unless they present entirely satisfactory evidence proving that they are not and never have been members of the Communist Party.

The White House and State Department, however, were not yet prepared to go to such lengths, and contented themselves with a stiff note to the Soviet government on August 25, 1934, warning that there could be "the most serious consequences" if it did not "take appropriate measures to prevent further acts in disregard of the solemn pledge given by it to the Government of the United States."

As always, the Soviets had a ready answer. When pressed on the matter by Bullitt, Litvinov simply claimed that the Soviet government had no jurisdiction over the Comintern, which, though technically correct, was a typical piece of Russian prevarication.

In fact, of course, the United States was never in any danger from the activities of the Comintern. The real threat to the nation's security came from the establishment of "legal" Soviet espionage agents working out of the Soviet embassy under diplomatic cover, to replace or augment the "illegals" in the Soviet trading company Amtorg, who had been operating for more than a decade.

With recognition, the Soviet intelligence agencies—notably the NKVD and the GRU, military intelligence—commenced the all-out espionage war with the United States that continues to this day, despite *glasnost.* Tyler Kent was one of their first foot soldiers, albeit a maverick mercenary rather than a dedicated recruit.

In the early days, the war was very much a one-sided affair. Although the Soviets undoubtedly assumed that the United States would operate both legals and illegals within the USSR, a naïve Bullitt wrote to Hull, "We must never send a spy to the Soviet Union." It would in any case have been difficult to do so, for at that time the United States possessed no intelligence agency apart from the very small Army and Navy intelligence departments. There simply was no machinery for espionage. Even the "Black Chamber," the American code and cipher bureau, which had been set up with British assistance during the First World War, had been disbanded in 1929 by Henry L.

Stimson, then secretary of state, reportedly with the memorable words "Gentlemen do not read each other's mail."

In early 1935, both military and naval intelligence departments reviewed the information accumulated by their respective attachés during the previous year. It had been slim pickings for the assistant naval attaché, Marine Captain Nimmer, and for the assistant military attaché for air, Lieutenant White. The military attaché, Lieutenant Colonel Philip D. Faymonville, had produced just enough material to convince Washington that he should remain on station—but what no one knew at the time was that he had obtained it only by supplying the Soviets with U.S. military secrets.

Nimmer left Moscow on February 8, 1935, taking with him the six-man Marine Corps contingent and thus leaving the embassy devoid of security guards. White and his four-man air crew remained, in their role of ambassador's pilot and support group. Their life was not as easy as it sounds: they were housed in a leaky, drafty shack that served as hangar, offices, workshop, and supply room, with internal temperatures regularly plunging below zero in winter.

But White's ordeal did not last much longer. After the plane was severely damaged in a heavy landing at the Leningrad airfield, the Soviets refused to allow a replacement to be flown in. Stalin's rash concession to Bullitt had become an irritating nuisance: other ambassadors had demanded equal treatment, and the officials of the NKVD had scarcely been able to contain their indignation that a capitalist enemy should be allowed to fly over sacred Russian soil, undoubtedly on spying missions. The accident gave them the perfect opportunity to call a halt. It was also a clear signal to Bullitt personally that the honeymoon was over. In the early summer of 1935, Lieutenant White and his men were shipped Stateside.

Bullitt stayed for almost another year, but his heart was no longer in the job. Day by day, his disillusionment grew as he was faced with unavoidable evidence of the true character of Stalin's regime. The biggest and until then most brutal and revealing incident had come on December 1, 1934, with the murder of Sergei Mironovich Kirov in Leningrad. Kirov, the able and popular party boss in Leningrad, had been shot by an unstable young man named Nikolaev, who was said to have committed suicide shortly afterward. The killing was at first passed off as the work of an unbalanced man embittered at being expelled from the party, or as a *crime passionnel*—Kirov was supposed to have been having an affair with Nikolaev's beautiful former wife. But to most observers, there was little doubt that the murder had been engineered by Stalin.

Kirov had been seen as a possible rival, the only man in the Soviet Union capable of unseating the Georgian dictator. His death was therefore inevitable. But what really opened the eyes of many former sympathizers like Bullitt was the way in which Stalin capitalized on the killing to strengthen his hold on the country.

On hearing of Kirov's death, Stalin immediately took a special train to Leningrad, accompanied by his closest lieutenants in the party leadership, Molotov, Voroshilov, and Zhdanov, and a horde of secret police. On arrival, Stalin hit the Leningrad NKVD chief, Filipp Medved', in the face and told him he was personally taking over the investigation.

Five days later, the Soviet news agency, Tass, announced that of thirty-nine Leningraders arrested for alleged involvement in the assassination, thirty-seven had already been executed, and that of thirty-two alleged plotters arrested in Moscow, twenty-nine had been shot. Dozens of other "plotters" were executed in other parts of the Soviet Union, as old scores were settled and anyone who was in any way opposed to Stalin was removed. Thousands of Leningrad party members, including all those who had been associated with Kirov, were arrested and transported to Siberia—a strange way of avenging his death.

The great terror of the thirties had begun. It would accelerate through 1935, to explode in the purges of 1936 to 1939. By the time it ended, not long before Stalin's cynical pact with Hitler, uncounted millions would have died, with millions more exiled to the gulags of Siberia and Kazakhstan. No one living in the Soviet Union in those times could have been unaware of what was going on, or of the evil nature of Stalin's regime. It certainly destroyed any vestiges of faith for William Bullitt, though he did not stay to witness the trials, which began in August 1936.

Bullitt left Moscow forever on May 16, 1936, to become

ambassador to France. After eighteen years of advocacy on behalf of the Soviets, he became one of their most outspoken critics. Until the Munich agreement opened his eyes to Hitler, too, he urged France to form an anti-Comintern pact with Germany. In the Second World War, he even broke with Roosevelt over a profound disagreement on U.S. support for the USSR.

But Tyler Kent seemed to have no such qualms about cooperating with the Soviets, and went on happily supplying secrets to Tanya and her masters in the NKVD. At about this time, he started stealing copies of classified signals from the embassy code room. He claimed later that he had done so purely for his own satisfaction, as a sort of hobby. Given his arrogance and his strange personality, this may have been partially true. What is harder to swallow is his claim that he never showed the signals to Tanya. Since she had the run of his apartment, it is hardly credible that he could have believed she never saw them. Again, we must set his need for financial and sexual rewards against any protestations of innocence.

An incident in 1936 demonstrates the high regard in which the NKVD officials held Kent, and the importance they attached to keeping him happy. It also shows the trust they placed in Tanya, and indicates that she must have been a high-ranking officer running a successful operation.

Kent took his accumulated biannual leave as a thirty-day holiday in Western Europe. He went first to England, leaving Moscow at 7:00 A.M. on August 29, 1936, and arriving in London on the morning of September 1. Ten days later, he left for Italy; he spent three days in the north of the country before traveling on to Belgrade and then to Budapest, where he arrived on the morning of September 20. After three days in Budapest, he was taken ill and hospitalized with a mastoid infection, a serious and painful condition in the days before antibiotics. He was confined to a clinic in Budapest until December 2, but his stay was lightened by a two-week visit from Tanya, which must have been sanctioned or even arranged by the NKVD. Obviously, she was trusted enough to be allowed out of the Soviet Union without fear of her defecting. And Kent was considered valuable enough to merit such special attention.

THREE

Beavers and Bolos

THE EASE with which Kent was able to help himself to classified documents shows just how bad security was in Moscow. Shortly after the discovery of Kent's activities in London, a secret investigation of the Moscow embassy's security was set up by Assistant Secretary of State Breckinridge Long, General Sherman Miles, the recently appointed chief of G-2, the Army's intelligence department, and FBI Director J. Edgar Hoover. Special Agent Louis Beck of the FBI was sent to Moscow, working under cover as a courier temporarily assigned to the embassy as an internal messenger.

The seriousness of the situation hit Beck as soon as he arrived. He was horrified to discover that on only his second night in Moscow he was able to walk into the code room unchallenged. All the safes were open and code books lay on the tables, together with messages to be encoded and decoded.

The code clerk, a recent arrival named Robert Hall, showed a complete lack of interest in his work and even left Beck alone in the room for forty-five minutes. The door was open at all times, and Beck was one of several people allowed to wander in to talk to the clerks there, though State Department regulations laid down that the only people allowed to enter the code room of any embassy were code clerks and people with specific authorization. The one precaution was that Soviet messengers had to wait behind a barrier several feet from the code room door.

Morale among the three code clerks in the embassy was particularly low. They were all dissatisfied with their lives and conditions, and were consequently easy prey for subversion. There is no evidence that any of those working there during Beck's visit succumbed, but one man, James Lewis, was especially vulnerable, as he was living with a Soviet woman. He wanted to marry her, but was caught in a double trap: State Department regulations did not allow married men to serve as clerks in Moscow; if he did marry, he would be transferred back to the United States, but because of Soviet regulations he would have to leave his wife behind.

Confidential and coded messages were supposed to be destroyed with care after dispatch, but it was the custom in the embassy, Beck noted, for all the originals of confidential messages to be piled up together with the original drafts of the coded telegrams. When enough messages had accumulated, they were taken to the basement by a messenger to be burned. There was no guard, and no control was ever exercised to see that the messages were in fact destroyed. With both the original documents and the coded copies, the messenger would not only be in a position to know the contents of all confidential communications to and from the embassy, but would also have the necessary data with which to break the secret codes and ciphers.

But there was still more disturbing evidence of the lack of security. The Soviet employees habitually loitered in the basement—indeed, some of them lived there—and usually gathered to watch the bundles of confidential messages being burned at the end of the working day. "Paper bundles such as the bundles of confidential messages do not burn readily," Special Agent Beck noted, "and even after being in the fire for several minutes many messages still may be removed and read. Only the Soviets usually know whether the paper thrown into the fire is completely burned."

Soon after arriving at the embassy, Beck undertook the task of destroying the messages. While he was doing so, as part of normal routine, he had no difficulty in removing from the fire original messages written by the ambassador concerning the treachery of Kent, Sylvester Huntowski, and Henry Antheil.

Three main types of message were sent through the code room, each coming from a different department in the embassy: political messages from the ambassador's office, and those concerned with personnel and visas from the personnel department and consular section respectively. All telegrams, however, whatever their nature, were kept in the same binders. This meant that a vice consul, for example, asking to see a visa telegram would be able to read all the political and personnel messages in the same binder.

Telegrams were indexed in the file room, where they were summarized so that the clerks did not know their exact contents. But the clerks had to know how and where to file each telegram, and with a file number and a summary of its contents it was usually a simple matter to work out what was in a message. The file room was one of the most popular meeting places in the embassy, primarily because it was the source of the most interesting reading matter, especially those documents marked "strictly confidential."

Complete confidential messages were kept in binders in the code room, and were supposed to be available only to the code clerks and authorized officers. But binders were carried around the embassy by messengers and left lying on desks, where anyone interested could pick them up and read them. And when they were returned to the code room they were placed on a table outside the door, where again they could be picked up by anyone.

Morale and efficiency were not improved with the arrival in January 1937 of Joseph E. Davies as the new ambassador. If anything, the situation became worse, for Davies was a catastrophe from the moment he arrived in Moscow. Married to the former Marjorie Meriweather Post, one of America's wealthiest women, he had been awarded the position after his wife contributed $16,500 to Roosevelt's 1936 presidential campaign. This was nothing unusual, for at that time most ambassadorships were handed out as payment for services rendered. But Davies's total ignorance of Soviet affairs and blatant intention of using the post to further his political fortunes were so glaring that the day following his arrival the entire staff of Foreign Service officers prepared to resign en masse. They had been incensed by the way the ambassador and his wife treated all of them, apart from Loy Henderson and Philip Faymonville, like household servants. After reconsideration, they voted to give Davies a chance, but the relationship remained unhappy.

Bullitt had arrived full of hope, but had soon been disillusioned by the Soviet system. Davies never lost his naïveté. From the time he presented his letter of credence on January 25, 1937, until he departed on June 11, 1938, he was a willing victim of Soviet propaganda, relying for information not on his own staff but on newsmen. His primary adviser on Soviet matters was Walter Duranty of the *New York Times,* who was always regarded as Stalin's pet stooge. Within the embassy, his sole confidant was his military attaché, the "Red Colonel" Faymonville.

Although he could be relied on in matters where the interests of the United States were in conflict with the Soviet government's, in all other areas Davies totally swallowed the Soviet line. His blindness to the evils of the regime was such that after attending several sessions of Stalin's infamous show trials he wrote to both Hull and Roosevelt that in most if not all cases the sentences of death or exile were entirely justified. Fortunately for everyone, the Davies family spent little time in Moscow: after only two months, they took a three-month trip back to the United States, and much of their time in Russia was spent on their luxurious yacht *Sea Cloud,* which was usually berthed in Leningrad.

One instance of Davies's dissatisfaction with Moscow sheds an interesting light on Tyler Kent's relationship with Tanya. Although they spent so little time there, Mrs. Davies decided that Spaso House needed deep freeze equipment, so she contacted Birdseye Foods, whose founder, Clarence Birdseye, had pioneered this technique. Birdseye naturally decided such an important client should have the personal attention of the company's European representative, Robert Grosjean, a graduate of Princeton, 1932, the son of an international banker who was the Belgian ambassador to the United States. Grosjean, now a resident of New Canaan, Connecticut, and Brussels, recalls his Berlin-to-Moscow train journey with some amusement.

As he was settling into his two-berth sleeping compartment a very attractive, well-dressed woman, speaking English with barely a trace of a Russian accent, entered. She told him it was normal on Russian trains for unmarried couples to share overnight quarters. "When this occurs," she explained, "we must keep on the blue overhead light." Grosjean did not complain, and spent an enjoyable two days in her company.

As the train pulled into the station in Moscow, and they prepared to say goodbye, they heard someone coming through the cars, yelling, "Monsieur Grosjean!" Tanya, for the beautiful woman was, of course, Tatiana Ilovaiskaya, recognized the voice as that of Tyler Kent. Turning swiftly to Grosjean, she whispered, "Don't tell him where I boarded the train. He thinks I have been visiting my mother." Grosjean was happy to keep her secret.

Grosjean, incidentally, courted and married Davies's daughter Emlen, a marriage that lasted twenty-nine years before ending in divorce. Davies moved on from Moscow on June 11, 1938, to become ambassador in Brussels. Just before his departure, he met Stalin. His comments, at a time when the Soviet dictator's paranoia was resulting in the death and imprisonment of hundreds of thousands of Soviet citizens, shows that Davies had learned nothing during his mercifully short term as ambassador: "I have seen him; I finally had a talk with him; he is really a fine, upstanding, great man."

During Davies's tenure in Moscow, the agents of the "fine, upstanding, great man" kept up their efforts to subvert his staff with all their usual methods of persuasion. In the early summer of 1937, a friend of Kent's, Anthony J. Barrett, who was a civilian quartermaster's clerk in the military attaché's office, reported to his boss, Colonel Faymonville, that the NKVD had photographed him indulging in homosexual acts, and had given him seventy-two hours to provide them with copies of American military codes. If he failed, they had warned, he would be sentenced to a long term of penal servitude, despite his diplomatic immunity.

Henderson arranged for Barrett to leave the country as a special diplomatic courier within twenty-four hours, and thus the blackmail plot was averted. Faymonville, true to his reputation as the red colonel, was reported to have been disturbed that his Soviet colleagues would attempt to obtain U.S. codes.

Barrett's experience was not unique; other clerks would be sent home for similar reasons, demonstrating a serious and continuing security problem. FBI Special Agent Beck's report highlighted this, in a section headed "Practice of Sexual Perversion among Staff Members."

A few of the men attached to the American Embassy at Moscow refuse to associate with Soviet prostitutes but find a "love life" among themselves. One of the Code Clerks, Robert Hall, and the Ambassador's Secretary, George Filton, engaged in sexual perversion in the Code Room of the Embassy until Hall, mentally spent, resigned. Filton and P. C. Cheney, a forty-five-year-old clerk, have been seen by the reporting agent in passionate embraces and kisses which could lead to only one conclusion . . . Filton and Cheney are reported to be desperate in their desire to leave Moscow and Filton has confidentially indicated to the reporting agent that he might end his own life. He has even requested the State Department to transfer him at his own request and at a reduced salary to some other post . . . Since both Filton and Cheney have been in Moscow for approximately three years and neither of them have been able to lead normal lives both are psychopathic cases. In 1939 Cheney was given home leave primarily because he was on the verge of a nervous breakdown.

The reporting agent points out that Moscow is a most undesirable post of assignment for these persons since if their sex conduct came to the attention of the GPU it could readily be used as a lever to pry confidential information from them, this observation being particularly pertinent to the Ambassador's Secretary . . . He suggests that married couples be sent to Moscow for short periods, possibly one or two years. This is the policy reported to be followed by other governments in the selection of personnel for Moscow.

The problem, of course, was not confined to the level of clerks. In the first years of the embassy, Ambassador Bullitt,

himself bisexual, was a security risk, open to blackmail. He was
having an affair with his confidential clerk—later promoted to
third secretary—Carmel Offie. Bullitt took Offie with him on
his holidays, and had him assigned to Paris when he moved
there. Offie joined the fledgling CIA in 1948, but was fired four
years later when Washington police arrested him for picking up
young males in Lafayette Park. He went on to become a substantial figure in the American labor movement, but was killed
in a London plane crash in 1970.

Other highly placed security risks in the Moscow embassy
included Alexander Kirk, chargé d'affaires for fourteen months
between the departure of Ambassador Davies and the arrival of
his replacement, a smooth New York lawyer who was a friend of
Roosevelt's, Laurence Steinhardt. Kirk was "light in his loaf-
ers," in the current intelligence community slang, and in Berlin, where he was posted in September 1939, he had a long
affair with his confidential secretary, Philip H. Fahrenholz, who
was suspected by two State Department field inspectors of
supplying Kirk with narcotics. Kirk was therefore a double
security risk, though he was an extremely able diplomat and
nothing was ever recorded against either his or Bullitt's patrio-
tism.

For Kent, sex was not the only diversion from the boredom of
life in Moscow. His father had died in 1936, but there was no
inheritance; Mrs. Kent was left with an inadequate pension and
their home in Washington, D.C., which she turned into a rooming house for government employees in order to support herself. To supplement his income from the U.S. and Soviet governments—a necessity if he was to keep up his way of life, with
his car and dacha in Moscow and biannual trips around Europe
or to the States with no expense spared—Kent hit on an inge-
nious scheme. Largely through Tanya's contacts in Moscow,
Kent, Tanya, and Anthony Barrett began buying jewelry and
small gold and silver objects, which the men smuggled out of
the Soviet Union in diplomatic pouches.

Barrett's hurried return to the United States put an end to
his part in the racket, but not before he had made one last
killing. He described it to Kent, whom he addressed as

"Dearest Pucia," in a letter from 661 West 180 Street, New York City, on July 1, 1937:

. . . I have so much to relate to you Pucia that I don't know just where to begin and where to stop . . . In the first place, I want to tell you about the furs. The cape has made a tremendous hit here. There is no question about it. It has been appraised at $350.00, and it is Japanese mink and not Russian mink and is supposed to be a very fine fur at that. The fur coat is caracal and has been prized [sic] at $400.00 by the New York furriers who know the cost of things. The rings have all been appraised and at figures which will surprise you beyond anything you ever saw. A pair of ear-rings I bought in Leningrad have been appraised at 200% per more than the cost of the things at the rate of 5 rubles equal $1.00. This would be a tremendous killing. The sapphire ring I obtained from Tanya is considered a very fine one and would be worth anything from $75.00 to $100.00 cash on the barrel. The little ring with the clover leaf is also a very fine one and would cost about $65.00. My cost was $9.00 in Moscow from the old man . . . Judging from the cost of the little salt and paper [sic] cups which I bought made of silver, the belts would bring in abut $150.00 apiece.

My sincerest advice to you Pucia is to concentrate on this sort of thing and bring back as much of it as you possibly can. Your baggage is not inspected in New York at all. My trunks and other things were not touched AT ALL. I was sorry I didn't bring in more furs and silver things to sell and make money on . . . These are real big beavers [Kent's word for smuggled merchandise] . . . I wish I had more diamond rings and furs . . . I could have made at least $1500.00 clear profit on one diamond ring alone. What you can do is send stuff over to Helsingfors in the pouch and have them hold it there for you. Don't forget to concentrate on the jewelry and the furs. If you sell another coat like the one I bought, I advise you to buy it without asking any questions. This is one of the most expensive furs they export to this country from Russia. I am not kidding you Pucia. The beavers are all yours and don't be afraid of the customs here. Nothing will be opened. I wish I had known this before I left Moscow. Linen is good, but why fool around with items of this kind when furs and diamonds are more profitable. Better get Tanya busy on these items.

Other parts of the letter show that Kent was regarded by his friends—and doubtless by himself—as a sophisticated arbiter of taste:

My many friends have been giving a lot of parties for me here . . . They think that I have improved considerably. My suits have been commented upon by everybody. I go around kissing the women's hands and they get quite a kick out of this also. I have told my girl friend that I owe my improvements in taste and way of dressing to you. You are to some extent responsible for everything. She thinks you are grand. I told that also to your mother and she laughed. They don't think I am as provincial as I used to be.

In between showing off his European clothes and manners, Barrett had more serious matters to attend to; he was summoned to Washington for what we would now call "debriefing." But his description of this reveals much more about what was going on in Moscow:

. . . I had quite a conference with the fellows in Naval Intelligence. One of the fellows was Leahy the Chief of Naval Operations. I gave them an ear full and they thanked me very highly. Leahy was to address a crowd in Wash. about Russia and he was going to use my information in his talk. I see by the paper where he did . . . I had very little time to flay the bolos [Bolsheviks] in the War Dept. G2. The new head of the M/A division is very anti-bolo and told me he was well aware of everything . . . Regarding the question of the M/A's Office, Moscow, being *red*. I tried to feel them out about it and discovered much to my disappointment that Bullitt had done everything possible to have us FIRED from Moscow, because Lange and I were REDS. There was no reference made to anybody else, and when I learned this I was indeed very shocked. Imagine the damn fool accusing me of being a bolo. I got this direct from General Burnett who was in charge of the MID when Bullitt was in Moscow. He told me that even the Sec. of State had to interfere in the case and that Bullitt kept on requesting my removal from the Service every time he visited the U.S. Unfortunately, this charge was not made against Col. Faymonville, and I had to be the victim of it all. Are you surprised or not? I am sure these were all Offie's charges and ideas and he probably put it up to Bullitt at the time. Are you surprised to know that you have been going around with a red all this time? I wouldn't be a bit surprised if he didn't make Henderson believe the same thing. Do tell Henderson something if he should ask you something about it in the future.

Further indications of Kent's anti-Soviet views are provided in Barrett's comments on conversations with Mrs. Kent at this time, underlining yet again that his collaboration with the NKVD was not for idealistic or ideological reasons. The mention of the Nazi and fascist dictators is an interesting sidelight, given Kent's future connections:

Pucia, you should put your mother on a right track about the political situation in Europe. She thinks Hitler and Mussolini are just awful bandits, safecrackers and bomb throwers, but on the contrary she thinks that Russia is making wonderful steps toward the improving of people's welfare. I told her a few things and told her you had been my adviser on all these points. She was rather surprised to hear that her views didn't correspond with yours. I thought I told you about this. I have been reading these wonderful articles they write here in the Hearst papers. I am enclosing a few.

After signing off with the name "Tool" (or "Toop") in Cyrillic characters, Barrett returned to his primary interest with a short postscript: "P.S. the ear-rings I bought in Leningrad were sold to me as silver, and here they say they are solid gold. What a beaver!"

Barrett's hopes of a clerkship with the Foreign Service were quickly dashed. Loy Henderson told him that as long as the Soviet secret police held the incriminating photographs, he could never again hold a position of trust in U.S. government service.

Kent was able to take advantage of Barrett's advice on smuggling at the end of 1938, when he returned to the United States on his biannual leave. He was still persevering in his efforts to become a Foreign Service officer, and in Washington on January 9 he applied "for a waiver of the written Foreign Service examination which, it is understood, is to be given February 14th of this year. There is enclosed a memorandum setting forth briefly the preparation which I have made in anticipation of this examination." He listed the titles of books he had studied, including seven on American history, five on European history, three on international law, and four on economics. G. Howland Shaw, chief of the Foreign Service Personnel Division, informed him on January 18 that his request for a waiver had been granted.

Kent took the oral examination on February 14—and failed. He was interviewed by Loy Henderson, back in Washington on the European desk after five years in Moscow. Years later,

Henderson told a St. Albans friend of Kent's that he had scored 100 on the exam, but "I flunked him on personality." The result was hardly surprising, considering how much Henderson knew about Kent's character and how he had tried to get him fired back in 1934.

On his way back to the Soviet Union, Kent stopped off in New York City to call on Barry Farris, chief of foreign correspondents for the International News Service. Kent hoped that because of his knowledge of the place and the language he might be taken on as a correspondent in Moscow, but once again his hopes were dashed. The INS, a Hearst organization, was undergoing one of its periodic belt tightenings, and there were no openings for new staff. Back in Moscow, Kent soon found changes afoot that were to affect his life for ever. In more ways than one, his destiny became entwined with that of his friend Henry W. Antheil, Jr., chief code clerk in the embassy.

By late 1937, Antheil had decided that four years in Moscow were enough: plagued by ill health, he was sustained only by special diets and medications provided by embassy medical staff. During 1938, more than thirty signals were exchanged between Moscow and Washington, London and Berlin, as he tried to switch to another posting, but by the time he returned to America on leave in the spring of 1939, he seemed no nearer achieving his goal. Although men like Loy Henderson had long pleaded for duty tours of two and a half years for the Moscow mission, their advice went unheeded. Department of State civil servants had no personal knowledge of the debilitating conditions in the Soviet capital, and continued to insist on men serving out the full term of their contracts there.

Before returning to Moscow, however, Antheil was given a task by the State Department: to deliver new code books to overseas embassies. He was instructed to pick up two locker trunks, one small trunk, and two locked cases containing confidential documents, and to deliver specified codes and documents to embassies and legations throughout Northern and Central Europe. In London, which was one of the cities Antheil had been trying to get himself posted to, Ambassador Joseph P. Kennedy was so impressed by his efficiency that he requested Antheil be transferred to London.

Kennedy's request was granted on May 13, which meant that

a certain amount of reorganization was needed in Moscow. On June 20, Stuart E. Grummon, then the chargé d'affaires, made a request to Washington that the clerks Tyler Kent, Harry L. Anderson, and Eugene Pressly, together with the vice consuls Walter T. Costello and Edward McKee, "in whose loyalty the mission has confidence, be permitted to use the confidential codes." Receiving no reply, Grummon reduced his list to one, wiring State: "Request Department's telegraphic authorization for clerk Tyler G. Kent in whose loyalty the Embassy has confidence to use the confidential codes." The following day, he received a one-word reply: "Granted." Kent, who was still sleeping with Tanya and no doubt still lying abed mornings deciding what she would tell her NKVD masters, was now a code clerk handling the embassy's most secret and confidential messages.

But fate was by no means finished with him. In September, the Moscow embassy wired Kennedy that Antheil would not be moving to London after all. It seemed the embassy had changed its mind about releasing Antheil. In fact, it was Antheil who had changed his mind, or had had it changed for him by the NKVD: it was later discovered that he had deliberately avoided the London assignment by altering code signals. There could be several possible explanations of this, not the least of which is that the political situation had changed overnight on August 23, 1939, with the signing of the Nazi-Soviet pact.

A young third secretary in the German embassy, Hans von Herwarth, a founding member of the "mutual admiration society," which met at the American dacha, and a staunch anti-Nazi, was secretly passing information on German actions and intentions to Charles Bohlen, which Bohlen was sending back —through the code room, naturally—to Washington. These signals were of great interest to the Soviets; it may be that they did not regard Kent as a reliable enough source of information and wanted to ensure they got everything.

Antheil remained in Moscow, but found himself moving around Northern Europe on a series of detachments; he was by then considered the foremost code and cipher man in the European division of the State Department. In the spring of 1940, he was sent, in the guise of a courier, to reorganize code room operations in the embassy in Berlin. Shortly afterward, he was sent to Helsinki, Finland, to do the same for the embassies and legations in the Baltic.

On June 15, 1940, he was flying back to Helsinki aboard an Estonian airliner after a trip around the Baltic states. That day, Stalin decided to move in on Lithuania, Latvia, and Estonia, an operation he had been planning for some time to protect his northwestern flank against attack by Hitler. The Red Army marched into Lithuania and staged incidents on the borders of the other two states; the Soviet Navy blockaded Estonian and Latvian ports; and just after lunch, Soviet SB-2 fighter aircraft attacked two Estonian airliners. One of them crashed into the sea just north of Tallinn, killing everyone aboard—including Henry Antheil. Estonian fishermen hurried to the scene and began picking up floating debris, but a Soviet submarine suddenly appeared and took all the recovered objects. It was never determined whether these included the U.S. diplomatic pouch that was being carried by Antheil.

Secretary of State Cordell Hull hailed the dead courier as a hero. But a few days later, when Antheil's Helsinki colleagues repacked his footlockers to ship them back home, they found irrefutable evidence, including code books and other documents, that he had been a longtime Soviet agent. What was more, there was evidence that he had been altering signals sent to and from the embassy. Washington immediately sent a courier to Moscow to fetch the "true readings," the original messages, for comparison with those Antheil had altered.

Sometime later, a State Department officer told the FBI that a large collection of signals had arrived in Washington. It would have taken several days to check them out, but that day, or possibly in the night, the true readings were burned in the fireplace of a room on the fourth floor of the State Department building. The officer thought this may have been done to protect the department's public image. Nothing was ever mentioned in the press about Antheil's disloyalty, but Robert T. Crowley, one of America's foremost authorities on the KGB and its predecessors, who has made a thorough study of the documents, including some not available to researchers, comments that "there were 'bear tracks' [signs of Soviet involvement] all over the case."

The FBI report on Antheil mentioned the agency's interest in the relationship between Kent and Antheil, but there is no record available to the public of what steps, if any, were taken to pursue the connection.

Meanwhile, in September 1939, Ambassador Kennedy was furious at losing the code clerk he had been promised and fired off an angry letter to Moscow. The result of this was that on September 13 Ambassador Steinhardt called Kent into his office and told him he was being transferred to London in place of Antheil. Kent was not pleased. He had no desire to leave Moscow at that time, especially for a London which was at war and expecting to be attacked at any moment by the bombers of Hermann Göring's Luftwaffe. He immediately cabled Henderson in Washington: "What chance transfer to Department?"

Henderson, hardly surprisingly, was not enthusiastic. On September 18, Kent received his reply—in the name of the secretary of state himself, so there could be no argument: "Your 13 September. Apparently no vacancies for person your qualifications in Department at present. (Signed) HULL."

Three days later, Washington notified Moscow that Kent's assignment to London was approved, with a salary of $2250—a cut of $250 dollars a year because living costs in London were supposed to be lower than those in Moscow. Kennedy was notified at the same time, much to his displeasure.

On Saturday, September 23, 1939, Kent left the Moscow embassy. But it was not till then that he reported an auto accident of six weeks earlier. On August 7, while driving through Moscow, he had knocked down a slightly inebriated Soviet citizen. On Kent's instructions, the embassy settled the case in October for $75 without waiving his diplomatic immunity. Why did he take so long before saying anything about it? Robert T. Crowley suggests that the NKVD may well have taken Kent in for questioning and used the accident—a serious offense under Soviet law—to force him into some form of cooperation. After his arrest in London, Kent told his interrogators that he had destroyed the classified documents he had stolen from the embassy in Moscow. Or had he exchanged them for his freedom, or partial freedom?

Perhaps not unconnected to this mystery is a discrepancy concerning the date of Kent's actual departure. Embassy records state that he left at 5:25 P.M. on September 23. Usually, when a mission member left for a new posting, he was accompanied to the station by a friend or mission member. In an unpublished memoir, however, Kent states that he "boarded the Red Arrow . . . in early October." This would certainly have fitted with his known arrival date in London. What about the missing days not taken up by the trip? Did Tanya or another woman delay his departure? Or was he detained by the NKVD, possibly for briefing on his future role in London?

When Kent's train crossed the Finnish border, like most travelers returning from the Soviet Union he noted "the emergence into civilization from an oppressive land." That night, he gorged himself on the vast smorgasbord at the Hotel Societitshuset (now known as the Socis) in Helsinki, considering it, as it no doubt was, his best meal since he had last eaten outside Russia. Next morning he crossed the Baltic to Stockholm, where he stayed, as always, at a first-class hotel—in this case the Grand, one of Europe's most famed hostelries, with a superb view across the harbor and its ten thousand skerries, as the islands there are known.

Now that he was back in the West, Kent wasted no time in reestablishing his connections in high society. In Stockholm he was shown the sights by a daughter of the shipping magnate Axel Johnson—better known as Big Axel to distinguish him from Little Axel Johnson, president of the Svensk-Amerikansk shipping line. Big Axel headed the Johnson Line, which ran passenger-carrying freighters to the east and west coasts of both North and South America. That night, Kent dined with Big Axel and his daughter in the Johnson mansion at Karlavagen 37.

Again, Kent's two-day stay in Stockholm leaves us with certain mysteries. When his flat in London was searched, his address book and diary were found to contain the unexplained note for an address in the Swedish capital: "Floragaten 1, through kitchen, 8 P.M." Of course, this may have been a romantic or sexual assignation. But it is interesting to note that the Soviet embassy in Stockholm is almost adjacent to Floragaten 1.

After two days in Stockholm, Kent departed from the central

station for Bergen, Norway. He shared a compartment in the train with a blond, stolid man known as Ludwig Matthias, a native of Germany but for some years a naturalized Swedish subject. Matthias was managing director of the Ultramare Trading Company of Eriksbergsgaten 20, Stockholm. He was also, as it happened, a suspected German secret agent and probably a double agent working for the NKVD, too.

On arrival in Bergen, Kent and Matthias checked into separate rooms at the Hotel Norge, and the following morning they boarded the S.S. *City of Newcastle* for the two-day voyage to northeast England. According to Kent's story, as told to MI5 in London during his interrogation, Matthias handed him a box shortly before landing, explaining that it held cigars. Saying that he might be held up at customs and immigration because of his German birth, he asked whether Kent could carry in the box for him as a favor, presumably to avoid his having to pay duty. Kent said he agreed, and told Matthias he would be staying at the Cumberland—then the newest luxury hotel in London and the biggest in Europe, overlooking Hyde Park at Marble Arch. Matthias could collect his parcel from him there.

As expected, Kent, with his diplomatic passport, number 405, was whisked swiftly through immigration at Newcastle, and on to the London-bound train, with Matthias's "cigar box" safely stowed in his unopened baggage—a time bomb that would lead to his own destruction.

Shortly before his departure from Moscow, Kent had handed a locked briefcase to one of the other clerks, asking him to put it in the embassy safe for the time being. He said he would later request that it be sent on to him in London in a diplomatic pouch. The case remained in the safe, where it was found in 1940 by two Foreign Service inspectors visiting Moscow while Kent was in London awaiting trial. Suspecting it might contain stolen documents, they carefully opened it in the presence of Ambassador Steinhardt without breaking the lock. It contained four photographs of Tanya—two framed portraits and two in the nude—a nude photograph of an actress from one of the smaller Moscow theaters, a photograph of a naked, copulating couple (neither member of which was identifiable), a letter from the International News Service of New York relating to his efforts to get a job as a Moscow correspondent, two boxes of visiting cards and a printing plate, a copy of the first page of an embassy memorandum referring to his automobile accident, a Finnish dirk, a Colt police .38 caliber revolver with a holster and cartridges, and an antique pornographic book, *Le Portier des Chartreux,* published in London in 1788. The box was shipped back to Washington, where it became a State Department curio. All in all, it was a fitting postscript to Kent's stay in Moscow and an apt summation of his character.

FOUR

The Bore War

TYLER KENT reported for duty at the embassy in London on Thursday, October 5, 1939, twelve days after he had officially left Moscow. Elsewhere in Europe that day, other events were taking place that had far greater international significance, and that would, ultimately, influence his own conduct. The last remnants of the shattered Polish Army surrendered as Hitler flew to Warsaw to review the victory parade of his forces. Meanwhile, in Moscow Stalin was preparing for his take-over of the Baltic states by concluding a "mutual assistance pact" with Latvia, which gave him naval and air bases and the right to station 25,000 Soviet troops in the country. He had already forced a similar agreement on Estonia, and was "negotiating" with a reluctant Lithuania an agreement whereby no fewer than 75,000 Soviet troops would be stationed on Lithuanian soil. That same day, Foreign Minister Vyacheslav Molotov invited

Finland to send someone to the Soviet capital "for an exchange of views on political matters of mutual interest"—matters that within a few weeks were to lead to the Winter War.

In France, the last of 158,000 British troops were landing to join their French allies facing the Germans, whose all-conquering Tenth Army was being rushed back from Poland to the western front. In Britain, as the Chamberlain government announced the immediate call-up of another 250,000 men, it seemed certain that the land war between Germany and the Allies was about to erupt.

The war at sea had already been raging for over a month: more than 156,000 tons of British shipping had been sunk by German U-boats, a total of more than twenty ships. Among them was the passenger liner *Athenia*, torpedoed without warning on September 3 with the loss of 112 lives, 28 of them American passengers. The aircraft carrier H.M.S. *Courageous* went down in the Atlantic with a toll of 500 dead. The Royal Navy believed it had destroyed some twenty U-boats, one third of those ready for action at the start of hostilities.

On October 5, Winston Churchill, then serving in Neville Chamberlain's Cabinet as first lord of the Admiralty, sent a message to President Roosevelt commenting on the action of the Congress of American Republics. At a meeting in Panama two days earlier the organization had proclaimed a "zone of safety" around the western hemisphere south of Canada, ranging from three hundred to six hundred miles in width. No warlike acts were to be committed within this zone. Churchill said he liked the idea of keeping all submarines out of the area and that Britain would comply with any American request to do so. But he was not so happy about keeping British surface ships out, unless the United States undertook the policing of the zone.

German warships, including the powerful pocket battleships *Admiral Scheer* and *Admiral Graf Spee*, were then operating within the area covered by the zone of safety. They were inflicting serious casualties on British shipping by attacking merchant ships carrying vital cargoes to Britain, and the Royal Navy was in the process of forming "hunting groups" to track them down and destroy them. Churchill concluded this, his second cable to Roosevelt, by assuring him: "We wish to help you in every way in keeping the war out of Americas."

It is possible that this was one of the first messages, perhaps even the very first, to be encoded by Kent after his arrival in London, assuming he went to work right away. We have no way of knowing when he first saw it; if it was not on the day it was sent, it was certainly very shortly afterward. We do know that it alerted him to the fact that Churchill and Roosevelt were communicating with each other, and raised the question in his mind as to why the first lord of the Admiralty and the president of the United States should be dealing directly with each other. It was a question that was to have a significant effect on the course of his life.

The London that Kent encountered was already vastly different from the peacetime city, with precautions and preparations against air raids and invasion visible everywhere. Carl and Shelley Smith Mydans, a photographer and a reporter for *Life* magazine, arrived at about the same time. The city appeared to them neat and clean, though what little traffic there was on the streets was interspersed with military vehicles.

Three signs of war, or of waiting for war, that particularly struck Shelley were the sandbags piled neatly in front of glass windows, which were themselves crisscrossed with brown paper strips to keep them from shattering in bomb blasts; the trenches that had been dug—and were still being dug—in the public parks; and, a rarely remembered feature, shoulder-high poles planted at many street corners with boards about a foot square fixed to their tops, coated with a special yellow paint that would change to red in the event of a gas attack.

Carl's recollections, based on his diary entry for the Mydans' first days in London, tell much about life in the city in October 1939:

After checking in at the Dorchester we found an apartment in Athenaeum Court overlooking Green Park already laced with trenches. That first night on foot through the blackout, which made Paris in blackout seem like a highly lighted city, we managed to find the Odeon and saw the movie *Nurse Cavell*. The next day we registered with the police at Caxton Hall, listing our new residence in Westminster and putting ourselves on record to receive through the mail our

food ration cards. That night Shelley and I walked through the blackout looking for a restaurant . . . Figures in crowded wartime London streets loomed out of the blacked-out world. Suddenly some of
these shadowy figures lighted themselves with flashlights from behind. They were all young women and their sudden flashing movements were dramatic attention-getters, for they were all wearing un-
commonly thin dresses. I let Shelley walk ahead and stopped before
one of them. She lighted herself again and said "Paris! I'm from
Paris!" and so the prostitutes from Paris joined the war effort in
London.

Prostitutes apart, the Mydans' observations of London's
streets are an accurate indication of British concerns at the
time. In the five weeks since the declaration of war, there had
not yet been time for anyone to realize that the "phony war,"
or "bore war" as it was sometimes called in Britain as a pun on
the Boer War in South Africa forty years earlier, would last
another seven months before exploding into the reality of
blitzkrieg. Everyone expected Hitler to attack at any moment,
since his Polish campaign was finished, and his treaties with the
Soviet Union, backing up the Nazi-Soviet nonaggression pact,
meant he could release battle-tested troops from the east to
fight in France.

Although there was no panic and morale was high, the British people were understandably obsessed with the dangers of
war, whether real or imagined. No one had any experience of
mass bombing, apart from reports of what had happened in
Guernica and Barcelona during the Spanish Civil War, and in
Japanese attacks on Shanghai and other Chinese cities. In the
event, the imagined horrors of mass air raids were far worse
than the genuinely terrible actuality. The "experts" of the
Committee of Imperial Defence, basing their calculations on
casualty rates from the First World War and updated but inaccurate estimates of German air power, predicted upward of
600,000 deaths from bombing in the first sixty days of war, with
at least 100,000 killed in London during the first month.

Because of these dire predictions, preparations for disaster
had been thorough. Antiaircraft gun sites ringed the cities, and
barrage balloons—giant inflatables set to foil low-flying bombers—floated above them like tethered silver whales. The entire
population of Britain had been issued gas masks. Communal

and private air-raid shelters had been constructed everywhere. Every house had been provided with a hand-operated stirrup pump for fighting fires caused by incendiary bombs. Short-term prisoners had been released from jails all over the country and given five shillings, the equivalent then of about $1.25, as pocket money. More than 1.5 million children, tagged with brown-card luggage labels pinned to their clothing, had been evacuated from towns and cities to find instant foster parents in country districts. Historic treasures, including the coronation chair from Westminster Abbey, and art objects from galleries and museums, had been removed to safety, along with those animals from the London Zoo which had not already been put down. Around 140,000 patients had been moved or sent home as London's hospitals were cleared, ready for casualties.

As it happened, there were no bombs anywhere in Britain until November 13, when the Germans attacked the remote Shetland Isles. The first air raid on London did not take place until August 25, 1940. From then on, the blitz was real and dreadful enough, but the only bombs to explode anywhere in mainland Britain during 1939 were those planted by the IRA, which was then in the midst of a vicious campaign. Six weeks earlier, an IRA bomb had exploded in Coventry—the Midlands city that was to be the target in November 1940 of the Luft-waffe's most devastating single air raid—killing five people and injuring fifty.

No doubt this terrorist act was welcomed by Kent, who from the time of his arrival in England until his death on November 20, 1988, never had a good word to say about the British, their system, or any single Briton. The IRA, on the other hand, was lavishly praised in his unpublished memoirs:

The British prosecutors at Nuremberg should have blushed for shame when convicting Nazis of crimes infinitely less heinous than those committed over the centuries by the British against the Irish. May the heroic IRA boys in Maze prison in Belfast in 1981 accomplish the same ends as their forebears of 1919! The British have gotten away with centuries of genocide in Ireland continuing even to the present day [1981]. Perhaps that is because there never has been an appreciable number of Jews in the unhappy country [Ireland], therefore the powerful international Jewish propaganda organizations have never taken up the hue and cry of Genocide and Violation of

Human Rights with respect to British rule in Ireland, thus demonstrating that the vaunted Jewish "humanitarianism" is limited to
members of the tribe of Israel and is by no means as altruistic or
international in character as their leaders claim.

Admittedly, Kent wrote this many years later, but the basic
attitude and beliefs, regarding both the British and the Jews,
were already deeply ingrained in his character by 1939. They
go a long way toward explaining his actions, and certainly can
be seen to have played a great part in his disastrous choice of
friends in London.

As he had told Matthias, Kent checked in at the Cumberland
Hotel while he searched for more permanent accommodations. Two days later Matthias appeared at the reception desk,
rang through to his room, then went upstairs. He reappeared
in company with Kent, carrying a package measuring about ten
inches by sixteen. They walked through to the adjoining
lounge and had coffee, unaware that the two men in dark suits
who sat at the next table were from Scotland Yard's Special
Branch. When they finished their coffee and went on to the
restaurant of the Park Lane Hotel in Piccadilly for dinner, they
were followed by two different officers.

The Swedish police suspected Matthias of being an agent of
the Gestapo or the Abwehr, German military intelligence, and
had cabled the Yard of his departure from Stockholm for London. He was under surveillance from the moment he stepped
ashore until his departure several days later. By associating
with him, Kent had brought himself to the attention of the
Special Branch and of MI5, the Security Service. From that
moment, he was a marked man.

Although MI5 later told Ambassador Joseph Kennedy that
Matthias was a Gestapo agent—by which they presumably
meant that he worked for the SD, or Sicherheitsdienst, the SS
intelligence and security service—he remains a mystery figure.
Microfilmed records of the Gestapo, the SD, and the Abwehr
contain no trace of his name. If he was indeed a secret agent,
the most likely conclusion is that he was working for the Soviets, either the NKVD or the GRU, military intelligence.

. . . .

The London embassy that Tyler Kent joined in 1939 was headed by Ambassador Joseph Patrick Kennedy, a Boston multimillionaire and father of nine children. With his freckled face, red hair and a temper to match, his blue eyes constantly alight behind his glasses, Kennedy had enormous energy and abrasive charm and was an inveterate womanizer. The grandson of an Irish immigrant and son of an East Boston saloonkeeper and politician, Joe Kennedy had had a meteoric career. A mere two years after graduating from Harvard in 1910, he owned his own bank, and he made his first million dollars soon after.

He had been opposed to the First World War—his isolationist sentiment and "peace at any price" ideology were already evident—and was technically a draft dodger; he had worked in industry though three out of every five of his Harvard classmates went into the armed services. He was still under thirty and earning the huge salary, for those days, of $15,000 a year as assistant manager of Charles Schwab's Fore River shipyard in Quincy, Massachusetts, when he first met and crossed swords with the charismatic assistant secretary of the Navy, Franklin Delano Roosevelt.

The United States Navy had ordered four battleships for the Argentine Navy, and when payment was not forthcoming, Kennedy told Roosevelt he could not have the ships until the money was received. Not long afterward, four naval gunboats arrived, loaded with Marines, who forcibly took possession of the ship and turned it over to the Argentine sailors. The shipyard was eventually paid, but Kennedy was left in no doubt that he had met a tough trader. Although the two men were to be associated politically for much of their lives, they were never friends; in spite of his enormous wealth, the Irish-Catholic Kennedy was perhaps jealous of the patrician Roosevelt.

During the 1920s, Kennedy earned tens of millions of dollars. He was one of the few speculators who actually made money during the Crash of 1929 and the Depression that followed. As a sideline, he bought into the Hollywood motion picture industry, and acquired a beautiful mistress, the actress Gloria Swanson. In 1933, seeing that the fourteen-year alcoholic drought was about to end, he obtained exclusive importation rights for leading brands of Scotch, and at the same time secured permits to manufacture whiskey in America for "medicinal purposes"—whiskey he could sell for nonmedicinal consumption as soon as the Eighteenth Amendment, Prohibition, was repealed. The profits simply added to a growing fortune made from banking, shipbuilding, movies, real estate, oil, and diverse investments.

Kennedy was always active in Democratic politics, though he had flirted with the Republican Party in 1920, when he accepted membership of New England's oldest Republican organization, the Middlesex Club. His wife, Rose, daughter of the leading Massachusetts Democrat, John Francis (Honey Fitz) Fitzgerald, and his own father, an honest but powerful figure in the Massachusetts Democratic Party, soon brought him back where he belonged. In the 1924 presidential election, he supported Massachusetts-born Burton K. Wheeler, then a liberal Democrat, who became a senator from Montana. But in 1932, following the Depression and the debacle on Wall Street, he opted to back his old acquaintance Franklin Delano Roosevelt.

Kennedy gave $50,000 to Roosevelt's campaign, probably the largest single contribution, and raised another $150,000 from his affluent friends. He also accompanied FDR on the *Roosevelt Special*, the railroad train that took the candidate and his closest supporters on a thirteen-thousand-mile tour of the United States. In return, in 1934 he was appointed chairman of the Securities and Exchange Commission. It was an inspired choice: the commission was designed to watch Wall Street, and Kennedy, a Wall Street maverick, knew all the ins and outs of illegal stock manipulations. As the cynics said at the time, "Set a thief to catch a thief." Kennedy was indeed a sharp trader—many of his operations did not carry his own name, but that of Edward R. Moore, his friend and associate—but there has been no indication of anything illegal under the rules of the time. Had the SEC been in existence while he was playing the market, however, it might have been a different story. Kennedy served as chairman of the SEC for a year, and was then in limbo for two years, carrying on his political activities from his vast mansion.

For the presidential campaign of 1936, Kennedy provided more money, and a book, *I'm for Roosevelt*, ghost-written for him by the *New York Times* columnist Arthur Krock, who was paid $5000 for his five-week stint. Kennedy's reward this time was the chairmanship of the U.S. Maritime Commission in 1937, but Roosevelt, well aware of Kennedy's own presidential aspirations, would have preferred to remove him from the scene of political action to a post outside America. As it happened, Joe Kennedy had ideas of his own in this direction.

In the late summer of 1937, he learned that the ambassador to Great Britain, Robert W. Bingham, was dying of cancer in Baltimore's Johns Hopkins Hospital. Bingham's job, he decided, was the one for him. Apart from any other considerations, no fewer than four previous ambassadors to London's Court of St. James's—John Adams, James Monroe, Martin van Buren, and James Buchanan—had later become president.

The ambassadorship to the Court of St. James's has always been the most prestigious post in the American diplomatic service. In addition to furthering his own presidential ambitions, Kennedy hoped that the appointment would bring the social distinction he had been unable to secure for himself and his family among Boston's Brahmins. At Harvard, he had been denied admission to the college's socially superior clubs like the Fly and the Porcellian—Harvard had no fraternities—because of his Irish-Catholic background. In 1922, social snubs had led him to move the family from the Boston suburb of Brookline to the elite town of Bronxville in New York's Westchester County, where society was somewhat more open than on Beacon Hill. Now, he believed the London post would secure their entry into the very highest levels of British society.

One story of how Kennedy obtained the post provides an amusing example of his obstinacy and determination. He got word of his desire to Roosevelt via the president's son James, who had been a minor business associate of his for some years. But FDR at first refused to take the suggestion seriously—the idea of an Irish Catholic representing the United States in London seemed almost ludicrous. When James convinced him that Kennedy was serious Roosevelt asked his son to bring Kennedy to the White House. There, according to the younger Roosevelt, he said to an incredulous Kennedy, "Joe, take your pants down." Kennedy demurred. Roosevelt insisted. Finally, Kennedy removed his coat, slipped off his suspenders, and stood in shirt and undershorts, his trousers around his shoes. Thirty-nine years later, James vividly recalled the incident:

Father said, "Someone who saw you in a bathing suit once told me something I now know to be true. Joe, just look at your legs. You are just about the most bowlegged man I have ever seen. Don't you know that the ambassador to the Court of St. James's has to go through an induction ceremony in which he wears knee breeches and silk stockings? Can you imagine how you'll look? When photos of our new ambassador appear all over the world we'll be a laughingstock. You're just not right for the job, Joe."

Without batting an eye, Joe looked at him and said, "Mr. President, if I can get permission of His Majesty's government to wear a cutaway coat and striped pants to the ceremony, would you agree to appoint me?"

"Well, Joe," said Father, "you know how the British are about tradition. There's no way you are going to get permission, and I must name a new ambassador soon."

"Will you give me two weeks?" Joe asked.

Father agreed to that. Joe pulled up his pants and his dignity and went on his way, leaving Father chuckling contentedly.

Within two weeks, Joe was back with an official letter from the British government granting him the tradition-breaking permission. He'd called Father's bluff and Father laughed and agreed to name him ambassador to England.

To the experienced political observer, such a story may sound ingenuous to say the least. Certainly, the British Foreign Office took a much more jaundiced view, as expressed in a minute of March 11, 1940, by T. North Whitehead, who had completed a tour of duty in Washington the previous October:

One of the most important problems which Mr. Roosevelt has had to face during his eventful tenure of office has been the inefficiency, & even dishonesty, of many American civil servants, executive officers & politicians. This difficulty has been aggravated by the facts that the influence of an Administration is partly dependent upon a "spoils system" of appointing senior civil servants, & also Mr. Roosevelt's New Deal has involved an abnormal number of appointments. These appointments have, traditionally, to be farmed out amongst those groups with whom the Administration wishes to stand well. The East Coast Irish are such a group & are of great importance to a Democratic Administration. At the same time they represent about the most dirty group of politicians in the country. For this reason Mr. Roosevelt has been under the necessity of playing them down, to the great annoyance of the Irish. Particularly the most prominent Irish politician in recent times, Mr. Farley (at times Mayor of Boston & Governor of Massachusetts) has been held off important positions in the Administration to his great grief. [Whitehead was confusing James Farley with James Curley.] Mr. Farley controls large blocks of Irish votes by the simple process of buying them at the public expense. To pacify the East Coast Irish Mr. Kennedy was given his present appointment.

Whatever the reasons behind it, the American press was virtually unanimous in praise of the appointment. Kennedy received hundreds of letters from friends and well-wishers, but a letter from his friend Boake Carter, a reputable reporter, sounded an ominously prophetic note:

You are a man of courage. You possess that great faith that so many Irishmen have—the faith that no matter what he tackles, he can't be licked . . . but the job of Ambassador to London needs not only honesty, faith, sincerity and an abounding courage—it needs skill brought on by years of training. And that, Joe, you simply don't possess. Do not think of me as unkind in saying that. On the contrary, I'm trying to save you some heart aches. I do not condemn the trolley car driver because he cannot pilot a plane . . . I do not condemn Kennedy, the organizer, the businessman, because he is not a trained diplomatic surgeon. But I say this to you in all sincerity from the bottom of my heart—it takes a mighty big man to know when a job is too big for him . . . [Y]ou tempt all the Gods of the world in diving into the Court of St. James as a expert. Joe, in so complicated a job, there is no place for amateurs . . . [I]f you don't realize that soon enough, you are going to be hurt as you were never hurt in your life.

Carter, of course, was right. Save for family tragedies, the failure of his ambassadorship, leading to his being dropped from public service, was to be the most painful experience in Joe Kennedy's long life.

It was a warm, sunny March 1, 1938, when Ambassador Joseph Patrick Kennedy, accompanied by most of his personal staff, descended the gangplank of the S.S. *Manhattan* in Southampton. According to Page Huidekoper, an attractive, high-spirited Baltimore girl then working as Kennedy's personal assistant, there was a stunned look on the face of the embassy's most senior Foreign Service officer waiting there to greet them. "You see," she said later, "Herschel Johnson came from a distinguished Carolina family and he was frightfully proper and wildly protocol conscious . . . Having received a cable that all those wild Irish characters were turning up, he was terrified that they'd all be chewing gum."

Besides Huidekoper, Kennedy's personal staff, whose salaries were all paid out of his own pocket, were a bright and lively bunch. Arthur Houghton came from Hollywood's Motion Picture Association, the Hays office—"I have to have somebody over here I can have a laugh with," Kennedy wrote to Joseph Breen, head of the Association. "I hate like hell to take him away from you but, my God, London is cold, dreary and foggy during the winter." Houghton was to fulfill a role similar to the one later played by Dave Powers for President John Fitzgerald Kennedy, that of companion in pleasure. Harvey Klemmer, formerly a writer with Joe Kennedy at the Maritime Commission, would serve as speech writer. Harold Hinton, on leave from the *New York Times*, had been recommended by Kennedy's close friend Arthur Krock, the powerful *Times* Washington columnist. James Seymour, another friend from the Hollywood-Swanson era, was Kennedy's number two private secretary. Kennedy's principal private secretary and closest personal aide was Eddie Moore, his longtime Wall Street associate, who joined him later in March, sailing across the Atlantic with his wife, Mary, accompanying Rose Kennedy and the younger children.

In March 1938, the Kennedy family moved into the ambassador's thirty-six-room residence at 3 Prince's Gate, Knightsbridge, one of the smartest districts in London. The imposing six-story town house, its cream-painted stucco front embellished with elegant pillars and porticos, had been a gift to the United States from the financier J. P. Morgan. Built midway through Queen Victoria's reign, it stood facing Hyde Park, almost opposite the old Household Cavalry barracks, a little over a mile from Grosvenor Square. Sadly, the beautiful house and its immediate neighbors were destroyed by German bombs during the war, and an expensive but anonymous apartment block now stands in its place.

Almost at once, Joe Kennedy's hopes of social advancement were fulfilled. Shortly after their arrival, he and Rose spent a weekend with the king and queen at Windsor Castle, where he met two men with whom he would become vitally involved, Prime Minister Neville Chamberlain and Foreign Secretary Lord Halifax, a former viceroy of India. While dressing for dinner, Joe turned to his wife and summed up his satisfaction: "Well, Rose, this is a helluva long ways from East Boston!"

The following year, on March 12, 1939, Kennedy's star reached its highest point on the international scene when Roosevelt asked him to represent the United States at the coronation in Rome of Cardinal Eugenio Pacelli as Pope Pius XII.

The Kennedys were well received by both the press and public in Britain—indeed, at the start Kennedy's was possibly the most popular ambassadorial appointment ever. The children, in particular, were a smash hit. Along with the younger sons and daughters already with their parents there was Joe Jr., who had graduated from Harvard in June and taken a year off before starting law school, and Jack, who had obtained permission from Harvard to travel and observe diplomacy at first hand while continuing his studies in political science. By the summer of 1938 the entire family was in London. *Life*, published by Joe's friend Henry Luce, commented:

If Joseph Patrick Kennedy ever gets to be president he will owe almost as much to his children as to the abilities which earned him nine million. His bouncing offspring make the most politically ingratiating family since Theodore Roosevelt's. Whether or not Franklin Roosevelt thought of it beforehand, it has turned out that when he appointed Mr. Kennedy to be Ambassador to Great Britain he got eleven Ambassadors for the price of one. Amazed and delighted at the spectacle of an Ambassadorial family big enough to man a full-size cricket team, England has taken them all, including extremely pretty and young-looking Mrs. Kennedy, to its heart.

Joe made the front pages of Britain's popular newspapers within a few days of his arrival, when he made a hole-in-one at the 128-yard second hole at Stoke Poges Golf Club in south Buckinghamshire. A skeptical Joe Jr. and Jack cabled: "Dubious about the hole in one." From then on, he was seldom out of the society pages as the family plunged headlong into the social whirl, frequently traveling by private train to events like the Derby and Royal Ascot, yachting at Cowes, tennis at Wimbledon, and the Henley Regatta.

The ambassador and Rose were regular weekend guests at Cliveden, the stately home of Lord and Lady Astor overlooking the most beautiful reach of the Thames, near Maidenhead, acknowledged as the most influential political meeting place in the country between the wars. Virginia-born Nancy Astor, the first woman ever to sit in Parliament, presided over a group known as the Cliveden Set, which became synonymous with appeasement during the Hitler years.

Joe Kennedy was very much in sympathy with the attitudes of the Cliveden Set—as, indeed, were the majority of Britons until 1939. Most of Britain's leaders as well as millions of ordinary citizens had fought in the trenches in the First World War. They had an understandable horror of repeating the hell of battlefields like the Somme, where the British Army lost sixty thousand men between sunrise and sunset on the first day alone—fifteen thousand more than the U.S. Army lost during the whole war in Vietnam. Between July and November 1916, the dead from both sides on the Somme amounted to 1.15 million. No one wanted to see such carnage again, and at first Kennedy's outspoken support of appeasement seemed unremarkable, except that it was highly political. Ambassadors are not supposed to dabble in politics, but Joe Kennedy never seemed to understand this. It was a failing that would lead to his downfall.

The signs of impending trouble were evident from the first days of Kennedy's tenure, with his "coming out" speech to the Pilgrims Society, a group devoted to improving Anglo-American relations. When he submitted the text to the State Department for clearance, Hull deleted the sentence "The United States has no plan to seek or offer assistance in the event that war—and I mean, of course, a war of major scope—should break out in the world." He was left to offer a warning against an automatic assumption of American neutrality, but immediately went on to nullify this by also warning against any assumption that the United States would not remain neutral, which he believed was "just as dangerously conceived a misapprehension as the other."

During the crisis over Czechoslovakia in 1938, culminating in the Munich agreement under which Chamberlain and the

French prime minister, Edouard Daladier, gave in to Hitler's
territorial demands, Kennedy lent his unstinting support to
Chamberlain. Less than three weeks later, on October 18, he
made his most controversial speech, at the Navy League's Trafalgar Day celebration. It was the first time the honor of ad-
dressing the league had been conferred on an ambassador, and
Kennedy made the most of the opportunity to press his plea
"to do business with Hitler:"

It has long been a theory of mine that it is unproductive to both
democratic and dictator countries to widen the division now arising
between them by emphasizing their differences, which are self-appar-
ent. Instead of hammering away at what are regarded as irreconcil-
ables, they can advantageously bend their energies toward solving
their common problems and attempt to re-establish good relations
on a world basis. The democratic and dictator countries differ ideo-
logically, to be sure, but that should not preclude the possibility of
good relations between them. After all, we have to live together in the
same world, whether we like it or not.
   The nations of the world have always embraced many forms of
government, races, and religions. Surely we should be able to sur-
mount a difference in political philosophy.

Roosevelt was understandably irate when he read Kennedy's
speech, for it was a clear contradiction of his own doctrine of
"quarantining" the dictators with economic sanctions, declared in a famous and controversial speech on October 5,
1937. He was even more furious when he learned that it had
been vetted in advance by an ambivalent State Department.
   But Kennedy was unrepentant. He remained unmoved three
weeks later, when Hitler unleashed his thugs on the remaining
Jews in Germany and Austria on November 9 and 10 in the
most savage pogrom since the Middle Ages. During a night and
day of organized terror, at least 7500 Jewish-owned stores, 29
warehouses, and 171 houses were destroyed, 191 synagogues
were razed by fire and a further 76 physically demolished, 11
Jewish community centers, cemetery chapels, and similar
buildings were torched and another 3 gutted. More than thirty
thousand Jewish men were rounded up and thrown into con-
centration camps. At least 236 Jews, among them 43 women
and 13 children, were killed during the pogrom itself, with
more than 600 permanently maimed. Hundreds more died

over the next few weeks in the camps, bringing the death toll to around 2500. The Nazis derisively dubbed it Kristallnacht, the Night of Broken Glass.

After Kristallnacht, which took place in the full glare of international publicity, there could be no doubt in anyone's mind about the true nature of the Nazi regime. Roosevelt launched into a public rebuke at his five hundredth regular press conference on November 15, saying, "I myself could scarcely believe that such things could occur in a twentieth-century civilization." He also recalled Ambassador Hugh R. Wilson from Berlin, the strongest measure possible short of breaking off diplomatic relations.

Joe Kennedy, though appalled by the violence, said nothing to change the message he had given the German ambassador in London, Herbert von Dirksen, less than a month before. In a conversation on October 13, he had stressed his "understanding and sympathy" for Germany, and, according to Dirksen's report, "repeatedly emphasized the sympathy which the average American felt for the German, and which is greater than his liking for the average Englishman. Today, too, as in former conversations, Kennedy mentioned that very strong anti-Semitic tendencies existed in the United States, and that a large proportion of the population had an understanding of the German attitude toward the Jews." Kennedy did create a plan calling for mass resettlement of the German Jews—not in the United States, of course, but mainly in those areas of Africa which were uninhabited by whites.

As 1939 carried the world inexorably toward war, Kennedy continued to press for the west to do business with Hitler. He was not deterred by the Nazis' occupation of Czechoslovakia. But he was alarmed by Chamberlain's apparent desertion of the cause of appeasement and his inexplicable decision to guarantee Poland against Germany. Now, Kennedy's attitude, and his public utterances, began to change. The new outlook would destroy his popularity in Britain and eventually his diplomatic and political career. Convinced that war would come, he indulged in what the British regard as the unforgivable sin: defeatism.

Back in Washington on a visit in March 1939, Kennedy

walked into the State Department office of William Bullitt, then ambassador to France, during an interview Bullitt was giving to Joseph Medill Patterson, publisher of the anti-administration *New York Daily News,* and his Washington correspondent Doris Fleeson. Bullitt later recounted the ensuing events to Harold Ickes, secretary of the interior, and his wife, Jane, over dinner:

He [Kennedy] cheerfully entered into the conversation and before long he was saying that Germany would win, that everything in France and England would go to hell, and that his own interest was in saving his money for his children. He began to criticize the President very sharply, whereupon Bill took issue with him. The altercation became so violent that Patterson finally remarked that he suspected he was intruding, and he and Doris Fleeson left, but Joe continued to berate the President. Bill told him he was disloyal and that he had no right to say what he had before Patterson and Fleeson. Joe said that he would say what he Goddamned pleased—or words to that effect. Joe's language is very lurid when unrestrained, as it was on this occasion. Bill told him that he was abysmally ignorant on foreign affairs and hadn't any basis for expressing his opinion. He emphasized that so long as Joe was a member of the Administration he ought to be loyal—or at least keep his mouth shut. They parted in anger.

Joe did not keep his mouth shut, either in America or back in Britain. Nor did he alter his pro-German stance. When a group of powerful American corporations, including General Motors, Ford, Chase National Bank, Du Pont, and Standard Oil of New Jersey sent a GM vice president, James Mooney, to Berlin for financial talks, he took a personal interest in their plans. Mooney talked with Helmut Wohlthat, the Harvard-educated commissioner of Göring's Four-Year Plan, and Emil Puhl, German member of the Bank for International Settlements, about Germany's need for enormous loans of gold bullion. He then suggested to Kennedy that he meet with Wohlthat and Puhl in Paris. Roosevelt heard of Kennedy's plans and told him not to go, whereupon Kennedy arranged to meet Wohlthat in London on May 9. After their meeting, they agreed to get together again in Düsseldorf in September.

His opinions soon became a topic of conversation in London dining rooms. Sir Harold Nicolson noted in his diary for June 14, 1939:

Dine with Kenneth Clark. The Walter Lippmanns are there: also the Julian Huxleys and Winston Churchill as the guest of honour. Winston is horrified by Lippmann saying that the American Ambassador, Jo [sic] Kennedy, had informed him that war was inevitable and that we should be licked. Winston is stirred by this defeatism into a magnificent oration. He sits hunched there, waving his whisky-and-soda to mark his periods, stubbing his cigar with the other hand.

"It may be true, it may well be true . . . that this country will at the outset of this coming and to my mind almost inevitable war be exposed to dire peril and fierce ordeals. It may be true that steel and fire will rain down upon us day and night scattering death and destruction far and wide. It may be true that our sea communications will be imperilled and our food supplies placed in jeopardy. Yet these trials and disasters, I ask you to believe me, Mr. Lippmann, will but serve to steel the resolution of the British people and to enhance our will for victory. No, the Ambassador should not have spoken so, Mr. Lippmann; he should not have said that dreadful word. Yet supposing (as I do not for one moment suppose) that Mr. Kennedy were correct in his tragic utterance, then I for one would willingly lay down my life in combat, rather than in fear of defeat, surrender to the menaces of those most sinister men. It will then be for you, for the Americans, to preserve and to maintain the great heritage of the English-speaking peoples. It will be for you to think imperially, which means to think always of something higher and more vast than one's own national interests. Nor should I die happy in the great struggle which I see before me, were I not convinced that if we in this dear, dear island succumb to the ferocity and might of our enemies, over in your distant and immune continent the torch of liberty will burn untarnished and (I trust and hope) undismayed."

Before long, reports of defeatist statements made by Kennedy at private dinner parties and other social gatherings were flooding into the Foreign Office at such a rate that a special file was opened to accommodate them. At the same time, the antisubversion section of MI5 began keeping an eye on his activities and compiling its own file on the ambassador who was rapidly coming to be regarded as an enemy, although he represented a friendly power.

When war eventually came, on September 3, 1939, Kennedy found it hard to understand why his Cliveden Set friends, who had consistently supported an appeasement policy, were suddenly giving their total support to the war effort. He switched his own stance to advocating a negotiated peace—which might be regarded as nothing more than appeasement under another name—and even tried to persuade Roosevelt to act as a go-between. His reporting of the situation became more and more biased and unreliable as he did everything he could to bring Roosevelt around to his own point of view.

On September 11, in a "triple-priority" telegram "strictly confidential and most personal for the Secretary and the President," he told of an hour spent alone with the king and queen, during which the king had said that "the one problem which is desperately worrying him is that within a relatively brief period, possibly three or four weeks, Poland will have been liquidated by Herr Hitler and then certainly a proposal will be made by him to France and England to put a stop to this war and to arrive at some understanding."

Kennedy reported that the king had implied that the British government was extremely worried because they "know that if the war continues or if a Government is maintained on a war basis, it signifies entire social, financial, and economic breakdown and that after the war is over nothing will be saved." This was an accurate and honest summary of Kennedy's personal beliefs and fears about war. But it was a shamefully dishonest and inaccurate report of the position of the British government.

Kennedy added that he had also had a long talk with Sir Samuel Hoare, former foreign secretary, secretary of state for air and first lord of the Admiralty, and now home secretary and lord privy seal. Hoare, aptly known in British political circles as Slippery Sam, was also concerned about the possibility of peace calls from Hitler after a period of terror bombing by both sides. Pointing out that the Luftwaffe had twice as many bombers as the RAF, and would undoubtedly bomb British aircraft factories to halt production, he implied—or at least Kennedy inferred—that since no British government could openly negotiate for peace, the Americans might be able to save everyone's face by doing it for them.

"This occasion may never arise," he wrote, "but, having been quite a practical person all of my life, I am of the opinion that it is quite conceivable that President Roosevelt can maneuver himself into a position where he can save the world although I have not been of this opinion up to the present.''

Roosevelt squashed the proposal instantly, cabling back the same day that ''as long as the conditions which exist at present in Europe continue to exist, the Government of the United States see no occasion nor opportunity for the American President to initiate any peace move. Any move for peace which the United States Government initiated that would make possible a survival or a consolidation of a regime of force and of aggression would not be supported by the American people.''

In spite of Roosevelt's rejection, Kennedy went right on pressing for a negotiated peace, and redoubled his efforts to keep America from any involvement in the war. As he did so, his personal stock in Britain fell close to zero, and the much-prized invitations to social events dwindled to a mere trickle. Eighteen months after his triumphant arrival in London, his mission was doomed to failure. Kennedy's unpopularity both in Washington and in London hung like a pall over the embassy that Tyler Kent joined in October 1939.

Joe Kennedy was the first ambassador to occupy the recently acquired embassy complex in the heart of Mayfair at 1 Grosvenor Square, a red brick building now used by the Canadian high commission, opposite the site of the present U.S. embassy. Before then, the embassy had been housed in several buildings in Victoria Street, midway between the Houses of Parliament and Buckingham Palace. When the State Department decided to put all its London operations under one roof, it purchased from the Duke of Westminster's Grosvenor Estates the lease of a recently completed apartment block built on the site of three stately eighteenth-century houses that had been demolished in 1935.

The basement, first, and second floors were remodeled into suitable office spaces; the apartments on the upper floors, with the State Department's typical disregard for security, were rented out, with an entrance at number 3. Kennedy's spacious rooms were on the second floor, with French windows opening on to a small balcony overlooking the square. Kennedy detested the elegant pale blue décor: ''If a fairy didn't design this, then I never saw one in my life," he wrote acerbically to Jimmy Roosevelt.

London has always been the biggest United States embassy, a mark of the special relationship between the two great allies. In 1939, the staff, American and British, numbered about seventy-six, including thirteen Foreign Service officers, clerks, messengers, and other help. Soon after the outbreak of war, the number increased to about two hundred. The chancery pecking order, with salaries, was: Ambassador Kennedy ($17,000); Herschel V. Johnson, counselor of embassy ($9000); John G. Erhardt, first secretary and consul-general ($8200); Rudolf E. Schoenfeld, first secretary ($7200); William Butterworth, senior second secretary ($5000); four other second secretaries ($4500 each); Alexander V. Dye, commercial attaché ($9000); James Somerville, Jr., assistant commercial attaché ($5400)—he had the longest embassy service time, having been first appointed on February 23, 1935; Lloyd V. Steere, agricultural attaché ($7000); assistant agricultural attaché ($4000).

Tyler Kent, like most of the other clerks, was paid the standard salary of $2250, considerably less than the most junior Foreign Service officer, a discrepancy that, with his background and character, must have irked him considerably.

Consul General Erhardt supervised the activities of eighteen consuls and vice consuls in London and twenty-eight consuls and vice consuls in fourteen British cities, all of them save Birmingham ports of entry and departure.

In addition to the diplomats, there were also the service attachés and their staffs. The military attaché and military attaché for air was Brigadier General Sherman Miles, a West Point graduate of 1905, who became head of G-2, Army military intelligence, shortly after Kent's arrest. He was to play a major role in improving security in U.S. embassies, and it was he who saw to it that FBI Special Agent Louis Beck was sent to investigate the Moscow embassy in 1940. In London, Miles had four assistant military attachés for air and three assistant military attachés. The naval attaché and naval attaché for air was Captain Alan G. Kirk, U.S.N., with a staff of one assistant naval attaché and assistant naval attaché for air, and four assistant naval attachés. Alan Kirk later served as chief of operations for

the North Atlantic Fleet and as director of naval intelligence for
the years 1940 to 1941. From 1949 to 1951 he served as ambassador to the USSR.

Shortly after the start of the war, a special FBI agent was sent
to London under the cover of "legal attaché." His role was not
concerned with embassy security; he was to work with Scotland
Yard.

Tyler Kent quickly settled into the routine of coding and decoding, working round the clock, seven days a week, in eight-
hour shifts, a regimen initiated by Kennedy at the beginning of
September. At the end of his first week in London he moved
out of the Cumberland Hotel to a small flat, and a little later,
during the winter, moved again to a two-room flat at 47
Gloucester Place, about half a mile from the embassy, where
the landlady, Mrs. Welby, charged him £5 a week plus the cost
of cigarettes and London newspapers.

The code and file rooms where Kent worked were on the
embassy's second floor. The entry to the code room was
through the file room, which held a number of locked cabinets
containing encoded and decoded signals. The code room itself
housed a large desk with several typewriters and stacks of paper and carbon paper, and a safe, in which all code books were
supposed to be locked when they were not actually in use. Each
code clerk was given two keys, one to each room. Standard
operating procedure specified that a clerk should lock the door
of the file room behind him once he had entered, then unlock
the code room door and lock that again after he was inside.
Usually there were two clerks on duty at the same time, but
occasionally at night and on weekends or holidays there would
be only one.

Kent's assignment was to take all outgoing embassy signals,
usually bound for the State Department in Washington, and
encode them in the code or cipher designated by the sender.
With incoming signals, he was responsible for decoding the
messages and sending them on to their intended recipients.
Consequently, every signal that passed through the code room
in either direction—and these included signals from other embassies and legations in Europe, which were routed through

London for transmission to Washington—was either handled by Kent or was easily available to him.

The problems of slack security did not begin or end with Kent and his contemporaries. As recently as 1988, communications in the Moscow embassy were seriously compromised by the slackness of many Foreign Service officers and some ambassadors. In 1939, State Department communications security had been virtually nonexistent for many years. Even before the First World War, it was generally known that all its codes had been broken by any nation with code-breaking facilities. Toward the end of that war, an Army code clerk, James Thurber, the future *New Yorker* cartoonist and satirist, noted that most State Department codes dated back to the era of Hamilton Fish, secretary of state under President Ulysses S. Grant in the 1870s.

One incident from before the First World War illustrates perfectly the general attitude. The American minister in Bucharest couldn't be bothered with twirling the dial of the legation safe, so he kept his code book under his mattress. One day he discovered it had gone; reports filtered back to him that it had been taken to the Czar's Foreign Ministry. Too embarrassed to inform Washington, he simply waited until he had accumulated a large stack of signals, then took a train to Vienna, where he decoded them and answered them by using the embassy's code books.

In the late 1930s, the embassy in Rome used a safe with keys rather than a combination. An Italian national serving as an internal messenger made a wax impression of the lock, had keys made, and stole the code books, which soon reached the Berlin headquarters of the Abwehr. Field Marshal Erwin Rommel used these stolen code books to his advantage against American troops in north Africa in 1942 and 1943.

In Kent's time, State Department codes were named by the colors of the code book bindings: red, blue, green, and so on, or by letters. The most used was "gray," which had been adopted toward the end of the First World War and was well known throughout the international diplomatic community.

Kent himself described the codes then in use, in a letter dated February 16, 1964, to Joseph P. Kennedy's biographer, Richard J. Whalen:

The codes used in the U.S. diplomatic service in 1939 and up to May 20th, 1940 (to my knowledge), were as follows:

> Gray code—non-confidential
> Brown code—confidential
> A, B, C, D, codes—all confidential

My recollection is that D code was the most confidential at that time, although my memory on that point is not positive.

In the case of the 4 letter codes, the tables were changed every 3 or 4 months, that is to say, the arrangements of the letters in the five-letter groups were changed. In the case of the codes, the text was encoded twice; once in a basic five-letter group which did not change, and then a second time in another set of five-letter groups which changed as I indicated above.

For some reason, Kent did not include the strip cipher, which was introduced in 1939 and was then considered the department's most secure system. Unlike a code, in which a group of letters or numbers, or indeed words and phrases used with different meanings, represent other words, phrases, or even complete sentences, a cipher changes each letter or number in a message. At its most simple, letters of the alphabet are moved backward or forward—the letter B may stand for C, O may stand for P. At its most complex, the letters are jumbled in an apparently random fashion, often several times and changing constantly so that no letter ever represents the same letter twice. During the 1930s, sophisticated machines were developed, such as the German Enigma and the Japanese Purple, that were able to create ciphers so complex, they could be broken only by the invention of computers. Although the American Army and Navy started using machines, the State Department did not begin to use ciphers, as opposed to codes, until 1939, and even then continued to rely on manual systems. The result was that the strip cipher proved only slightly more difficult to break than the color and letter codes.

Although each embassy had its own huge safe, usually located in the chancery basement because of its weight, military and naval attachés preferred to keep confidential material in their own safes, just as they preferred to use their own codes, ciphers, and transmission facilities wherever possible.

. . . .

During his time in Moscow, Kent had acquired the habit of stealing copies of all the signals that passed through the code room. In London, he continued the practice. Although security in the embassy was better than it had been in Moscow, it was still child's play for Kent to help himself to top secret messages. "One of the ways in which this was done," he recounted gleefully in an interview in 1982, "was simply that I took copies which were surplus and were to be discarded, burned in an incinerator. That was one source. Another source was that Ambassador Kennedy was having copies of important political documents made for his own private collection, and part of my function was to make these copies. And it was quite easy to slip in an extra carbon."

With no Tanya on hand to share the contents with, Kent went on harvesting the embassy's signal traffic for various reasons. Partly, no doubt, it was for his own satisfaction, like that of any collector of stamps or books or paintings. It must also have been partly to nourish his need to possess secret knowledge and thus assert, if only to himself, his superiority over those lesser beings who were in authority over him. But it is impossible to avoid the thought that he may still have been collecting information for the NKVD. Though there is no evidence that he ever passed anything to them directly in London, it is known that several of his friends and associates outside the embassy were Soviet agents or collaborators, willing or unwilling.

Among the documents Kent stole were messages from MI5 to the FBI concerning a man named Armand Labis, who also used the name Feldman and other aliases. Although they did not say so in any of these messages, MI5 suspected that Labis was in fact Kent's NKVD contact man and paymaster. Labis, a Russian jew, was essentially a link man and a channel for money. He operated under commercial cover, initially with the Far Eastern Fur Company, of Shanghai and London, but in the mid-thirties, MI5 discovered that he was working in North America, supposedly for the Soviet Petroleum Company and for the trading and shipping organizations Amtorg and the notorious Morflot. His specialties included the supplying of forged passports and green cards, which gave permanent resident status to aliens in the United States. In 1938, Labis left

America for Britain. He was picked up after Kent's arrest and interned in Canada, where he remained after the war, living in Montreal.

MI5 was unable to prove a direct link between Kent and Labis, though the suspicion was strong enough, when added to Kent's other connections, to lead it to classify him as a Soviet agent. What is certain, however, is that after reading all the signals traffic from Ambassador Bullitt in Paris and Anthony Drexel Biddle, Ambassador in Warsaw, added to what he already knew about Laurence Steinhardt's messages from Moscow, Kent concluded that America's senior diplomats wanted war with Germany. And as he collected more of Churchill's telegrams to Roosevelt, he decided that the president and the first lord of the Admiralty were plotting to bring the United States into the war.

Despite his own travels, Kent had become an isolationist and noninterventionist. He began considering how he could pass on to the American public what he believed. The best and most effective way was through Congress, but for this he would need all the evidence he could lay his hands on. At last he had a good reason for collecting. The 1940 presidential election would give him an opportunity to change the course of history, and in so doing to ensure himself a place in the halls of fame. What a blow that would be against all those who had tried to belittle him and deny him his proper place in society.

FIVE

"The Best Caviar in All London"

IN ADDITION to his belief that Churchill and Roosevelt were intent on dragging a reluctant America into war, Kent also drew a second conclusion from the correspondence of the two leaders—a conclusion every bit as erroneous but every bit as explosive as the first. He decided that the president and the first lord of the Admiralty were plotting together to unseat the peace-loving Chamberlain and put the warlike Churchill into 10 Downing Street in his place. Countering this called for action in Britain—a difficult proposition for an American embassy employee, especially under the restrictions imposed for the war. However, Kent soon found useful allies in a White Russian refugee and a member of Parliament, both with extreme right-wing and anti-Semitic views.

By now, Kent had largely given up his hopes of a Foreign Service career, or of a translator's position in Washington. Not wishing to spend the rest of his life as a clerk, he turned back to thoughts of securing a newspaper job in Moscow, where his fluency in both oral and written Russian would be useful. With this in mind, he cultivated his contacts in the press world, keeping in touch with Spencer Williams, former Moscow correspondent for the *Manchester Guardian,* now living in London, and seeking out Ferdinand Kuhn, of the *New York Times* London bureau, and Hiroshi Clarke Kawakarni of Japan's Domei news agency. Through the firm of W. H. Smith, the British newspaper suppliers, he subscribed to *Pravda* and *Izvestia.* And in order to keep up his conversational Russian, he planned to make contact with London's White Russian community.

He was helped in this by Mrs. May Straker, the Viriginia-born wife of a Russian chemist who was now a naturalized British subject. Mrs. Straker, who got in touch with Kent after seeing a brief note in the diplomatic column of *The Times* announcing his arrival from Moscow, adds another question mark to our knowledge of his relations with the Russians. Very early in their acquaintanceship it transpired that she had been a schoolmate of Kent's mother, but since she apparently did not know it at the time, this could not have been her reason for contacting him. So why did she? Did she simply want to hear the latest news of life in Russia? Or was she instructed to put him in touch with the Soviet-influenced members of the White Russian community?

Many Russian refugees who had fled at the time of the revolution still had relatives in the Soviet Union or depended for their income on business ties there. Such people were easy prey for the NKVD and its predecessors, which made a habit of persuading many of them to carry out low-grade espionage tasks under threat of reprisals against their families or friends in the Soviet Union. In this way, some of the most unlikely prospects, often violently anticommunist in their beliefs, became reluctant collaborators with Soviet spymasters in their host countries.

Whatever Mrs. Straker's motives, we do know that she introduced Kent to the White Russian community, many of whose members were known to be under Soviet influence, and that, having done so, she never saw him again. Again, there may be a simple explanation—perhaps she found she did not like him, or he may have offended her in some way—but it does seem odd that an old friend of his mother's should neither have seen him socially again, nor, later, even have visited him in prison when his mother was desperately worried about him.

The White Russian community into which May Straker introduced Kent was smaller and less colorful than its counterparts in Paris, Berlin, or Shanghai. Informal social activity centered on the Russian Tea Room, a café-restaurant at 50 Harrington Gardens, immediately opposite the South Kensington tube station. With polished wooden furniture, paneled walls, and an open fireplace, it looked, said an Englishwoman of the time, like "the sort of café you could visit unescorted without jeopardizing your reputation." Although it served piping-hot lemon tea from a huge silver samovar in Russian-style glasses instead of the traditional English teacup, the name Tea Room was something of a misnomer, since it was also described as serving the finest champagne and "the best caviar in all London," together with vodka and Russian dishes like riaptchiki.

The proprietors were Admiral Nikolai Wolkoff and his aristocratic wife, Vera, a former maid of honor to the Czarina. The admiral, an erect, white-haired figure, sporting imperial whiskers and a Vandyke beard, had once been the Czar's aide-de-camp, and was the Imperial Russian naval attaché in London at the time of the Bolshevik revolution. Stranded in London with no money and no prospects, he had been set up in the café business by well-to-do British friends.

The Wolkoffs had three daughters, Anna, Alexandra, and Kyra, and one son, Gabriel, who had made a good career in business. They had become naturalized British subjects in the summer of 1935. The most dominant personality of the four was undoubtedly thirty-six-year-old Anna, who liked to call herself "de Wolkoff," in the style of a French aristocrat.

Born in St. Petersburg in 1903, Anna was short, dark-haired, and dumpy. Two photographs published in the *Sunday Express* of November 10, 1940, give two different impressions of her appearance: in one, wearing Auxiliary Fire Service uniform, she looks stern and utterly unfeminine; the other, taken sometime earlier, shows a not unattractive woman. According to the MI5 agent Joan Miller, Anna "displayed the intensity of manner which is often associated with persons of a fanatical disposition," and a Russian princess who was prominent in émigré affairs recalls that Anna's aggressive manner made her very unpopular among the White Russian community; at charity meetings she "wore a monocle and banged the table."

Anna's most violent outbursts were reserved for Jews and communists. Like Hitler, she equated one with the other, considering Bolshevism to be a Jewish plot and blaming Jewish revolutionaries such as Leon Trotsky (born Lev Bronstein) and Karl Radek for the downfall of the Russian Empire and her family's misfortunes. She felt particular resentment that, after a lifetime of distinguished service to his country, her father should end up running a café. But her attitude to the Jews went back way beyond Hitler and Trotsky. "I was brought up on that, ever since I was a child," she testified at her trial. "Every Russian, especially of my standing, hates Jews. I was literally suckled on it."

At the outbreak of war, Gabriel objected strongly to the anti-Semitic activities of Anna and their father, and even wrote to the admiral urging him to give up attacking the Jews because of the effects such attacks might have on the war effort. His appeal was wasted. Both Anna and the admiral considered that Britain's entry into the war was a grave mistake engineered by the Jews and their supporters, and that Chamberlain should accept Hitler's peace overtures. Although they were in no way anti-British, they were vocally pro-German.

Shortly before the start of the war, Anna had taken a holiday on the Continent while recuperating from an operation. In particular, she had wanted to visit those parts of Czechoslovakia which had been grabbed by Hitler in March. She stayed with the Princess of Lichtenstein and was to have met Konrad Henlein, the Sudeten Nazi leader, but had to be content with his deputy, Karl-Hermann Frank, when Henlein was called to Berchtesgaden to confer with Hitler. On her return, she wrote a report for her friends in Britain displaying her profound dislike for the Czechs, and saying that she thought Hitler had been entirely justified in seizing what remained of Czechoslovakia after the Munich settlement. Her dislike also extended to the Poles, who she believed had been made hopelessly arrogant by Chamberlain's unconditional guarantee: this, she said, had been very ill advised, since without it the Poles might have fallen in with Hitler's wishes without a fight.

"She took herself and her causes very seriously indeed," wrote Joan Miller. "It was difficult to get close to her, as she was filled with mistrust, but once she'd accepted you, Anna was capable of impulsive and generous acts. In spite of her upbringing, she was a good cook, and this skill, I imagine, helped to keep the restaurant in business."

Anna's principal occupation, however, was not the restaurant but haute couture: in her late twenties she had established a dress design salon in Conduit Street, just off Bond Street. The business was very successful—she even had a color named after her, "Anna Blue." Her clientèle included the Duchess of Gloucester and Wallis Warfield Simpson, the future Duchess of Windsor. Her introduction to royalty may have originated in her youth, for she is said to have attended a private school where she became friends with Princess Marina of Greece, who married King George V's youngest son and became Duchess of Kent.

The winter of 1939–1940 was the coldest in the British Isles for many years. On January 17, the Thames in London froze over for the first time since 1888; ten days later, the worst storms of the century swept the country. Amid the blizzards, public services were strained to the limit and transport was almost halted; on one occasion the Edinburgh-London express train pulled into Euston station twenty-four hours late on a journey of 405 miles. With fuel shortages, power supply difficulties, and the introduction of food rationing on January 8—weekly limits of four ounces of butter, twelve ounces of sugar, four ounces of uncooked bacon or ham, and three and a half ounces of cooked ham per person—life in Britain was less than comfortable, Kent, however, was pleasantly warmed and cheered by the fireplace in the Russian Tea Room and the company— and sometimes the beds—of his new friends.

Anna Wolkoff quickly became the center of his new social life. There is no hard evidence that she and Kent were lovers, though with his tomcat morals and obsession with sex it is hard to believe that he did not add her to his list of paramours. Certainly, she visited his room on many occasions, and when the weather cleared they spent frequent weekends together in the country or on the south coast. To make this possible, he had bought her car from her, or at least had the registration transferred to his name, since as a diplomat he was entitled to special gasoline coupons while civilians were banned from using their cars and had been ordered to lay them up for the duration of the war.

It was through Anna Wolkoff that Kent met Irene Danischewsky, at an Anglo-Russian reception in late December 1939 or early January 1940. A beautiful, curvaceous redhead, she was born Irene Mairinov twenty-nine years earlier in Moscow, but had been brought to England, at the age of four, at the outbreak of the First World War. She was now the wife of thirty-five-year-old Alexander Danischewsky, a naturalized British subject born in Russia, a director of the White Sea and Baltic Trading Company, which imported and refined tar, pitch, turpentine, and pine oil from the Soviet Union at its works in Managers Street, Limehouse, alongside the West India Docks. This was a family company founded in the early years of the century by Israel Danischewsky and his son Paul, which operated through Leningrad and Archangel and, later, out of Bergen in Norway.

Irene soon became Kent's mistress. Although she could rarely get away from her husband in the evenings, she was able to go to Kent's flat during the daytime, when he was working the midnight-to-8:00 shift at the embassy. For Kent, this was extremely convenient; he could see Anna and his other women friends in the evenings when working the shift from 8:00 A.M. to 4:00 P.M., and at night when he finished at midnight. Irene remained blissfully ignorant of the others until after Kent's arrest, when she was told of the competition by Inspector Pearson. Even then she refused to believe it, and remained Kent's most devoted friend, visiting him in prison during his entire period of confinement and corresponding regularly with his mother. One curious factor about Kent's relationship with Irene, considering his political and racial attitudes, is that the Danischewskys were Jewish. Kent's bigotry, like that of many men throughout history, seems to have stopped at the bedroom door.

. . . .

The people Kent met through Anna Wolkoff were by no means all Russians. Because of their former standing in the diplomatic community, the Wolkoffs had a limited entrée into London's society. Among their friends was Don Francesco Maringliano, Duke del Monte, a lieutenant colonel of cavalry and assistant military attaché in the Italian embassy, described by Kent as "about forty-five, shortish, thickset, dark hair and complexion." Anna and an English friend named Enid Riddell took Kent to meet him over dinner at L'Escargot, then the most fashionable French restaurant in Soho. After dinner, they moved on as guests of del Monte to the Embassy Club in Bond Street, which had been the Duke of Windsor's favorite night spot when he was Prince of Wales and the world's most eligible bachelor.

Kent was naturally delighted to associate with someone of del Monte's standing both as an aristocrat and as a diplomat. And del Monte must have been delighted to associate with Kent, but for very different reasons. Italy did not enter the war until June 10, 1940; despite Mussolini's friendship with Hitler, it remained officially neutral until then. The Italians still maintained embassies in countries that were at war with Germany, and, together with Spain and other pro-Nazi nations, were able to help their Axis partner by providing valuable information on those countries. As assistant military attaché, del Monte's primary function was collecting intelligence. And Kent, of course, was in a position to supply high-grade confidential material.

The connection with del Monte was to prove fatal to Kent's ambitions. But it was another friend of Anna's who was to have the greatest influence on Kent's future, and who must have seemed the most valuable contact he could have made for revealing the supposed Churchill-Roosevelt plot to unseat Neville Chamberlain.

Captain Archibald Henry Maule Ramsay was introduced to Anna in late 1938 or early 1939. Born in 1894, Ramsay, a slim, elegant man of medium height with a hawklike nose and trim mustache, his remaining hair sleeked back with brilliantine, was the Conservative member of Parliament for the Scottish constituency of Peebles and Southern Midlothian. He came from one of Scotland's oldest and most distinguished families: he was the eldest son of Lieutenant Colonel Henry L. Ramsay of the political department of the India Office, the grandson of General Sir Henry Ramsay, KCSI, CB, and a great-nephew of the twelfth Earl of Dalhousie.

Educated at Eton and Sandhurst, he was posted to the 2nd Battalion of the Coldstream Guards and in 1916 was severely wounded in France, where he was awarded Britain's third highest medal, the Military Cross. He was invalided out of the army in 1919. While recuperating on leave in London, he had married the Honourable Ismay Lucretia Mary Preston, daughter of Jenico, fourteenth Viscount Gormanston, and widow of Lord Ninian Crichton-Stuart, MP. They set up their London home in an elegant Victorian house, 24 Onslow Square, in a fashionable area of South Kensington, though Ramsay preferred when possible to stay in the family's Kellie Castle in Arbroath, Scotland, with its excellent shooting and fishing.

From the mid-1920s onward, Ramsay established himself as one of Britain's most virulent anti-Semites, speaking regularly at Rotary Clubs and similar gatherings around the country. While he expounded on the evils of communism in a standard speech entitled "Red Wings over Europe," he continually stressed the Jewish aspects of Bolshevism. At the same time, for good measure, he also accused Jewish millionaires of taking over Britain.

The depth of Ramsay's anti-Semitism was demonstrated in 1940, when he appeared as a witness at Anna Wolkoff's trial and was questioned by the solicitor general, Sir William Jowitt.

"You believe, do you not—you may be right or wrong; I am not concerned to argue it—that this country is absolutely under the heel of the Jews?" Sir William asked.

"I do," Ramsay replied firmly.

"You believe it has been under the heel of the Jews, at any rate since before the last war?"

"Yes."

"And you believe the Jews were responsible for provoking both the last war and this war?"

"Yes."

"And you believe that the Jews are embarked upon a conspiracy to try to destroy and discredit the Christian faith?"

"Yes."

"And that as one of the steps in that conspiracy they want to bring about universal chaos and disorder?"

"Yes."

"And that is why it is that they are anxious to promote wars wherever they go?"

"That is one of the reasons."

"Is there any other reason?"

"Making money."

"And you regard it as a very great disaster that a Christian nation, with great traditions such as our nation has, should be under the heel of the Jews?"

"Of the first magnitude."

The catalogue of hate sounded so extreme as to be incredible, coming from a man in Ramsay's position. To make certain he could not be accused of putting words into the witness's mouth, Sir William gave him chance to challenge any misrepresentation.

"I have tried to state your views fairly," he said, "and I hope I have succeeded."

"You have—most fairly," Ramsay acknowledged.

Ramsay's loudly stated opinions did not damage his political career—indeed, they may even have enhanced his prospects at a time of economic disaster. In the 1931 general election, he contested Peebles for the Conservative and Unionist Party and inflicted a devastating defeat on the sitting Labour MP, J. C. Westwood, taking 65 percent of the total vote. Westwood's predecessor, incidentally, had been Sir Donald Maclean, father of the Donald Maclean who defected to the Soviet Union with Guy Burgess in the great spy scandal of 1953.

Ramsay was not an outstanding success in Parliament—his most notable post was as a member of the Potato Marketing Board—but when the Spanish Civil War broke out, he became Britain's premier opponent of the antifascist International Brigade, constantly asking leading questions about it in the House. He claimed that the British press was presenting "General Franco's enemies as liberal and Protestant reformers, instead of the anti-God revolutionaries they were."

As a result of his pro-Franco agitation, he was offered the chairmanship of the United Christian Front Committee. In that role he sent out thousands of letters to leading Britons, apprising them of what he saw as the true facts concerning the war in Spain and urging Christians of all communities to join in combating the "Godless Red Terror that threatened Spain then, and . . . all Europe, Britain included." He persuaded a number of other organizations to cooperate with him in anticommunist work, including the National Citizens Union, the British Empire League, the Order of the Child, the British Israel World Federation, and the Economic League. They met in a committee room in the House of Commons, but other MPs, even those of his own party, kept well clear.

During this period, Ramsay introduced two bills that outraged the political opposition, some of his own party, and large segments of the press. The first was the Aliens Restriction (Blasphemy) Bill, which would have prevented aliens residing in Britain from attending international communist congresses. The second, the Companies Act Amendment Bill of December 13, 1938, would have made it compulsory for shares "in newspapers and news agencies to be held in the actual names of the holders, instead of the names of nominees, a common practice among British publishers." On the face of it, this second bill was an admirable attempt to introduce openness and accountability; a similar law (Title 39 U.S. Code Section 233, Section 34.38) had long been in effect in the United States. But one must suspect that Ramsay's motives were more concerned with revealing Jewish interests than with defending the freedom of the press.

Ramsay was a prominent supporter of the Anglo-German Fellowship, a respectable organization that had many distinguished figures among its members—as well as Kim Philby and Guy Burgess, who joined in order to establish their conservative credentials. Ramsay was also a founder member of the Link, a less wholesome and more extreme association to promote Anglo-German friendship. Within two years, the Link had grown to thirty-five active branches, with a total membership of 4329. Its official organ was the *Anglo-German Review*, an overtly pro-Nazi publication that was a mouthpiece for Hitler's propaganda minister, Joseph Goebbels.

Even the Link was not extreme enough to satisfy Ramsay, however, and in May 1938 he formed his own association, the

Right Club. Unlike the Anglo-German Fellowship and the Link, both of which operated openly, the Right Club was from the beginning a strictly secret society. As such, it had a certain schoolboy flavor to it; its emblem, designed by Ramsay himself, was an eagle disposing of a viper, representing "the communist and Jewish element in British society." This was made into a silver badge, which was given to each of the members, about 100 men and 150 women, in a red leather case. There were four classes of membership—the highest was "warden"; the lowest, "fellow"—depending on the entrance fee paid. The warden fee was £25, the equivalent of about $125, a substantial amount in prewar Britain.

The list of members, which was seized by MI5 at the time of Kent's arrest, has recently been discovered in a London lawyer's safe. One of the founding members—number eight on the list—was William Joyce, the American-born Irishman who traveled to Germany shortly before the war to offer his services to Hitler and found fame, or infamy, as Lord Haw-Haw, broadcasting Nazi propaganda to wartime Britain. He was hanged as a traitor at Wandsworth Prison in 1946. Among the others were the Duke of Wellington and three other peers of the realm, including Lord Redesdale, father of the celebrated Mitford sisters, plus four sons of peers, the Russian Prince Galitzine and no fewer than twelve members of Parliament. The Duke of Wellington, a descendant of the legendary Iron Duke who defeated Napoleon at Waterloo, was chairman of a committee that coordinated the activities of pro-German, anticommunist, and anti-Semitic organizations like the Right Club, the Link, and the Anglo-German Fellowship.

Kent, of course, was an enthusiastic member, though, strangely, his name does not appear on the list. But the most active and most committed member, after Ramsay himself, was undoubtedly Anna Wolkoff, who described herself variously as Ramsay's aide-de-camp and his political secretary. Anna was secretary of the club, and its headquarters was in her flat above the Tea Room, reached through the restaurant via a door to the left of the entrance, opening on to a narrow staircase.

In retrospect, the activities of the Right Club seem harmless enough, even slightly ridiculous. But in those politically unsophisticated years, with the Nazi threat growing stronger every day, it was taken very seriously by the security services. Its original intentions were to infiltrate the British Establishment, fan the existing prejudice against the Jews and hatred of communism, and promote an understanding with Hitler. Until September 1939, those ambitions were all perfectly legal, however distasteful they were to those who did not share the members' views.

With the coming of war, the situation changed completely. The Anglo-German Fellowship collapsed, and the Link was immediately disbanded. "Naturally, we closed down on the declaration of war," its chairman, Sir Barry Domvile, said. "That was essential, the King's enemies became our enemies. We had done our best for better Anglo-German relations and with the outbreak of hostilities there was no more to be done. All the branches are closed." The Right Club, however, remained very much alive, though it went underground, and was an obvious vehicle for the genuine menace of fifth-column subversion as it turned its attention to ways, all of which had become strictly illegal, of obstructing the war effort.

Throughout the autumn and winter of 1939 and into the spring of 1940, groups of well-to-do right-wing extremists gathered behind the blackout curtains of Anna's flat to lament the state of the country and to plot ways of persuading the government to agree to peace terms with Hitler. There were frequent discussions, led by Anna, about what to do if this goal failed and about which of their opponents should be hanged from lampposts when the Germans invaded.

Something of the tone of Right Club meetings can be gauged from the poems and songs composed by Ramsay. His favorite, apparently intended to be sung to Elgar's tune used for "Land of Hope and Glory," ran as follows:

> Land of dope and Jewry,
> Land that once was free;
> All the Jews praise thee,
> While they plunder thee.
>
> Poorer still and poorer
> Grow thy true-born sons,

Faster still and faster
They're sent to feed the guns.

Land of Jewish finance,
Fooled by Jewish lies,
In press and books and movies
While our birthright dies.

Longer still and longer
Is the rope they get
But, by the God of battles,
T'will serve to hang them yet.

The original of this screed, written in pencil on House of Commons letterhead, has the note "Composed on the day Great Britain declared war on Germany."

This and other verses in a similar vein were printed and distributed in public places by members of the club. But their main efforts went into the "sticky-back campaign." As Joan Miller recounted, "They used to sneak about late at night in the blackout. groping for smooth surfaces on which to paste the pro-German, anti-Semitic notices they carried." The most used of those proclaimed, simply, "This is a Jews' war." Other even more childish practices included using greasepaint to deface ARP (Air Raid Precautions) posts, casualty stations, and posters and—most daring of all—going to cinemas to boo and jeer at Winston Churchill when he appeared on newsreels.

However ludicrous all this seems to us fifty years later, the Right Club took these activities in deadly earnest. Anna even issued elaborate instructions for members to ensure the success of the sticky-back campaign:

Walk on dark side of road. Prepare your sticker in advance; it will stick the better and you will not miss your object. Don't stop walking while sticking if possible. Look out for dark doorways; Police usually stand in them at night. Stick on Belisha Beacons [pedestrian crossing posts], lamp posts, Church Boards, Hoardings, Bus Stops, Phone Kiosks. Don't stick on walls as the glue is not strong enough for rough surfaces.

Use the grease paint on: Notices indicating next casualty station,

A.R.P. Notices, Advertisements on Hoardings, White or pale painted walls and columns. As danger signal talk of the weather, for instance. Colder from the East means someone is approaching from the right. Read your road indication by torch light and memorize at least two streets in advance.

Take turns in sticking, look-out and route reading. As we leave this house we do so in pairs at a few seconds' interval and are strangers until we meet at midnight at Paradise Walk.

Surely no schoolgirl ever organized an illicit midnight excursion from the dorm with greater seriousness or more relish. Paradise Walk, incidentally, is a small side street just off the Chelsea Embankment near the Royal Hospital, home of the Chelsea Pensioners, about a mile south of Anna's flat.

A larger and more significant sticker that Anna posted up around London was headed "New Year's Resolution." It read:

Your New Year's Resolution. We appeal to the working men and women of Great Britain to purchase the new Defence Bonds and Savings Certificates thus keeping the war going as long as possible. Your willing self-sacrifice and support will enable the War profiteers to make bigger and better profits and at the same time save their wealth from being conscripted. Lend to defend the rights of British manhood to die in a foreign quarrel every twenty-five years. Don't be selfish. Save for shells and slaughter. Forget about the slums, the unemployed, the old-age pensioners and other social reforms your money could be invested in. Just remember that your savings are much more wisely spent in the noble cause of death and destruction. Be patriotic. Come on, the first million pounds.

Kent claimed at his trial that he had not met Ramsay until March 1940, but that is difficult to believe, because he had been close friends with Anna since at least the end of 1939 and had attended Right Club meetings. What is certain is that they got on well together. They must have found that they had a great deal in common, in spite of Kent's lowly position in the embassy: both were immaculate dressers, fond of good clothes; both came from good backgrounds; and their political outlook was almost identical.

Anna went often to Kent's flat—she had her own key, and was sometimes there alone, using his typewriter—and before long Ramsay was a frequent visitor, too. Watchers noted that Ramsay was also left alone in the flat at times and also used the typewriter. Kent showed both of them the documents he had collected from the embassy, and allowed them to browse through them as they pleased. He was delighted to find that Ramsay agreed with his own conclusions.

Two documents in particular caught Ramsay's interest: messages from Churchill to Roosevelt sent on January 29 and February 29, 1940, concerning shipping. The first read:

PERSONAL AND SECRET FOR THE PRESIDENT FROM NAVAL PERSON
I gave orders last night that no American ship should, in any circumstances, be diverted into the combat zone round the British Isles declared by you. I trust this will be satisfactory.

This message, which reported one of the few decisions made by Churchill without proper consultation with the War Cabinet, was modified next day:

I trust that the information I gave you last night about the orders sent to British ships will not be made known until measures have been concerted which will remove appearance of discrimination. It has been pointed out to me that my signal to fleet can only be maintained if measures are taken to ensure in advance of their departure that United States ships carry no objectional [sic] cargo. Moreover, in exceptional cases it may be necessary to divert United States ships if we have definite ground for suspicion against them. It would be most helpful if some arrangement could be reached with Lothian on these lines and meanwhile all publicity avoided.

These telegrams referred to the stopping and searching of neutral ships by the Royal Navy, to ensure that they were not carrying "contraband" cargoes for Germany—goods and materials that would help the German war effort. Suspect vessels were escorted to a British port, where they were searched from stem to stern before being allowed to proceed. The German Navy carried out similar stop-and-search operations: in one celebrated case in October 1939, the U.S. freighter *City of Flint*, bound for Liverpool and Glasgow from New York carrying agricultural tractors, fruit, grain, leather, and wax, was seized by the battleship *Deutschland*. For three weeks, a German prize crew tried to sail the ship, disguised with a false name and false colors, to a German port. Their remarkable voyage, which included several days spent hiding from the Royal Navy and the RAF in the Soviet arctic port of Murmansk, ended when the

Norwegian Navy apprehended the fugitive vessel and returned it to its rightful owners.

While U.S. carriers were unhappy about such actions by Germany, they particularly resented their ships being stopped and detained by the British. For one thing, it raised memories of 1812, when similar actions by the British had been largely responsible for sparking war between the two nations. In the mid-twentieth century these feelings were exacerbated by the great rivalry that then existed between Britain and the United States for prime position in the world maritime trade, and, of course, by the agitation of the isolationist, anti-British lobby.

Tension between London and Washington over this policy was already high because of interference with U.S. mail aboard transatlantic ships and an announcement by the British government that it intended to stop buying tobacco from America and obtain it from Turkey and Greece instead. In January 1940, relations almost reached breaking point. The Royal Navy stopped the American freighter *Mooremacsun* on the high seas, forced it into a British port, and refused to allow it to sail again, or to release its cargo, without a "navicert," a naval certificate signed by the owners or their agent guaranteeing that the cargo was not bound for an enemy port nor for a neutral country for possible transshipment to Germany.

Roosevelt and his advisers, urged on by both isolationists and interventionists, felt the British were sailing way out of line with this case, and protested strongly. On January 22, Secretary Hull called in Ambassador Lord Lothian.

"Increasing tension and a feeling of resentment are steadily rising in this country," he told him, "due to a multiplicity of what are considered here as excesses by the British government in prescribing and carrying out war restrictions on trade and finance. There is a feeling that your government is ceasing to show any consideration to my government and the people of this country."

Lothian's argument that Britain was fighting for its survival cut no ice with the courtly but determined Tennessean. "That is not the question," he replied, "but whether your government is not doing itself much more harm than good—a fact which I strongly believe."

For the United States, it was a matter of principle: since its inception, it had followed a policy of freedom of the seas, whereby American merchantmen could take their cargoes into any country, in peace or in war, in the absence of special considerations such as the neutrality laws of the 1930s. But for Britain, the blockade of Germany was a matter of life and death. Dependent as always on imports of food and raw materials, the British were fighting for their very existence as German U-boats torpedoed the British merchant ships, which were its lifeline, and German warships stopped neutral ships bound for Britain. To allow similar cargoes to be delivered unhindered to Germany would have been suicidal.

Churchill's messages of January 29 and 30 were therefore extremely important. What he was telling Roosevelt was that Britain would make an exception for America: unlike those of other neutral nations, American ships would not normally be stopped and searched. In the first message, sent before the Cabinet had been consulted, Churchill offered an unconditional promise covering all American vessels. Chamberlain and the other ministers, however, were less trusting and less magnanimous. They quickly reminded the first lord of the Admiralty that he did not have the authority to make such promises, and insisted on the two vital provisos contained in the revised message: the United States would have to guarantee that no ships left its ports carrying forbidden cargoes, and the special concession to American ships would have to be kept secret from other nations, which would naturally demand equal rights of free passage, thus negating the blockade.

Roosevelt replied to Churchill that he thought the matter was "working out satisfactorily." But he added, "I would not be frank unless I told you that there has been much public criticism here. The general feeling is that the net benefit to your people and to France is hardly worth the definite annoyance caused to us. That is always found to be so in a nation which is 3000 miles away from the fact of war."

Churchill's response came in the second message in which Ramsay was interested:

STRICTLY PERSONAL AND CONFIDENTIAL FOR THE PRESIDENT FROM NAVAL PERSON

Very many thanks for your most kind letter of February 1. Since on January 29 I gave orders to the fleet not to bring any American ships

into the zone you have drawn around our shores, many of the other
departments have become much more concerned about the efficiency
of the blockade and the difficulties of discriminating between various
countries. The neutrals are all on them and they are all on me.
Nevertheless, the order still stands and no American ship has been
brought by the Navy into the danger zone. But you can imagine my
embarrassment when Moore McCormack Line actually advertises in
Norway that they do not have to worry about navicerts or Kirkwall
[the British naval base in the Orkney Islands to the north of Scot-
land], and when all the Scandinavian countries complain of discrimination in American favour. I wonder if there is any way in which the
Moore McCormack Line could be persuaded, in addition to accepting
navicerts as a general rule, not to carry mails for Scandinavia until the
arrangements we are trying to make at St. John, New Brunswick, or
elsewhere, are ready. All our experience shows that the examination
of mails is essential to efficient control as only in this way can we get
the evidence of evasion. I do hope that I may be helped to hold the
position I have adopted by the American shipping lines availing
themselves of the great convenience of navicerts which was [sic] an
American invention and thus enable American trade to proceed without hindrance.

It is matter of great pleasure to me to keep you informed about
naval matters, although alas I cannot have the honour of a talk with
you in person.

Kent was interested in these documents as proof—as he saw
it—of collusion between Churchill and Roosevelt to draw
America into the war. Ramsay was interested in them for the
same reason, but even more so because he believed they
showed Churchill going behind the back of Chamberlain and
the Cabinet. The normal channel for all communications between the president and the British government was the Foreign Office, and Churchill appeared to be usurping the authority of the prime minister and the foreign secretary by dealing
directly with the president. What Ramsay did not, indeed could
not, know was that Churchill had from the very first acted with
the full knowledge and approval of the Cabinet, including,
naturally, Chamberlain himself.

By the spring of 1940, Kent had decided that the Roosevelt-
Churchill correspondence must be made public in America,
with the aim of preventing Roosevelt from being nominated
for an unprecedented third term as president. It might not

even be necessary for the signals themselves to be revealed: in an overwhelmingly isolationist United States, the mere fact that the two statesmen were in secret communication might well be sufficient to scotch the nomination, or if that failed, to lose him the election.

Kent faced a problem, however, in getting the signals out of Britain. He suspected, quite correctly, that the diplomatic pouches were being surreptitiously opened and that he would be in big trouble if he were caught smuggling secrets. He considered resigning from the Foreign Service, but if he did, his correspondence would definitely be opened by the British postal censors.

Ramsay seemed to be the answer to Kent's dilemma. He could show the signals to Chamberlain, thus confounding Churchill's supposed plot, and he could use his parliamentary privilege to reveal them on the floor of the House of Commons. American reporters would pick them up from there. In the event, Ramsay was arrested before he had done either: he had delayed making any announcement in order to accumulate more signals and thus strengthen his case. But the sudden eruption of the land war in Europe on May 10, coupled with the resignation of Chamberlain in favor of Churchill, meant that he had left it too long.

Soon after Kent had shown the two signals to Ramsay and Anna Wolkoff, Anna asked to borrow them. Assuming that she wanted them for Ramsay, Kent willingly handed them over. "I was quite surprised," he confessed many years later, "when she returned and handed me three glass negatives which were copies of the two signals, along with the copies I loaned her. I was somewhat perturbed, but didn't say anything." What happened to the prints made from those negatives has never been properly established. They were certainly not given to Ramsay. But there is convincing circumstantial evidence that she passed them to her friend the Duke del Monte of the Italian embassy, who relayed them to Germany via Rome.

Kent may have been perturbed at the thought that the signals had been photographed. But the idea of their being passed to the Germans may not have been entirely unwelcome to him; he always did prefer the Germans to the British, and had not yet given up all thoughts of a post in Berlin. On February 27, he wrote to Alexander Kirk, whom he had known in Moscow and who was now chargé d'affaires in the Berlin embassy, saying he had heard there was a clerk in Berlin who wanted a transfer to London, and that he, Kent, would be more than willing to be transferred to Berlin.

I am fully aware of all the adverse conditions of life in Germany, but I think that after my stay in Moscow I haven't much to learn about things of that sort. I am very much interested in Central and Eastern Europe and feel I would be much happier studying conditions in Germany than remaining here in London, where I have no particular interest. May I also humbly suggest that my background of Soviet conditions in Germany and of the Russian language may at some future date prove of use to the Embassy inasmuch as Germany and Soviet Russia, to all appearances, will eventually league up against the Allies . . . I am quite expert in the use of codes and am quite willing to continue in that work . . . I also know German quite well.

I have not taken the matter up with the people here because I first wanted to learn your reactions to the proposition.

Considering what Kent had done during his time in Moscow, it is appalling to imagine the damage he could have done in Berlin. Fortunately, it was not to be. Kirk replied on April 6, apologizing for the delay, which had been because "I wanted to canvass the situation here." However, it seemed that the man who had wanted a transfer to London no longer wanted to leave Berlin, so there was no place for Kent. But Kirk concluded: "I appreciate very much that you should care to join our group . . . I shall keep you in mind."

The letters to and from Kirk were found in Kent's flat at the time of his arrest. This was the first Kennedy or Johnson knew of his request, and the ambassador was understandably angry. But by then, it was the least of the black marks against Tyler Gatewood Kent.

SIX

Knight's Black Agents

KENT BECAME A MARKED MAN only two days after his arrival in London, when Ludwig Matthias called on him at the Cumberland Hotel. But if he had not come to the attention of MI5 then, he would have done so soon after, when he began mixing with the Wolkoffs and their friends from the Russian Tea Room. The White Russian community in London was a natural breeding ground for spies, and the Security Service kept a close eye on it—so much so that its files list no fewer than 135 former Russian nationals who were, however reluctantly, relaying information to the NKVD in order to protect members of their families still living in the Soviet Union.

Even Admiral Wolkoff was listed as being under Soviet influence, as was Mrs. Straker, who had introduced Kent to White Russian circles. Like many of those who dispensed charity for the Russian Red Cross, May Straker was targeted by the NKVD because she knew which exiles were in desperate straits and therefore likely to be more open to persuasion. Indeed, according to MI5, both the Russian Red Cross and the Russian Refugee Committee were controlled by the NKVD. E. Sabline, president of the Russian Refugee Committee, had been marked down in the early 1920s as having Soviet connections. People like Mrs. Straker were considered merely low-grade Soviet assets, but Sabline was rated much more highly. As a former Imperial chargé d'affaires in London, he was one of the most distinguished members of the White Russian community and still moved in exalted circles. He is reported, for instance, to have had several meetings with Sir Alexander Cadogan, permanent under secretary at the Foreign Office, when, no doubt, questions of British policy toward the Soviet Union were discussed.

Irene Danischewsky's family were believed to be even more heavily involved than most, first with GPU and then with the NKVD. In addition to having family in the Soviet Union, the Danischewskys depended on Soviet concessions for their livelihood; virtually all of their not inconsiderable income came from trade with the USSR. It is not possible now to establish with any certainty whether they were members of the same family, but British Foreign Office files list two Danischewskys with interesting records. One was described in 1918 as a Bolshevik agent in Norway, where the family had strong business connections. The other, K. K. Danischewsky, was a high-ranking member of the Soviet hierarchy, who had returned from exile in Siberia in 1917 to become a member of the Revolutionary Military Council. He became a member of the All-Russian Central Executive Committee, served on the Collegium of the Commissariat for Foreign Trade, and was head of the Soviet Union's timber export development. The British Foreign Office notes say he was "well educated and of good family . . . a moderate communist and believed to be honest."

The Danischewskys were, in fact, under regular observation in London by MI5, since their Concordia Works and warehouses in the docks were believed to employ one or more members of the Soviet organization Morflot, whose activities included shanghaiing Soviet seamen who had jumped ship to live in England. The sailors were lured on to Soviet ships with the promise of Russian food, vodka, and sometimes letters from their families back home. Once aboard, they were never seen again. Morflot also abducted other Soviet citizens who did not wish to return to their homeland.

By the spring of 1940, therefore, Kent had brought himself to the attention of the British security services in four different areas: the suspected German agent Ludwig Matthias; the Wolkoffs and their émigré circle, with its NKVD connections; Captain Ramsay and the Nazi sympathizers of the Right Club; and the Danischewskys with their suspected Morflot involvement. It is hardly surprising that MI5 should have started taking a keen interest in him and his activities.

Britain's secret services in 1939 and the early part of 1940 were divided into two main bodies: MI5, the Security Service, and MI6, the Secret Intelligence Service. Although their initials stand for Military Intelligence, departments 5 and 6, neither had any direct connection with the War Office or military intelligence as it is understood by an army, navy or air force. Following the old British tradition of secrecy at all costs, until quite recently their very existence was never officially acknowledged.

MI6 works to and for the Foreign Office, and is responsible for running agents and espionage worldwide and for counter-espionage outside the United Kingdom and the British Commonwealth. The jewel in its crown in 1940 was the so-called Government Code and Cypher School, generally abbreviated to GCCS, which from the start of the war was based at a mid-Victorian Gothic brick mansion, Bletchley Park, some fifty miles north of London and about midway between the universities of Oxford and Cambridge, from which it drew most of its senior staff. In spite of the number of professors and other distinguished academics working there, it was not, of course, a school but the British center for cryptanalysis. Its main work was concerned with deciphering foreign radio traffic collected by the Radio Security Service, known as MI8, and its greatest triumph, achieved with the initial help of Polish and French intelligence services, was the breaking of the German Enigma machine ciphers. MI6, through a combination of GCCS technology and old-fashioned secret agents, was to play a significant part in the case against Kent.

But the real work was carried out by MI5, which was then responsible for combating espionage, political subversion, and sabotage not only in the United Kingdom but also throughout the Commonwealth, with the exception of the dominions of Canada, Australia, New Zealand, and South Africa, which were independent and self-governing and therefore had their own intelligence and security services. MI5 answers to the Home Office, and works closely with the Metropolitan Police's Special Branch, formed in 1887 to replace the Special Irish Branch and the port police, and is responsible for fighting all political crime.

At the start of the Second World War, MI5's headquarters occupied two floors in Thames House, now the headquarters of ICI, the giant chemical corporation. A heavy gray stone building on the corner of Millbank and Horseferry Road on the north bank of the river, Thames House faces the Archbishop of Canterbury's London residence, Lambeth Palace, first built in 1207 and modernized in 1484, on the other side of Lambeth Bridge. Since the location as well as the title was a heavily guarded secret, MI5's address was usually given as Room 055, The War Office, Whitehall, SW1, or Box Number 500, Parliament Street Box Office, SW1.

Inevitably, the "Fives," as MI5's officers are often called in the jargon of the international intelligence community, surrounded themselves with an aura of mystery and deception, as did their counterparts, the "Sixes." They created a secret world of fantasy and flimflammery, where nothing was what it seemed. As in a bad spy thriller, false names and addresses abounded, and assigned military ranks rarely coincided with reality. The director general of MI5 from its foundation in 1909 until he was fired by Churchill in 1940, "Major General" Sir Vernon Kell, had actually retired from the army in 1924 as a colonel, and many of his men who styled themselves captain or major had never served in the armed forces at all. In any case, rank counted for little. Sir Claude Dansey, for example, operational chief and éminence grise of MI6, used his genuine rank of lieutenant colonel—except when he was operating under one of his many exotic aliases. But for two years during the war, Dansey's assistant was Sir James Marshall-Cornwall, the senior full general of the British Army, who was quite happy to work under his command.

For MI5 in particular, a certain amount of mysterious glamour was essential if it was to maintain the myth of the all-seeing, all-powerful organization whose tentacles stretched around the globe. Eighteen months before the start of the war, its entire staff numbered only twenty-eight. As war became inevitable, and German and Austrian refugees flooded into Britain, bringing the fear that among them might be some who were actually Nazi spies, MI5 embarked on a frantic recruitment campaign, drawing in a mixture of good, bad, and indifferent officers. In the process, organization suffered severely, but somehow the service managed to get itself in order so well that not a single enemy agent remained uncaught, and the only ones who continued to operate had been turned and were being used against their former masters.

Unfortunately, MI5 was not so successful against British agents of the Soviet Union, such as Kim Philby, Guy Burgess, Donald Maclean, and Anthony Blunt. But those particular chickens did not come home to roost until after the war, when the Soviet Union changed from an ally to the principal enemy. Ironically, throughout the 1920s and well into the 1930s, MI5's primary concern had been with the threat of Soviet communism. It was not until the late thirties that it recognized the threat caused by the rise of Hitler, and even then many Britons, particularly in the upper and middle classes, continued to regard the Nazi dictator as a bulwark against Bolshevism.

This attitude governed MI5's recruitment policies after the First World War, resulting in a service drawn almost entirely from the British Establishment—albeit its slightly seedier elements. It was not the only influence; there were other reasons that partially explain Kell's reputation for snobbery and class prejudice. Following the Armistice in 1918, most wartime MI5 officers returned to civilian life, and Kell's budget was sharply slashed. Since he could afford to pay his staff only the most miserable salaries, he turned to two types of recruit: young regular army officers who were paid by the War Office, and young men who had unearned private incomes. This meant, inevitably, that they came from well-connected and well-to-do families, with a background of expensive schools and universities.

Kell forbade the recruitment of known homosexuals or Roman Catholics—the former because of his prejudice and a realization of the security risks involved, the latter because he believed that the Vatican had the world's best espionage organization, and he did not want MI5 to be infiltrated by the Pope's agents. His prejudices did not extend to women—he employed several young women, such as Jane Sissmore, a former barrister who became one of his finest interrogators—but he did insist that they be pretty and have good legs.

Vernon Kell, born in 1873, was a powerful personality, and with his square jaw and clipped mustache looked every inch the perfect commander. His father had been an officer in the South Staffordshire Regiment, which Kell himself joined as a young man, and his mother was the daughter of an exiled Polish count, with relatives strewn across Europe. He was a brilliant linguist, fluent in German, French, Italian, Polish, Russian, and Chinese, and had traveled widely before returning from the Far East and action in the Boxer Rebellion with his health shattered by dysentery and asthma. Because of his disabilities, he was posted to the War Office in 1904. Five years later he was offered the post of director of the home section of the newly formed Secret Service Bureau, then labeled MO5, charged with investigating and countering espionage in the United Kingdom. In spite of the grand title, Kell's new section consisted of himself and one clerk. It was entirely through his own efforts that by 1914 it was already a sizable and efficient outfit, ready for its massive expansion to a staff of more than eight hundred during the war.

Despite his conventional appearance, Kell had a taste for the unorthodox verging on eccentricity; his chauffeur-driven Invicta automobile flew a pennant emblazoned not with a major general's two stars but with a tortoise, to signify the slow-moving nature of MI5's operations. Inevitably, his personality not only dominated the organization but also dictated its character. Most recruits were men and women he had himself approached after meeting them socially, and he made a point of personally interviewing every candidate in great depth until the rapid increase for the Second World War made this impracticable.

The man who was to be Tyler Kent's nemesis, and who would ensure that President Roosevelt's highly vocal isolationist opposition was denied the explosive issue of an alleged secret plot to take America into the war, was introduced to Kell at a dinner party in 1924. Kell took a liking to him and asked him to come to his office next day, where to his astonishment the young Maxwell Knight found himself being invited to join MI5.

Charles Henry Maxwell Knight, born September 4, 1900, was a tall, handsome man with immense charm and all the social graces. He was also a remarkably complex character, able to divide his life into watertight compartments, keeping the quiet, nature-loving introvert quite separate from the bright, confident man-about-town. Born into an impoverished family—his father, a lawyer, had squandered his inheritance on a series of mistresses and frequent trips to the south of France—Knight was educated on H.M.S. *Worcester,* a combination of first-class public school and training ship for merchant navy officers. At the age of seventeen, he volunteered for war service and became a midshipman in the Royal Naval Reserve, serving on armed trawlers and merchantmen.

By the end of the war in 1918, Knight had had enough of the sea, and turned his back on a career as a ship's officer, with the result that his uncle, who held the family purse strings, cut him off without a penny. Undismayed, he began earning a meager living teaching Latin and games at a school in suburban Putney, which he was doing when he met Vernon Kell.

While still in the RNR, Knight had sailed to New York, where he had enjoyed a short period of shore leave. He was fascinated by America, and had been able to sample a little of the high life, thanks to the patronage of a rich American who took him and a few companions under his wing and showed them the town. There, he had his first taste of jazz. It was love at first sound, the beginning of a lifelong affair. Jazz became one of the three great passions of his life, along with spy hunting and natural history; he even learned to play the drums, saxophone, and clarinet with great skill. He claimed, later, to have had lessons with the great Sidney Bechet, though this was almost certainly an exaggeration if not a fantasy.

Although his income from teaching was extremely small, he had a taste for the pleasures of London's night life, where he could enjoy dancing with beautiful women and listening to jazz bands. This was made possible by the social contacts he had retained from his days on H.M.S. *Worcester,* who were glad to invite him to parties as a "deb's delight," a young man with impeccable manners who could be relied on as a dancing partner for debutantes. He was also, as it happened, a safe partner, for although he was eventually married three times and lived with at least two other women, he never consummated any of his relationships. There has been speculation that he was a suppressed homosexual or bisexual, but no one has been able to produce any evidence to support these suppositions. It is far more likely that he was sexually impotent, sublimating his sex drives in his work and his hobbies.

Knight's love of natural history began when he was a child, during long periods spent living on his rich uncle's country estate in South Wales when his father's money had run out yet again. A shy, introverted boy, he wandered the fields and woods and seashore studying the wildlife he found there, finding it easier to relate to animals, birds, and bugs than to people. In later life, he learned how to handle people brilliantly, but he never lost his love for animals, and as often as not would be carrying mice, lizards, or grass snakes in his pockets even while working. His homes were always full of living creatures, from parrots and monkeys to ferrets and bush babies.

In 1946, though still serving in MI5, he started a satisfying new career as a radio naturalist and became nationally famous for his BBC broadcasts. In addition to contributing to adult programs, he was a much-loved figure to a whole generation of children as "Uncle Max" on *Nature Parliament.* He began writing nature books, which proved much more successful than the two rather mediocre thrillers he had published in 1934 and 1935, and regular articles for such magazines as *Country Life* and *The Field.* Ten years later, at the age of fifty-five, he resigned from the Security Service and devoted himself full time to what had been his favorite hobby.

Knight took to life in MI5 with great enthusiasm, and soon

proved that Kell's legendary intuition in choosing suitable recruits had not failed him. He was a natural. One of the first
cases MI5 was involved with after he joined was in many ways a
precursor of Tyler Kent's attempt to prevent Roosevelt's re-
election by publishing his correspondence with Churchill. In
1924, the aim was to prevent the re-election in Britain of Ramsay MacDonald's Labour government, and the correspondence
was a secret instruction from Grigori Zinoviev, president of the
Comintern, to the Communist Party of Great Britain, concerning the use of supposed communist cells in British Army units
as part of a planned revolution.

MI5 pronounced the letter genuine, and it was published in
The Times and the *Daily Mail* on October 25, 1924, just four days
before the general election. MacDonald's government had
been planning to sign a new treaty with the Soviet Union,
providing for a massive British loan. Publication of the Zinoviev letter, with its exhortations to revolution, ensured that
Labour's chances were swept away in a landslide defeat. The
resulting government, headed by Stanley Baldwin, included
Winston Churchill, who had switched to the Conservatives
from the Liberals, as chancellor of the Exchequer.

No doubt Churchill—and Max Knight—recalled the effects
of the Zinoviev letter sixteen years later when faced with the
possibility of revelations that might be damaging to Britain's
friend Franklin D. Roosevelt. Controversy has raged ever since
about whether the letter was a fake—but real or a forgery, it
totally destroyed Ramsay MacDonald's chances. What, then,
would be the result of the accusation, however false, that Roosevelt was plotting to drag the United States into another European war?

One of the principal experts who had declared the Zinoviev
letter genuine, Captain Guy Liddell, MC, was working at the
time in Scotland Yard, where he had been in charge since 1919
of Special Branch's intelligence and antisubversion activities,
in close cooperation with Kell. In September 1931, MI5 took
over this side of Special Branch, and in the process acquired
Lidell, who went to work in B (Counter-Espionage) Division.

Lidell, then probably the best-informed intelligence officer
in Britain on matters concerning communist subversion and

the Communist Party of Great Britain, was short and slightly built, the remaining hair on his balding scalp slicked down. He was both shy and extraordinarily vain, with a disconcerting manner of avoiding eye contact with those he was interviewing by staring into the distance over their heads. But he had a keen intellect, and was both liked and admired by his juniors. Even Kim Philby admitted that he was "an ideal senior officer for a young man to learn from . . . [H]e would murmur his thoughts out loud, as if groping his way towards the facts of a case, his face creased in a comfortable, innocent smile. But behind the façade of laziness, his subtle and reflective mind played over a storehouse of photographic memories."

Liddell, who had a modest private income, came from a noted family—each of his two brothers had also won the coveted Military Cross during the Great War—and was married to the madcap Calypso Baring, daughter of Lord Revelstoke. Like Liddell himself, Revelstoke, head of the Baring Brothers merchant bank, had strong Irish connections; he lived on Lambay Island, near Dublin. The Barings also had strong links with America: Warren Delano, a cousin of President Roosevelt's, had married into the family and was a partner in the firm.

Liddell's marriage to Calypso was extremely stormy and a constant source of worry to him, until it was dissolved, in 1943, after she deserted him and set up home in Florida with her half brother. During the thirties and early forties, she spent more and more time in America, leaving him to find solace in his work and in art and music. He was rated as probably the best amateur cellist in Britain, gave regular musical evenings, and was a serious collector of paintings. One of the pictures he bought from his friend Anthony Blunt, who was an eminent art historian and became keeper of the queen's pictures—in addition to his role as a Soviet spy in the wartime MI5—was alleged to have been a forgery, but in general his judgment was excellent.

His judgment of people was usually excellent, too. He was particularly good at spotting and encouraging talent, and it was not long before he recognized Max Knight's potential and began grooming him as a case officer, one who recruits and directs agents. Knight's big chance came when he was put in charge of placing agents in the Communist Party, to counter its subversive activities. Setting a precedent for his later investigation of the Right Club and the trapping of Tyler Kent, he found an attractive young woman to spearhead his penetration of the communist web.

Olga Gray was a honey blonde of twenty-five, convent-educated, a keen hockey player with a good body and a good mind but an insecure personality. Her father, who was killed in the First World War, had been night editor of the *Daily Mail* in Manchester, and her mother was a personal friend of Mrs. Neville Chamberlain's in Birmingham. Knight persuaded Olga to enlist in the CPGB and become a voluntary worker for the Friends of the Soviet Union as a first step on what would be a seven-year mission. Midway through this time, she was hospitalized with a nervous breakdown, but Knight wooed her back into service, and she went on to become so successful at convincing the communists that they entrusted her with a secret mission. She was asked to carry funds to Indian comrades in Bombay—where Knight's contact turned out to be the leader of the jazz band at the Taj Mahal Hotel. On her return she was given an important post at party headquarters in King Street, and asked to set up and run a "safe house" for the NKVD. For this, Knight provided the flat, which belonged to MI5, with the result that visiting Soviet agents were unwitting guests of the British Security Service.

As a result of Olga Gray's painstaking efforts, Knight knew the CPGB's every move and was able in 1937 to smash a spy ring stealing top secret plans from the government's ordnance factory at Woolwich Arsenal, and to jail its Moscow-trained leader, Percy Glading. The Woolwich Arsenal case solidly established Max Knight's reputation for antisubversive and antiespionage operations. But it blew Olga Gray's cover. Fearful of retaliation by the CPGB or even from Moscow agents, she accepted a false name and disappeared. She had married an RCAF officer, and went to live in Toronto. In the late 1980s, she was still alive and well there, and still nervous about revealing her true identity.

The huge success of the Woolwich case, and the whole operation against the CPGB, which continued through other Knight agents working inside the party, made Knight a star in MI5. He

was given complete charge of operations against political subversion, with a self-contained, ultra-secret section of his own
under the designation B5(b).

The section had its own premises, away from the rest of MI5,
in a flat in Dolphin Square, a huge modern development facing
the Thames between Vauxhall and Chelsea bridges, a little over
half a mile from Thames House. The flat, at 308 Hood House,
belonged to the brother of Knight's second wife, Lois, and the
doorbell carried her maiden name, Miss Coplestone. As the
section grew, MI5 bought another flat in an adjoining block, 10
Collingwood House, to accommodate other staff members,
leaving Knight and his secretary in Hood House. Both flats
were kept strictly secret; Knight never allowed agents to visit
there, insisting that meetings with them take place either in the
lobbies of second-rate hotels or in other MI5 flats kept for the
purpose. Members of the public who came forward with information were usually interviewed in the offices of the Special
Branch at New Scotland Yard or in Room 055 at the War Office.
When Kell moved the rest of MI5 to Wormwood Scrubs prison
a week before the start of the war, hoping that this less central
location would give more safety from bombing, Knight and his
staff stayed put in Dolphin Square.

In keeping with the cloak-and-dagger atmosphere he so enjoyed, Knight used pseudonyms both in and out of the office,
including Captain King, Mr. Kay, and—most typically—M.
This last was not, in fact, an official code name, but was simply
short for Maxwell. Nor was it, as has been suggested, the basis
for Ian Fleming's spymaster in the James Bond books. Forbidden to use the genuine C, the official designation of the chief of
the Secret Intelligence Service, Fleming cheekily changed it to
M for Menzies, the real name of the man who was C. Nevertheless, Knight encouraged all his staff to call him M, and no doubt
hugely enjoyed seeing this used by Bond.

Max Knight's search for another bright and beautiful undercover agent to penetrate a suspect organization would take two
years. In the meantime, he had plenty to occupy his time. With
the rise of Hitler in Germany and a fascist movement in Britain
led by Sir Oswald Mosley, he was concerned with the possibility of subversion from the right as well as the left, and began
infiltrating agents into profascist and pro-German organiza-

tions. At the same time, he had several agents working under cover against the communists, including the mystery writer John Dickson Carr, the future Labour MP Tom Driberg, and Bill Younger, a member of a famous brewing family.

Driberg and Younger were recruited as students at Oxford University, which had attracted a great deal of attention on February 9, 1933, when a Union debate ended by approving the resolution "This house will not fight for King and Country." Aware that the university's October Club harbored many communist students, Knight sought reliable young men to spy on their fellows. Some of them stayed on in the service afterward.

Derek Tangye, another writer who joined the wartime MI5 as its press officer, recalled Knight telling him: "The Russians are very patient. They will recruit a young man at university with communist views, tell him to dissociate himself from the party, watch him, and keep him on ice for years. Then one day they will come to him and say: 'Now we want you to do this.' " These were astute words, prophetic even, but sadly Knight seems to have confined his actions to Oxford, paying no attention to Cambridge, where precisely such recruiting was taking place, to devastating effect.

Knight's staff tended to be young, lively, and sophisticated, fond of the good life, as he was, and mostly well bred. There was also a strong literary element, particularly during the war, when his assistant was Lord Clanmorris, who wrote excellent detective stories as John Bingham. Knight himself had given up writing after his two third-rate thrillers, *Crime Cargo* and *Gunman's Holiday*, but Younger wrote good poetry under his own name and thrillers under the apt pseudonym of William Mole; Driberg was a successful journalist; and John Dickson Carr was a hugely successful author both under his own name and others, notably Carter Dickson. With the war, Bill Younger's stepfather, Dennis Wheatley, added his talents to the team. It was fitting that they should call themselves Knight's Black Agents, a literary pun on Macbeth's speech:

> Good things of day begin to droop and drowse,
> Whiles night's black agents to their preys do rouse.

. . . .

While visiting Wormwood Scrubs a few weeks into the war, Knight spotted a beautiful, smartly dressed young woman lunching in the canteen, the former inmates' mess hall. After keeping an eye on her for a little while and making a few inquiries about her background, he relayed a luncheon invitation through Bill Younger. The young woman was Joan Miller, a former employee of the Elizabeth Arden beauty salon's display department now working for the dashing former car-racing ace Lord Cottenham in MI5's transport section. Joan was already aware of Max Knight, one of the most glamorous figures in the business, and accepted the invitation with alacrity. Forty-five years later she vividly remembered that first meeting:

At twelve-thirty I went into the canteen and saw Maxwell Knight at a table for two in the corner of the room. He got to his feet as I approached; even before he spoke, I was conscious of the charm this smiling man possessed—charm of a rare and formidable order. His voice, which I found hypnotic, confirmed the impression. By the end of that first lunchtime session I was captivated. M, at that time, must have been about twice my age; it's possible, I suppose, that I had been subconsciously on the look-out for a "father figure"—my own, an amiable, rather weak man who liked to gamble, hadn't exactly come up to scratch as a parent—but there was a great deal more to my feeling for M, even at this early stage.

The luncheon was a success for Max Knight, too. Before it was finished he had invited Joan to dine with him that evening, at the Authors' Club in Whitehall Court—a suitable rendezvous for such an assignation, since it was immediately beneath the original headquarters of the Secret Service. Elated at having found a possible successor to Olga Gray, Knight told Joan about the aims and methods of B5(b), and explained that he wanted her to infiltrate an extreme right-wing organization called the Right Club. She would be introduced to the club by another of his agents who was already in place, a middle-aged lady who always reminded Joan of Agatha Christie's Miss Marple. She called herself Mrs. Amon, though in fact her name was Marjorie Mackie.

Knight had already infiltrated two other agents into the Right Club, an attractive Belgian girl named Helene de Munck and one of his case officers, Philip Brocklehurst, but Marjorie

Mackie had reported that the club was "on the look-out for a recruit from the War Office," which clearly indicated that the members were up to no good. It also provided an excellent opportunity for Knight to plant someone like Joan, and thus to repeat or even surpass his great triumph in the Woolwich Arsenal case.

SEVEN

M and the Mata Hari of Dolphin Square

JOAN MILLER'S FUTURE was settled long before the dinner with Knight at the Authors' Club was over. "I was ready to agree to anything put forward by M," she wrote later, "and also tremendously excited by the prospect of getting to grips with work rather more exacting than anything I'd had to deal with in the transport office. I was already benefiting from M's ability to instill confidence and enthusiasm in his subordinates."

But confidence and enthusiasm were not enough for the job Knight had in mind for her. Before she could pass herself off as a suitable recruit for the Right Club, Joan Miller had a great deal to learn, both about B5(b) and about fascism and the extreme right in Britain. Max Knight set out to teach her and to turn her from a bright young secretary into a first-rate secret agent.

The process began the very next day, when Joan moved out

of the prison and into 10 Collingwood House, Dolphin Square, which she was to share with Knight's case officers. She was not popular with them, partly no doubt because of her strong personality, but also perhaps because they were jealous. "She completely dominated Max," John Bingham later told Knight's biographer, "and she quickly became a person of considerable influence. I know we were all slightly afraid of her, for we only needed to get on her wrong side and she would put the boot in for us with Max."

One unexpected bonus of Joan's new position was that Knight taught her to drive, and used her as his chauffeur. This meant that she had access to a car, with no problems over strictly rationed fuel, and a permit saying she had full War Office permission to use it and should not be questioned, as she was on War Office business. With taxis in very short supply, this was especially useful late at night, when she was doing the social round of the London night spots.

From the first, Knight was clearly attracted by more than her potential as an agent, and it was not long before she became his mistress in every way apart from sex. As in all his other relationships with women, he failed to consummate the affair. Joan was extremely puzzled by this; as a very attractive young woman with a fair amount of experience and several conquests behind her, she found it hard to understand how Knight could woo her so ardently and then shy away from physical lovemaking. She noted that he seemed to enjoy and even seek out the company of good-looking young men, and speculated on the possibility that he might be a homosexual.

Whatever his shortcomings as a lover, however, Knight was an excellent teacher. He soon explained the political background to her, and tutored her in the byways of deception. One of his maxims was "If you're going to tell a lie, tell a good one and, above all, stick to it." To show her how a really dedicated agent worked, he got out the files of the Woolwich Arsenal case and took her through it, step by step.

"I was deeply impressed," Joan recalled later, "by the vigilance and perseverance shown by Olga Gray, who kept her wits about her through the whole dangerous course of the undertaking, and never lost her credibility with the other side."

Joan was fascinated by what she learned:

The Woolwich Arsenal files were as full of intrigue as any work of fiction specially constructed to satisfy the avid thriller-reader: plots and plans, illicit photographs of naval guns, shifty foreigners, fateful attaché cases deposited in left-luggage compartments, conspicuous brown paper parcels passing from one impassive conspirator to another at Charing Cross Station. And, at the centre of it all, an MI5 agent keeping tabs on everyone around her and keeping her head at the same time. With the example of Olga Gray in front of me, and above all with Max's encouragement, I managed to ignore the perfectly reasonable qualms that assailed me whenever I envisaged myself in a similar role. Max easily convinced me of the value of the work; it was only my own competence I had doubts about.

To complete her training, Max instructed her in the various techniques of watching and searching, including such useful items as the mechanics of breaking open a locked trunk. He also arranged for her to have lessons from the police in the art of burglary, and, from "a very special department of the Post Office," on how to open and reseal letters. And besides the expensive flowers he showered upon her while persuading her to leave her own flat and move in with him, he gave her several more exotic but useful presents, such as an elegant, leather-covered cosh, lined with lead, from Tom Hill in Knightsbridge, and a small gun, "a sort of stocking gun really, but none the less lethal for that."

Thus equipped, Joan was ready to undertake her first mission as an agent. As a sort of trial run, she was involved in a surveillance operation on a leading member of the CPGB, an Indian lawyer named Rajani Palme Dutt, who had been expelled from Oxford in the First World War for spreading subversive propaganda, and whose brother had formed the first communist cell in Cambridge in 1931. Knight instructed Joan to break into his flat and retrieve compromising documents that he believed Palme Dutt stored in a steel box under his bed. Aided by one of Knight's case officers, Guy Poston, she succeeded in picking the lock on Palme Dutt's door, entering his flat, and finding the box under the bed. To everyone's disappointment, it contained nothing more than a set of marriage lines dating from 1924. Nevertheless, the episode had been a useful graduation exercise, if nothing else, and Joan could now regard herself as a fully qualified secret agent.

. . . .

Early in 1940, on a blustery winter evening with the wind whipping snow through the London streets, Marjorie Mackie led Joan into the Russian Tea Room for the first time. The place was crowded and cheerful, firelight glinting on the steaming samovar and the polished wood. A hubbub of conversation filled the air as people delighted in shared complaints about shortages of food and other essentials and the irksomeness of the blackout. Alone at a corner table, erect and aloof, the white-bearded Admiral Wolkoff sat watching his customers.

Joan and Mrs. Mackie found an empty table, sat down, and ordered tea. After a little while, Anna Wolkoff came in and made her way across the room to speak to Mrs. Mackie—or Mrs. Amon, as Anna knew her. Mrs. Mackie introduced Joan as a friend of her son, who was at sea serving in the navy. Anna asked what she did, and Joan told her she worked at the War Office, adding with a laugh that her job was concerned with filing and was really terribly boring. Anna nodded once or twice, then spoke of something else. The bait had been laid: Joan could only hope that she had made a deep enough impression for it to be remembered and taken.

From then on, Joan took to calling in at the Tea Room at all hours of the day, sometimes alone, sometimes with an innocent friend. The admiral welcomed her, often joining her to talk about the old days in Russia, and gradually she became friendly with Anna, too, carefully dropping ever bolder hints suggesting she was opposed to the war and sympathetic to the fascist cause. She even invented a prewar romance with a Nazi officer to give substance to her claims. All the time, Anna listened, "wary and suspicious as a wildcat," giving away nothing of her own opinions beyond a smile of apparent approval. Presumably, at some of Joan's visits Tyler Kent must have been present, since he was also a regular visitor, but at that time she knew nothing of him.

Eventually, all the hard work paid off: Anna invited Joan to her flat to join a group of friends for one of her special omelets. Joan climbed the narrow stairs "with quaking knees." This was the test: she was about to be vetted. She was relieved to find Marjorie Mackie among the ten or twelve women gathered to meet her in the cramped living room, all senior club members and all much older than she. At their center was Ismay Ramsay. As they looked Joan up and down with the piercing scrutiny that well-bred ladies have employed on women younger or less fortunate than themselves since civilization first began, Mrs. Mackie spoke up for her.

"Joan has a great deal of common sense about political matters," she said. "She finds the War Office a bit of a bore."

"Actually, I'm not too keen on war, either," Joan added, going on to spout the sort of sentiments she knew would be well received: it was a disaster that the country should have embarked on war; the government should never have abandoned the policy of appeasement and was wrong to have opposed Germany's expansionist ambitions; and so on. She complained of feeling cut off from the sense of being morally in the right that made things tolerable for everyone else. The ladies listened and approved.

Joan discovered she had passed the test when, not long after, she was invited to join the Right Club and was presented with her eagle-and-snake badge in its smart red case. Knight told her Mrs. Mackie had reported that the club's plans were to persuade her to get herself transferred to a War Office department where she would have greater scope for sabotage. When Mrs. Ramsay suddenly invited her for tea, both Joan and Knight guessed she intended to put the suggestion to her.

Knight was jubilant. He had been watching the Ramsays for some time, waiting for the chance to catch them in the act of subversion. But nothing had happened. A tap on their telephone had produced nothing more incriminating than that their cook was helping herself to their supplies of sugar and butter. Now, however, there was the possibility of being able to trap Ismay Ramsay into making seditious proposals. All that was needed was to make sure it was done in front of witnesses.

Coached by Knight, Joan persuaded Mrs. Ramsay to take tea with her in a flat borrowed from MI5 officer Philip Brocklehurst, where two large Special Branch detectives were installed in a small, airless closet with equipment to make a sound recording of the conversation. The attempt turned into a farce. Recording would have been impossible with the windows open, because of traffic noise, but it was an exceptionally warm day. Joan managed to avoid opening the windows, but the room was uncomfortably hot, and an ill-at-ease Mrs. Ramsay confined herself to social pleasantries. When she left, two parboiled policemen fell out of the closet, without a word of evidence to justify their ordeal.

A few days later, Mrs. Ramsay repeated her invitation, and this time Joan had no alternative but to go to the Ramsay home in Onslow Square. With no witnesses and no record of the conversation—recording equipment had not yet advanced sufficiently for Joan to be inconspicuously wired for sound—Ismay Ramsay proceeded to make the most outrageous proposals, asking Joan to get herself moved to a job where she could steal secret material.

Knight could not move in on the Ramsays for this suggestion without blowing Joan's cover, but he could make use of it to enhance her standing with the Right Club. In the best traditions of the secret world, he provided her with ample supplies of "chicken feed"—genuine material from secret files, but of little real value to an enemy—which convinced them that Joan was indeed working for them.

This development was particularly timely, for it had suddenly become important to build up the Right Club's trust in Joan. Her original task had been simply to infiltrate the club in order to obtain a full list of members, who could then be rounded up when the time was right. Now, Knight ordered her to devote herself principally to keeping an eye on Anna Wolkoff. He had reason to suspect that Anna was involved in something far more serious than posting sticky-backed slogans in the dead of night.

Joan did as she was told, though she feared that Anna suspected her and might turn on her at any moment. Her fears proved groundless. Anna responded to her friendly attentions and was soon describing her as Captain Ramsay's assistant aide-de-camp. Indeed, she became so agreeable that at one point she gave Joan a present of a smart Worth dress in pink and blue. Joan accepted with mixed feelings. She found herself liking the other woman, despite Anna's character defects—her friends nicknamed her "Julius Streicher" after the Nazis' most notorious Jew baiter, the gauleiter of Nuremberg, and Joan thought there was "rather more than a hint of hysteria in her anti-Semitic outpourings."

The first positive evidence of Anna's other activities came from one of Knight's other undercover agents in the Right Club, Helen de Munck. While the war in Western Europe still hung fire, Helen was able to make periodic visits to her family in Belgium, which was then still a neutral country. Early in 1940, Anna asked her to carry a message to one of the Right Club's agents in Brussels, questioning the trustworthiness of another Belgian agent and asking about the progress of "our work in Belgium." Helen carried out this task successfully— after showing the messages to Knight—and thus earned Anna's trust, a trust that Max Knight and Joan Miller were soon able to exploit to uncover something more incriminating against Anna.

Anna often boasted to Joan about her contact with the Duke del Monte at the Italian embassy. On one occasion, she took Joan with her to post a letter through the front door of his house, hinting that she was using del Monte to pass messages to William Joyce, or Lord Haw-Haw, who had been broadcasting from Germany against Britain since September 11, 1939. Joan reported this to Knight, but without positive proof there was little they could do.

Then events played into their hands. Anna complained that she had an important coded letter for Joyce at the Rundfunkhaus in Berlin, "full of tips about the line he should take in his German propaganda broadcasts," but was unable to get it out of the country, as her friend the duke was ill. Joan thought quickly and told her she believed the trusted Helene had a friend in the Romanian legation and might be able to use the Romanian diplomatic bag. Helene was given the letter, which she took straight to Knight.

The next day, Anna was upset to learn that the letter had already gone to Helene's fictitious friend; she was eager to add a postscript to it. Helene retrieved the letter from Knight and called Anna, who came to her flat to make the additions, using Helene's typewriter, and rounding off with a drawing of the Right Club emblem and the letters PJ, for "Perish Judah."

The letter was in cipher, and Joan and Knight drove up to Bletchley Park, where the experts soon decoded it. It read:

Talks effect splendid but news bulletins less so. Palestine good but IRA etc. defeats object. Stick to plutocracy. Avoid King . . .

Here Krieghetze [warmongering] only among Blimps [diehard reactionaries]. Workers fed up. Wives more so. Troops not keen. Anti-Semitism spreading like flame everywhere—all classes.

Note refujews in so-called Pioneer Corps guaranteed in writing to be sent into firing line.

Churchill not popular—keep on at him as Baruch tool and war theatre-extender, sacrificer Gallipoli, etc. Stress his conceit and repeated failures with expense lives and prestige . . .

Butter rations doubled because poor can't buy—admitted by Telegraph—bacon same. Cost living steeply mounting. Shopkeepers suffering . . .

Regret must state Meg's [Joyce's wife, Margaret] Tuesday talks unpopular with women. Advise alter radically or drop. God bless and salute to all leaguers . . .

Acknowledge this by Carlyle reference radio not Thurs. or Sun. Reply same channel same cypher.

The postscript added by Anna was:

If possible, please give again, sometime in the week, the broadcast which the German radio gave in German about three months ago . . .

It is now very important that we hear more about the Jews and Free Masons. PJ

After making a copy, and some deletions, Knight and Joan handed the letter to one of their contacts—in fact, Marjorie Mackie's naval officer son, then home on leave—who really did have a friend in the Romanian legation. Not long afterward Joyce acknowledged receipt by mentioning Carlyle in one of his broadcasts. Anna told Joan she had heard this, so she knew her letter had reached Berlin safely. It had, however, been intercepted by the German censors and never given to Joyce himself, though he had been instructed to respond as though it had.

In communicating with the enemy, Anna had now committed a very serious offense. Knight could have moved in on her then, and obtained a conviction. But he chose to wait, knowing that by letting her run she would lead him to bigger game. The bigger game was Tyler Kent.

MI5 had been aware early in February that the Churchill-Roosevelt correspondence was being leaked. Soon after Churchill had signaled to Roosevelt on January 29 and 30 that American ships would no longer be stopped and searched, Italy, Spain, and other neutrals officially protested against the favoritism being shown to the United States, and demanded equal treatment. Churchill had specifically asked Roosevelt not to publicize the British offer just to avoid such complaints, and Roosevelt had complied. How, then, had the Italians and the Spanish come to know about it? The only possible conclusion was that they, or more likely the Germans, had somehow secured access to top secret British communications.

The first clue to how they were doing so came from MI8, the wireless interception service, which had picked up radio traffic between Hans Georg von Mackensen, the German ambassador in Rome, and the German Foreign Office in Berlin. When the GCCS cryptanalysts at Bletchley Park decoded one message, it turned out to be a paraphrase of the Churchill-Roosevelt messages. At first, no one in either GCCS or MI6 realized the significance of this find. That Churchill and Roosevelt were in communication was so secret that even when the messages reached the Foreign Office they were regarded as forgeries, until one of the tiny group of people in the know spotted them, recognized them as genuine, and raised the alarm.

Confirmation that the German embassy in Rome was indeed receiving secret documents came from an MI6 agent on the ground, an antifascist Italian journalist named Luigi Barzini. Barzini, the son of a noted Italian-American newspaper publisher and former editor of the New York daily *Corriera d'America,* was accredited to the Italian Foreign Ministry as a correspondent, and had many excellent contacts with officials who thought as he did. Some of these officials talked to him about a "fantastic influx" of American documents. Barzini immediately passed on the information to his British control. At the same time, another British agent, this one working for the Abwehr in Berlin, also reported that the Germans were obtaining the Churchill-Roosevelt messages.

On February 7, Guy Liddell wrote to Herschel Johnson, the U.S. embassy counselor, alerting him to the danger:

SECRET   Box No. 500,
                                                        Parliament Street, B.O.
                                                        London, S.W.1.

L.305.95.Dy.B   7th February 1940

PERSONAL & CONFIDENTIAL

Dear Johnson,
   I think the following information may be of interest to the State Department.
   I have heard from an informant whose statements have in other respects proved to be accurate, that at any rate just prior to the war and possibly still, the German Secret Service had been receiving from an American Embassy reports, at times two a day, which contained practically everything from Ambassador Kennedy's despatches to President Roosevelt, including reports of his interviews with British statesmen and officials. The source from which the German Secret Service got these documents is not definitely known, but is someone who is referred to as "Doctor," and our informant, who is in a position to know, is of opinion that the "Doctor" is employed in the American Embassy in Berlin.
   The above information, as you will realise, is extremely delicate and in any enquiries that you or the State Department think fit to make, we should be grateful if you would take every possible step to safeguard our informant.

   Liddell's letter appears to be a cunning mixture of truths and half truths, carefully designed to persuade the embassy and the State Department to start searching for the source of the leaks but at the same time disguising British sources and avoiding telling the Americans just how much MI5 really knew. As soon as he received it, Johnson contacted Liddell to ask for more details. In conversation, and off the record, Liddell was able to hint at what MI5 actually believed, nudging him in the desired direction by saying that, "as a matter of purely personal observation, he did not feel sure at all that Berlin was the place where the information was actually handed to German Secret Service agents." Johnson took the hint and told Assistant Secretary of State James Clement Dunn in Washington, in a letter stamped SECRET,

[I]t could not possibly have been done through anyone in the American Embassy at Berlin, as none of the Ambassador's confidential telegrams were ever repeated to Berlin . . . Moreover, with few exceptions, the Ambassador does not send copies of his confidential telegrams in code or clear to other missions in Europe. In this Embassy the number of people outside the code room who had any legitimate access to these telegrams was extremely limited.

However, whether the information, as alleged, reached the German Secret Service through somebody in the American Embassy in Berlin or not, it seems perfectly clear, if the basic fact is true, that somebody either in this Embassy or in the State Department is involved.

A few days later, Liddell sent someone—probably Max Knight—to give Johnson further information on the Berlin connection and to create another mystery. The British informant, he told him, was actually in the German Secret Service and was in touch with a man named Jankhe, who was on the staff of Hess, the deputy Führer of Germany. The British agent had been in Jankhe's office when a stenographer-interpreter who did the translations from English into German asked Jankhe if she could leave the office, as there was nothing in from America. Jankhe had replied, "No, the Doctor is not dictating this afternoon."

Johnson passed the new information on to Dunn, with the comment "I personally am not quite sure that the British are telling us all they know." Johnson had good reason for doubt, but since the British knew there was a traitor in the embassy, they also had good reason for caution. The identity of the mysterious Doctor has never been revealed, and there is always the possibility that he was a creation of MI5's imagination, intended merely as a subtle device for telling the State Department that the problems with communications security might be in the Washington code room. Since they were then reading both the German signals from Washington and American radio traffic, they were justified in having no faith in American security.

On the other hand, the Doctor could well have been genuine —and there was certainly a traitor in the Washington code room, with methods and motives remarkably similar to Tyler Kent's, though he was not identified until many years later.

There were several possible candidates for the role. But the most likely person was Dr. Hans Thomsen, the German chargé d'affaires in Washington. Hitler had withdrawn his ambassador in November 1938, in retaliation for the recall of the American ambassador from Berlin after the Kristallnacht pogrom.The "blond Viking" and "smart spymaster" Thomsen, a Ph.D., had been running the embassy ever since. On April 3, 1940, Thomsen sent a revealing cable to Berlin:

TOP SECRET   Washington, April 3, 1940
No. 527 of April 3   1:12 P.M.

A reliable and tried confidential agent who is very friendly with the director of the code room of the State Department reports as follows after having seen the relevant telegraphic reports:

1) Kennedy reports serious differences of opinion between London and Paris. The French were "fed up" and desired to loosen the ties with England. Laval was emerging as Reynaud's probable successor. In order to make France keep in with them, the English Government had promised her the Rhine-Ruhr district after final victory and after the division of Germany into constituent parts as before 1870.

2) Phillips reports a dispute between Mussolini and Ciano [Italian foreign minister]. Ciano who made no secret of his pro-Allied sympathies had been sharply reprimanded by Mussolini. Mussolini had declared that he would not dream of ever being disloyal to the Führer.

THOMSEN

The culprit in the code room was Joseph P. Dugan, a clerk there for thirty years. His perfidy was not exposed until 1956, after his death, with the publication of the tenth volume of captured German Foreign Office documents, covering the year 1940. Dugan's treachery was unwitting: he had been persuaded by a friend, an anti-British isolationist, to let him look at signals, particularly those between Ambassador Kennedy and the president. Thinking his friend was passing the information to isolationist contacts "on the Hill" who would help bring down Roosevelt, Dugan readily allowed his friend to read the signals and in some cases to make copies of them.

But instead of going to his isolationist contacts in Congress, the friend—who has never been publicly identified—went straight to the German embassy on Massachusetts Avenue, where he handed the signals over to be encoded at Dr. Thomsen's direction and cabled immediately to Berlin. Among the other signals passed by the friend with information gleaned from Dugan's office in the old Army, Navy, and State Departments building on Pennsylvania Avenue were those concerned with Kennedy's critical attitude toward Britain and its chances of survival, and his complaints about the ways he was being bypassed by Roosevelt's special envoys Sumner Welles and William (Wild Bill) Donovan. The latter went on to found the Office of Special Services, the OSS, based on Britain's Special Operations Executive.

Between October 22, 1939, and April 29, 1941, Thomsen sent six important signals to Berlin based on information originating with Dugan. The most damaging was the last, alerting the Germans to the startling fact that the United States had succeeded in cracking the Japanese diplomatic code. The Germans immediately notified the Japanese via their ambassador in Berlin, but the Japanese refused to accept the idea that the Americans could have broken anything but a few low-grade codes, and continued using what they still considered to be their unbreakable ciphers.

Over the following four months, the British intercepted several more signals from Rome to Berlin containing paraphrased Churchill-Roosevelt messages. The last, sent on May 23, three days after Kent and Anna Wolkoff were arrested and at almost exactly the same time as Ramsay was being picked up, was potentially the most damaging of all:

MOST URGENT   Rome, May 23, 1940—8:50 P.M.
TOP SECRET   Received May 23—10:00 P.M.
No. 955 of May 23   Pol. I M780g

For the personal attention of the Foreign Minister.

I am reliably informed by an unimpeachable source that on the 16th of this month the American Ambassador in London received telegraphic instructions from Roosevelt to deliver a message of reply to Churchill, which deals as follows with various requests presented by the latter in a personal letter to the President.

1) It would be possible to hand over 40 or 50 destroyers of the old type, but this is subject to the special approval of Congress which would be difficult to obtain at present. Besides in view of the require-

ments of national defense it is even doubtful whether they could be spared. In addition, in Roosevelt's view, even given approval, it would take at least 6 or 7 weeks before the ships could take up active duty under the British flag.

2) As regards supplying the Allied governments with the most modern type of anti-aircraft guns, everything possible was being done.

3) If British plenipotentiaries received appropriate instructions at once to discuss with the responsible authorities in Washington questions relating to the manning and supply of ammunition for anti-aircraft guns, America would be ready to give the most favorable consideration to the matter, always, of course, with due regard to the requirements of her own national defense.

4) The British plenipotentiary has already made contact with responsible American authorities regarding delivery of steel; the President believes that satisfactory results have already been achieved.

5) The President would examine Churchill's suggestion of a visit by an American squadron to an Irish port.

6) As Churchill knew, the American fleet was now concentrated at Hawaii, where it must in any case remain for the moment.

Finally, the President promises to define his attitude towards further questions in the Churchill letter as soon as he is in a position to do so.

I am sending the documentary evidence for this report by the next reliable opportunity.

MACKENSEN

After Kent's arrest, the flow of signals from Rome to Berlin stopped abruptly. The leak from London had been plugged.

It was at the end of February 1940 that Joan Miller first reported to Knight that Anna Wolkoff was talking about Tyler Kent as "an important contact." About a month later, Joan confirmed that Anna was devoting a great deal of time to Kent, and that she described him as being pro-German in outlook. What was more important was that she said he had given her "interesting diplomatic information of a confidential nature."

Knight began taking a greater interest in Kent, especially when he heard in mid-April from "another equally reliable source," presumably Marjorie Mackie, that Anna was claiming Kent had given her secret information about the battles off the coast of Norway. Hitler had ended the phony war with a bang

on April 9 by invading two neutral countries, Denmark and
Norway, and fierce battles were raging in and around Norway.
By twisting this information, Anna was able to create excellent
anti-British propaganda.

At the same time, Anna also began bragging to her friends
that Kent was telling her about confidential exchanges between
Kennedy and the British foreign secretary, Lord Halifax, and
that Kennedy had reported to President Roosevelt that conditions in Britain were so bad that serious internal trouble might
be expected at any moment. She also talked of Kent's showing
her, or telling her about, secret correspondence between Guy
Liddell and Washington concerning the purchase of radio di-
rection-finding equipment. This last piece of information must
have come as a particular shock to Knight and Liddell, since the
equipment was for pinpointing the position of radio transmit-
ters and was to help MI5 catch spies.

Joan also reported that "Tyler Kent was using the American
diplomatic bag on behalf of the Right Club for communicating
with contacts in the United States," and that he and Anna
Wolkoff had dined together at the Ritz. The dinner at the Ritz
may well have taken place, but the claim about using the diplomatic bag or pouch was a fabrication by Kent or Anna; Kent
had sent only one letter to the States since his arrival in London, telling his mother he had met May Straker.

For some reason, Knight still did not move in on Kent. Presumably he was hoping to accumulate yet more evidence, particularly on his contacts in Britain. On Saturday, April 13, his
watchers trailed Anna Wolkoff from Kent's flat to the studios of
a White Russian émigré photographer, Eugene (Nicholas
Eugenevich) Smirnoff, where she waited while he photographed two documents, one a single sheet, the other two
pages long, which she had borrowed from Kent.

Even then, Knight held his fire. During the first week in May,
according to a report he later gave to the American embassy,
he obtained a warrant and searched the home of "another
member of the Right Club who was known to be in communication with a British subject engaged in assisting the enemy in
Germany." Anna was alarmed by this, and gave what she described as her "most incriminating papers" to Kent, who told
her he would lock them away in a safe at the embassy. It was

presumably at this same time that Captain Ramsay handed over the red leather-bound ledger, its covers secured by a lock, to Kent for safekeeping, in the belief that Kent's diplomatic immunity would offer protection against searches by the police and the Security Service.

With the eruption of the war in France and the Low Countries on May 10, and the enforced resignation of Chamberlain in favor of Churchill as prime minister, the situation in Britain changed radically. Within a week, it had become desperate as the Nazi panzer divisions smashed their way through the British and French armies. Churchill flew to France on May 16 to see the position for himself, and cabled back to the War Cabinet emphasizing "the mortal gravity of the hour." Back home the next day, he worried about the possibility of France's making a separate peace with Hitler, followed by a mass invasion of Britain by air. Would there, he agonized, be "enough trustworthy troops in England," since virtually every trained soldier and every piece of modern fighting equipment was across the Channel?

In such a crisis, fears of the existence of a fifth column of Nazi sympathizers were inevitably magnified, fears that were energetically fanned by four German radio stations broadcasting propaganda to Britain. These broadcasts were intended to sow confusion and doubt. They threatened an imminent invasion, emphasizing the help the Germans expected to receive from "loyal" Britons opposed to the warmonger Churchill. It was impossible to tell how many people actually listened to the broadcasts, but they were advertised by stickers, leaflets, and posters distributed by supporters like Right Club members. Spy fever swept the country, along with demoralizing rumors of sabotage and of the landing of German paratroops. The collapse of Holland, Belgium, and then France was attributed to the treachery of pro-German collaborators, who had aided the enemy by securing bridges and spreading panic among the civilian population. The same, it was said, could well happen in Britain.

Faced with a potential crisis of confidence, Churchill called a special meeting of the War Cabinet to press for an extension of internment. Already, all aliens of German descent were locked away in internment camps: Even though most of them were refugees from Nazism, the government could not afford to ignore the possibility that the Nazis might have infiltrated agents among them, and there simply was not time to screen each one. Now, Churchill also wanted to imprison Britons whose loyalty might be in question.

For Knight and Liddell, it was time to blow the whistle on Anna Wolkoff and Tyler Kent.

Washington, D.C., November 17, 1933. President Franklin D. Roosevelt greets
William C. Bullitt, the U.S. ambassador to the USSR, just recognized by the
United States.

Spaso House, the U.S. ambassador's residence in Moscow, first occupied by Bullitt in 1934.

Mokhovaya House, Moscow, served as U.S. chancellery and residence for Foreign Service officers and clerks (1934–1953). Tyler Kent lived here for most of his tenure in Moscow.

Kent took this picture of Red Square and the Kremlin from his window in Mokhovaya House.

This heretofore unpublished photograph (ca. 1938) of the staff of the U.S. embassy in Moscow during Ambassador Joseph E. Davies's tenure was found in Tyler Kent's files. Included in the photo are: (middle row) Charles (Chip) Bohlen, third secretary (fifth from left); Loy W. Henderson, first secretary (eighth from left); Alexander Kirk, minister counsellor (tenth from left); Davies (twelfth from left); Lt. Col. Philip D. Faymonville (fourteenth from left). Kent was apparently absent.

The United States Embassy, Grosvenor Square, London. Joseph P. Kennedy, U.S. ambassador to the Court of St. James's (in doorway), and his embassy staff, including both American and British employees, taken shortly after Kennedy's arrival in March 1938.

London, March 3, 1938. Joseph P. Kennedy opens his first week as ambassador with a conference of his Foreign Service officers and personal staff members: (left to right) Kennedy; T. E. Brown, second secretary; Herschel V. Johnson, embassy counsellor; Harold Hinton, personal press officer; D. Jenks, consul general.

A grim-visaged Anna Wolkoff in her Auxiliary Fire Service uniform.

Captain Archibald Ramsay, MP, and Lady Ismay Ramsay attending the 1937 Eton–Harrow cricket match. The pro-German, anti-Semitic Ramsay retained his seat in Parliament through more than four years of wartime imprisonment.

Major General Sir Vernon Kell (left), director general of the British Security Service (MI5) from 1909 to 1940, and Captain Guy Liddell, director of MI5's B division, responsible for counterespionage.

Author's Collection

47 Gloucester Court, London. Kent's flat was on the second floor. It was here, on May 20, 1940, that Kent was arrested, in the presence of his mistress.

Author's Collection

Joan Miller, beautiful undercover agent of MI5's section B5(b), who infiltrated the Right Club and provided vital evidence against Kent, Wolkoff, and Ramsay. The photograph was damaged by a jealous rival.

Estate of Joan Miller

Max Knight, head of MI5's section B5(b), who masterminded the investigation and arrest of Tyler Kent. In this 1940 photograph, he is wearing a uniform to which he is not entitled as a cover, like his rank, for his MI5 operations.

Estate of Joan Miller

EIGHT

A Fool or a Rogue

AT 12:30 P.M. ON SATURDAY, May 18, the telephone rang in Herschel Johnson's office in the London embassy. When he answered, Johnson heard a familiar voice.

"Guy Liddell here, Herschel. Can you see one of my assistants at three this afternoon on a most delicate matter?"

Johnson agreed immediately. He had, of course, received Liddell's warning of the preceding February, and he and Liddell had been friends for several years. Although he always referred to the Englishman as a member of the "military intelligence branch of Scotland Yard," he almost certainly knew that Liddell was in fact director of MI5's B Division, responsible for counterespionage.

Johnson himself had played a shadowy role in the worlds of intelligence and security for a considerable time. There is evidence that as far back as 1915 he was the State Department's expert in this field, maintaining contact with the British on the activities of German agents and saboteurs in America. When Lieutenant Colonel Claude Dansey, then a senior officer in MI5, was sent to Washington in April 1917 to advise the U.S. government on setting up its first military intelligence agencies, he dealt initially through his friend Herschel Johnson. By 1940, Dansey—the most experienced and one of the most powerful intelligence officers in the world—had become operational head of the Secret Service and its chief in all but name. Dansey never lost touch with any of his influential friends and contacts, and it is unthinkable that he would not have kept up with Johnson.

Throughout the 1930s, Johnson was responsible for communicating with Guy Liddell on matters concerning the mutual security of Great Britain and the United States. When Liddell visited Washington in 1938, it was Johnson who gave him warm introductions to the State Department communications expert, Assistant Secretary Dunn, and others. With such a background, it seems likely that Johnson was posted to the London embassy in the critical year of 1938 specifically to handle intelligence and security coordination with the British. At that time, of course, America had no official intelligence agency.

Liddell's "assistant" showed up at 3:00 P.M. It was Max Knight, who wasted little time in getting down to business. "Information of a very serious nature has come to the attention of Scotland Yard," he began, keeping up the fiction that MI5 did not exist, "regarding the activities of Tyler Kent, an employee of this embassy.

"This will be a fairly long story," he continued, settling himself comfortably in his chair. He started by telling of Kent's meeting with Ludwig Matthias, the suspected Gestapo agent, back in October. Johnson, shocked that the Yard had not notified the ambassador at the time, told Knight he considered this "most unfortunate." He said, indignantly, that the embassy would never have allowed Kent to continue working in the code room if they had known he was under suspicion. Knight, completely unruffled, explained this away by saying they had wanted firmer evidence before making any accusation. He did not tell Johnson that he had said nothing at the time because MI5 did not trust Kennedy himself, and was compiling a dossier on him for the Foreign Office. He then gave detailed descriptions of the Right Club and the beliefs and activities of Captain Ramsay and Anna Wolkoff, and listed many of the meetings between Kent and Wolkoff.

According to Johnson's report, Knight told him that on April 22, 1940, it had become clear from things Anna Wolkoff had said that Kent had either shown her or told her about "correspondence which had been exchanged between a British government source and the United States Embassy on the subject of purchasing certain technical apparatus from the American government." Knight explained that this came from secret messages sent by Johnson himself to James Clement Dunn concerning the purchase of American radio interception equipment by British intelligence.

Knight went on to say that Anna Wolkoff had phoned Kent at the embassy on May 14, and they had talked in Russian. (Wolkoff later explained that she and Kent always used Russian when speaking over the phone because of a possible wire tap.) After listing several other instances in which Wolkoff had repeated information that only Kent could have provided, he told Johnson he planned to arrest Wolkoff in two days, on Monday, May 20, and that it would be most helpful if a simultaneous search could be made of Kent's flat. Johnson agreed with this and with the suggestion that nothing should be done before then that might arouse Kent's suspicions.

It was evening before Knight left the embassy. Johnson immediately phoned Kennedy at his residence in Windsor. To Roosevelt's disgust, the ambassador had been the first member of the diplomatic corps to move out of London and away from the danger of bombing after the outbreak of war. The ambassador was dining with Clare Boothe Luce, the successful playwright and future American ambassador to Italy, wife of his good friend Henry Luce. The meal was of more than social significance to Kennedy, since the Luces were actively promoting his presidential ambitions with a stream of favorable comment in their mass-circulation magazines. As Kennedy was occupied, and the phone lines were not secure, Johnson had to content himself with conveying the seriousness of the affair without citing names or details.

The next morning, under a cloudless blue sky, he drove the

twenty-three miles west to Windsor to give Kennedy a complete report. Before leaving London, he called the permanent under secretary at the Foreign Office, Sir Alexander Cadogan, who knew about the Kent affair in general terms but not in detail. What, he asked, was the position in British law concerning diplomatic immunity in respect of a clerk of Kent's status who was neither a Foreign Service officer nor a civil service employee? Cadogan promised, "I'll check this out immediately and get back to you." His answer came while Johnson was briefing the ambassador: Sir William Malkin, the Foreign Office's legal adviser, said there was no legal barrier to a search of Kent's flat, provided Kennedy approved. Kennedy agreed at once.

"I told Sir Alexander that the ambassador waived any immunity for Kent," Johnson later wrote in his report, "and would report the matter to the secretary of state immediately for confirmation and approval."

He then drove back to London and telephoned Knight at Dolphin Square. Knight hurried around to Johnson's flat to discuss the next day's operation. The warrants were already in hand, he said. Wolkoff would be arrested at about 9:30 A.M. and Kent's flat would be raided at about 11:00 A.M.

As Knight left Johnson's flat that afternoon, a greater drama was taking place elsewhere. News reached London after lunch that the German panzers had reached the Channel, and that the French armies to the south of the British Expeditionary Force had, as Churchill's private secretary John Colville put it in his diary, "melted away and left a vast gap on the British right." The Allies were facing a military disaster of the first order.

Churchill hastened back to Downing Street from Chartwell, his country home in Kent, where he had gone that morning for a few hours' sunshine while he wrote his first speech to the nation as prime minister, which he was to broadcast that evening. Speech writing was postponed in favor of an emergency War Cabinet meeting at 4:30, when Churchill tried to breathe fire into generals and politicians alike. "His spirit is indomitable," wrote Colville, "and even if France and England should be lost, I feel he would carry on the crusade himself with a band of privateers."

The Cabinet meeting over, Churchill turned to his speech at 6:00 P.M. Three hours later, he was on the air. He made no effort to hide the seriousness of the situation. After describing the German successes, he warned:

We must expect that as soon as stability is reached on the western front, the bulk of that hideous apparatus of aggression which gashed Holland into ruin and slavery in a few days, will be turned on us . . . After this battle in France abates its force, there will come the battle for our island—for all that Britain is, and all that Britain means . . . Side by side, the British and French peoples have advanced to rescue not only Europe but mankind from the foulest and most soul-destroying tyranny which has ever darkened and stained the pages of history . . . [B]ehind us—behind the armies and fleets of Britain and France —gather a group of shattered states and bludgeoned races: the Czechs, the Poles, the Norwegians, the Danes, the Dutch, the Belgians—upon all of whom the long night of barbarism will descend, unbroken even by a star of hope, unless we conquer, as conquer we must; as conquer we shall.

Today is Trinity Sunday. Centuries ago words were written to be a call and a spur to the faithful servants of truth and justice: "Arm yourselves, and be ye men of valour, and be in readiness for the conflict; for it is better for us to perish in battle than to look upon the outrage of our nation and our altar. As the Will of God is in Heaven, even so let it be."

While the prime minister's speech was notable as a rallying cry to the nation, its most important element—the call to "arm yourselves"—was primarily aimed at perhaps another audience beyond Britain's shores, across the Atlantic Ocean.

If the battle is to be won, we must provide our men with everincreasing quantities of the weapons and ammunition they need. We must have, and have quickly, more aeroplanes, more tanks, more shells, more guns. There is imperious need for these vital munitions. They increase our strength against the powerfully armed enemy. They replace the wastage of the obstinate struggle; and the knowledge that wastage will be speedily replaced enables us to draw more readily upon our reserves and throw them in now that everything counts so much.

• • • •

At midnight, Tyler Kent reported for duty as usual in the code room of the embassy, where he was working the shift from midnight till 8:00 A.M. He suspected nothing of the net that was closing around him. Two hours later, he was delighted when the night porter, a British citizen named Croft, brought him a large envelope addressed to Herschel Johnson from John Colville. Although he had no authorization to do so, he opened it and found, as he expected, a personal message from Churchill to Roosevelt—the "telegram for those bloody Yankees," which the prime minister had handed to his private secretary earlier. Picking up a pencil, he quickly scribbled down a copy for his own use.

The message, headed SECRET AND PERSONAL FOR THE PRESIDENT FROM FORMER NAVAL PERSON, read as follows:

Lothian [the British ambassador in Washington] has reported his conversation with you. I understand your difficulties but I am very sorry about the destroyers. If they were here in six weeks they would play an invaluable part. The battle in France is full of danger to both sides. Though we have taken heavy toll of enemy in the air and are clawing down two or three to one of their planes, they have still a formidable numerical superiority. Our most vital need is therefore the delivery at the earliest possible date of the largest possible number of Curtiss P-40 fighters now in course of delivery to your army.

With regard to the closing part of your talk with Lothian, our intention is whatever happens to fight on to the end in this Island and, provided we can get the help for which we ask, we hope to run them very close in the air battle in view of individual superiority. Members of the present administration would likely go down during this process should it result adversely, but in no conceivable circumstances will we consent to surrender. If members of the present administration were finished and others came in to parlay amid the ruins, you must not be blind to the fact that the sole remaining bargaining counter with Germany would be the fleet, and if this country was left by the United States to its fate no one would have the right to blame those responsible if they made the best terms they could for the surviving inhabitants. Excuse me, Mr. President, for putting this nightmare bluntly. Evidently I could not answer for my successors who in utter despair and helplessness might well have to accommodate themselves to the German will. However, there is happily no need at present to dwell upon such ideas. Once more thanking you for your good will.

With his private copy complete, Kent settled down to encode the message, ready for transmission. But the dramatic situation was about to take a comic turn worthy of Gogol's *The Inspector General.* He had completed only the first two lines before he was interrupted by an irate Rudolf E. Schoenfeld, the Foreign Service officer in charge of the code section.

Schoenfeld had given orders that he was to be notified immediately whenever a message for the president from Churchill came in while he was off duty. He had been phoned at home by the embassy duty officer, Vice Consul J. P. Palmer, at 2:00 A.M. about the message and had told him, "Hold it. I'll be right over." He got up immediately, dressed, and made the ten-minute walk to the embassy; like most officers and clerks, he lived within easy walking distance of the chancery to avoid public transit delays during air-raid alerts. He was furious on his arrival to discover that the message was already being encoded by Tyler Kent.

"Why, in view of my special request to hold it, was it sent to the code room?" he demanded.

Palmer explained that the night porter had received the message and had for some reason taken it directly to the code room before notifying him. Slightly mollified, Schoenfeld hurried to the code room and asserted his authority by taking the message away from Kent. But he had hardly finished reading it when the phone rang and a man announced as Captain William Elliot of the Admiralty informed him that the prime minister did not want the message sent and wished to have it returned to him before 6:00 A.M. Elliot said he would be coming over to pick it up.

Schoenfeld was deeply suspicious of this. "In view of the obviously dangerous implications of Captain Elliot's request," he wrote in his report on the affair, "I telephoned the Admiralty." It seemed that Schoenfeld's doubts were justified, for the night duty officer at the Admiralty, a Captain Burridge, denied any knowledge of the message or of Captain Elliot. Schoenfeld, no doubt believing he had uncovered some dark plot, rang through to 10 Downing Street and asked to speak to one of the prime minister's private secretaries. To his chagrin, he was told that Mr. Churchill had not yet moved into number 10; Neville Chamberlain, although he had resigned ten days before, was still living there. Churchill had graciously allowed him to stay on while he sorted out his affairs and found accommodations. The new prime minister was living in his old quarters at the Trafalgar Square end of Whitehall, Admiralty House.

Another telephone call found a Captain Pym, a secretary of the Imperial Defence Committee, who knew about Churchill's message, described its contents, and confirmed that it had been sent from Colville to Johnson. Pym also confirmed the existence of Elliot, gave a clear physical description of the man, and said he would be wearing a Royal Air Force uniform.

Elliot was, in fact, not a naval captain but Group Captain Elliot, RAF. In addition to his role as prime minister, Churchill was also minister of defense, and Elliot was a member of the small defense secretariat that had been set up to assist him in this role. He went on to become an air chief marshal, the equivalent of a four-star general. When he arrived at the embassy and presented his identification, Schoenfeld was relived to see that he fitted the description given over the phone by Captain Pym.

"Quite frankly," Schoenfeld told him primly, "I felt it necessary to check up on you. In these times one cannot be too careful. We are naturally obliged to safeguard the British government as well as ourselves."

Elliot agreed, interjecting, with a nod, "Fifth column activities." He explained that the prime minister was "rather unorthodox in his methods," and there had been a bit of a foul-up over the message. Churchill had said he wanted it recalled, without saying why, and had then retired to bed with orders that he was not to be disturbed.

Schoenfeld chatted with Elliot for a quarter of an hour, then handed over the message, together with Colville's covering note, against a signed receipt. Next morning, soon after Kent's arrest, the message was returned to Schoenfeld. It had not been altered in any way.

There is a simple explanation for Churchill's behavior over the message for Roosevelt. It seems certain that he had been informed about Tyler Kent and his impending arrest, most likely through his trusted confidant Major Desmond Morton, who maintained contact on his behalf with the Foreign Office and the intelligence and security services. Morton, a gregarious, hard-drinking Irishman, had survived a rifle shot through the heart in the First World War and had been awarded the Military Cross for bravery. In the thirties he became part of the intelligence establishment as head of the Industrial Intelligence Centre, and illegally supplied Churchill, during his wilderness years, with secret information about German armaments and capabilities, which fueled his attacks on Chamberlain and the appeasers. Morton's closest friend and contact in MI5 was Max Knight; the line to Churchill was therefore a very short one.

In addition to the state of the war and the increasingly delicate nature of the personal correspondence between Churchill and Roosevelt, there was another, even more pressing reason for MI5 to move in on Kent at this particular time. After a visit to the front in France during the previous week, Churchill had decided to begin sending the president copies of the daily telegrams on military operations, primarily compiled for the heads of the British dominions—Canada, Australia, South Africa, and New Zealand. The first telegrams to be copied for the White House were those for May 19. After that date, there could be no question of allowing Kent to remain where he was. The trap would have to be sprung without further delay.

Monday, May 20, was a cloudy day—the first after three whole weeks of unbroken sunshine and clear skies. Shortly after 9:00 in the morning, an eleven-year-old boy was waiting for his mother outside the Russian Tea Room in Harrington Road, South Kensington, where she worked as a cook. Fascinated, he watched as a police car drew up and four men in gray suits climbed out and entered the building. They soon emerged with Anna Wolkoff, obviously under arrest; they bundled her into the car and drove swiftly away. To a young cockney lad in wartime London, Wolkoff was a strange and sinister foreigner, a perfect type, with her arrogant manner and, sometimes, even a monocle, for a sensational storybook villain. There could be little doubt that he had just witnessed the capture of a spy—and indeed he learned later that it was really true. The scene impressed itself on his mind forever, planting an interest in espionage and covert operations that was to blossom into a grove of best-selling spy thrillers. The boy's name was Len Deighton.

At 11:10 A.M., Ambassador Kennedy went into his outer office and instructed Franklin Crosbie Gowen, second secretary in the embassy, that he was to accompany Max Knight to Tyler Kent's flat. "Bear in mind, Franklin," he told him, "that in case Kent says his rooms cannot be searched because of his diplomatic immunity, tell him to take the matter up with me."

Knight, with Detective Inspector Pearson and Detective Constables Scott and Buswell, arrived to collect Gowen at 11:15. Five minutes later, they were ringing the doorbell of 47 Gloucester Place, where an unsuspecting Tyler Kent was entertaining Irene Danischewsky in his bedroom.

Once the search of Kent's flat was completed and he had finished dressing, elegantly as always in his London-tailored suit, he was marched out the front door, hustled into the police car, and driven away. Knight phoned for a cab from the nearest stand, and he and Gowen loaded in the evidence and followed. They went not to a police station, however, but to the embassy, where, accompanied by the two detective constables, Kent was shut up in room 119 until midafternoon.

While Gowen stationed himself in the ambassador's anteroom, Knight took Kent's brown leather suitcase and cardboard cartons into Kennedy's office, where John G. Erhardt, the first secretary and consul general, and Herschel Johnson were waiting with the ambassador. The second-floor room was sparsely furnished; it held Kennedy's large desk, several chairs, a radio for receiving BBC domestic programs, and a shortwave set for those from farther afield. There was a large picture of Roosevelt on one wall, and a single group photograph of the ambassador's family on the desk. Two vases of fresh-cut flowers added a touch of color.

"Let's look at the evidence," Kennedy said as the suitcase and cartons were placed on the desk before him. He may have hoped that the British charges would prove to be exaggerated if not groundless. But any such hopes were immediately shattered as the suitcase and cartons were opened.

The sheer volume of papers was overwhelming; there were thirty file folders, plus hundreds of unsorted papers. Their

classification ranged from confidential to secret, and they included signals to Washington, from other embassies and legations in Europe, that were generally routed through London.
All told, there proved to be 1929 documents. It took until June
4 to check and list them all; the title-by-title list filled sixty-
seven closely typed pages. But their nature was immediately
apparent: they were all signals that had passed through the
London embassy code room from January 1938 until May 20,
1940, including of course the penciled copy of that very day's
message from Churchill to Roosevelt which had been found in
Kent's pocket.

A quick look inside a folder marked "Churchill" revealed
copies of six other most secret or top secret messages between
Churchill and Roosevelt. As if this were not enough, Kennedy
had to face the extreme personal chagrin of seeing a copy of his
own recommendation to Roosevelt, which he had added to
Churchill's desperate plea for help sent on May 15. Referring
to the request for the loan of forty or fifty old destroyers,
several hundred aircraft, antiaircraft guns, and ammunition,
Kennedy had said that he believed Britain was on the verge of
collapse, and added, "If we had to fight to protect our own
lives, we would do better fighting in our own backyard." Such a
disclosure of his defeatist, anti-British stance, presenting
Knight with clear evidence that he was actually trying to persuade Roosevelt to refuse Churchill's appeals, must have
pushed Kennedy's anger at Kent to boiling point.

The large, leather-bound volume fastened with a strong lock
remained a mystery for the moment, as Knight made no attempt to open it. But an unlocked tin box was found to contain
Kent's professional and social name cards and his address
book. In this were listed a number of names, addresses, and
phone numbers of people—mainly women—who were under
surveillance by MI5 and Scotland Yard's Special Branch, several of whom would subsequently be charged and convicted of
violating the Official Secrets Act. One address was that of the
suspected Gestapo agent Ludwig Matthias. A collection of personal correspondence included the "Dearest Pucia" letter
from Kent's former Moscow embassy friend, Anthony J. Barrett, which showed how they had both been involved in smug-

gling furs and jewels from the Soviet Union into the United States.

The two unauthorized sets of duplicate keys to the code and file rooms provided further evidence of Kent's misconduct and irregular intentions; he clearly wanted to be able to get into the rooms at any time, even if he were transferred to other duties. But the most disturbing pieces of evidence were the three glass photographic negatives of Churchill's messages to Roosevelt dated January 29 (embassy signal 265) and February 28 (embassy signal 490). The only possible reason for making negatives was to produce prints. But where were the prints now? Who had received them? The obvious answer was the Germans.

At this time, only Knight among those present in Kennedy's office was aware of the connections between Kent, Wolkoff, and the Duke del Monte. And only Knight knew that MI8 had picked up signals from Ambassador Hans Georg van Mackensen in Rome to the German Foreign Office containing paraphrases of the Churchill-Roosevelt messages. The United States was not directly informed of this intercept nor, until later, of the British success in breaking the German codes and Enigma machine ciphers, which enabled them to read such signals. The operation at Bletchley Park was one of the war's most jealously guarded secrets, and British intelligence not only mistrusted Kennedy but was also only too well aware that the State Department's communications and records department—not to mention its embassy code rooms—was as leaky as the proverbial sieve.

Even without such knowledge, however, Kennedy was thoroughly incensed at Kent's treachery. He was also irate at not being told of Kent's meeting with Matthias and the four-month investigation. Livid with rage, he looked across the desk at Knight and snarled, "Send the traitorous bastard in!"

Kent was propelled into the room by Detective Inspector Pearson. Kennedy glared at him.

"This is quite a serious situation you have got your country involved in," he said. "From the kind of family you come from —people who have fought for the United States—one would not expect you to let us down."

Kent received the rebuke calmly.

"In what way?" he countered.

"You don't think you have?" the ambassador queried. "What did you think you were doing with our codes and telegrams?"

"It was only for my own information."

"Why did you have to have them?"

"Because I thought them very interesting."

At this, Kennedy gave up in disgust and handed the questioning over to Knight. During the entire interview Kent remained, according to Kennedy, "cool, contemptuous, and arrogant," responding to questions with a sneer in his thin, nasal voice. The verbatim transcript vividly illuminates his attitude throughout.

"I am talking to you now by invitation of your ambassador," Knight began formally, "and not in any way in connection with matters which concern only Great Britain at the moment. The situation as I see it is this: I think it is just as well you should know you can be proved to have been associating with this woman, Anna Wolkoff."

"I don't deny that," Kent replied.

Knight began tightening the screw. "I am in a position to prove that she has a channel of communication with Germany," he continued; "that she has used that channel of communication with Germany; and that she is involved in pro-German propaganda, to say the least. As your ambassador has just said, you have been found with documents in your private rooms to which he considers you have no proper title. You would be a very silly man if you did not realize that certain conclusions might be drawn from that situation, and it is for you to offer the explanation, not us."

Kent said nothing. Knight picked up the leather-bound book and asked what it contained. Kent shrugged and said he didn't know.

"Who gave it to you?" Knight demanded.

"I think probably if you opened it you would find out," Kent drawled. Knight cut him short.

"By whom was it given to you?" he snapped.

"Captain Ramsay. What it contains I do not know, He asked me to keep it . . ."

Again Knight cut him short. "Don't you think it strange that a member of Parliament should come to you, a minor official in an embassy, and give you a locked book to take care of for him?" he asked.

Kent did not reply. After a moment, Knight pressed him for an answer. "Now seriously, doesn't it strike you as odd that a member of Parliament should bring you a locked ledger and ask you to take care of it for him?"

Again Kent shrugged and remained silent. But Knight was determined not to let him off the hook. When Kent finally said he didn't know why Ramsay should have entrusted the book to him, Knight told him he was "adopting a sort of naïve attitude that failed to deceive. You are either hiding something, or . . ."

Again Kent insisted that Ramsay had simply given him the book for safekeeping. Knight moved on. "Did you know that Captain Ramsay was associated with Anna Wolkoff?" he asked.

"Yes, if by 'associated' you mean that he knows her," Kent replied, still perfectly cool.

Knight was too professional to be pricked by Kent's supercilious manner. "There's no time to go into all these details here. There will probably be further opportunities on future occasions," he told him. Changing tack, he produced a piece of paper from his pocket. "Here is a letter that you wrote to Anna Wolkoff on March 21, 1940."

Kennedy was interested by this new piece of evidence. "May I see that?" he asked.

"Certainly," Knight replied, handing it over to him. Turning back to Kent, he said, "In that letter you write about coming back from the Easter holiday, at which time 'I hope to see you and make the acquaintances of more of your interesting friends.' Now, who are the 'interesting friends'?"

Kent replied that he had been talking about Captain Ramsay, whom he found interesting because "we had a sort of common view, to a certain extent."

Knight changed the line of his attack once more. "The first time that you came to my attention was in February of 1940," he told him, not strictly truthfully, "when your friend Anna Wolkoff was telling people that she had made an extremely useful contact with a young man at the American embassy. I am going to speak now extremely bluntly. I am afraid I must take the view that you are either a fool or a rogue, because you cannot possibly be in any position except that of a man who has either been made use of or who knows all these people. I propose to show you how. Now, on April 16, 1940, it was reported to me that Anna Wolkoff was telling some of her close associates in the Right Club—I presume you know what the Right Club is?"

"I have heard of it," Kent replied airily.

Knight turned to Kennedy again. "She was telling her associates a story which purported to be based on an interview you, Mr. Ambassador, had with Lord Halifax, and it concerned the landing of the Germans in Norway and the difficulties that had been encountered by the British Navy in connection with that. I believe I am right in saying that that is only a small indication, but it has some truth." He switched back to Kent, pressing harder. "I don't know how you are prepared to explain that Anna Wolkoff should know that, even if you claim that you didn't tell her."

Kent remained calm. "I don't remember what I said in conversation in April of 1940," he answered.

"You have a very good memory for what you have not said but not a very good memory for what you have said." Knight's irritation showed for a moment, but he swiftly controlled it and returned to the attack, displaying a little more of his hand, even though it contradicted what he had already said about the start of his interest in Kent. "I talked to you this morning about this man Matthias," he said. "Now, you were in a restaurant with Matthias on 8 October 1939. He then went and paid a short visit to your room at the Cumberland. On leaving, Matthias was carrying an envelope approximately ten inches by sixteen inches, which he was not carrying when he went into the hotel."

If Kent was rattled by this display of omniscience, he did not show it. "I certainly don't remember that incident at all," he claimed, and went on to the cover story agreed to by himself and Matthias. "I am guilty of one thing, and that is smuggling through the British customs a box of cigars, which I subsequently lost, and that was the object of his visit to my room."

Knight could hardly have been convinced by this explanation, but there was little he could do for that moment. He went on to reveal more of his knowledge, no doubt hoping to shake Kent's self-confidence. "On the April 16 incident I will give you some more details. I believe you had dinner with Anna Wolkoff at the Russian Tea Room on April 12?"

"I have had dinner there two or three times," Kent shot back. "I don't remember the dates."

"In a conversation you had with her on that occasion she claims that you gave her confidential information regarding the North Sea battles—the success had been greatly exaggerated and it was British propaganda designed to cover heavy British losses sustained in the air attack on Scapa Flow. Then followed further conversation on the version given your ambassador by Lord Halifax. On 21st of April, Anna Wolkoff visited you at your rooms, and just after she came out of there she was in possession of some information about correspondence which had been going on between officials in the British government and officials in the American embassy on the subject of the purchase of certain technical radio apparatus."

Kent vacillated. "There may be something on that in some of those papers. I don't know just what that refers to . . ."

Knight moved on to another area, asking Kent whether he had ever sent any communications to America in the diplomatic pouch. Kent said he had not, apart from a few letters to his immediate family. He also denied knowledge of the identity of Lord Haw-Haw, saying that all he knew of him was that he was "supposed to be some sort of Irishman."

Knight seemed not to be getting anywhere. After trying once more to get information on Ramsay's book, he returned to the stolen documents.

"It is not for me to discuss the question of your position with regard to these documents belonging to your government, because that is not my affair at all. But your explanation about this appears to me to be extremely unconvincing, and your explanations of every point raised are unconvincing."

By now, Kent was quite sure of himself and was thoroughly enjoying playing with Knight. His response was infuriating. "Well, give them to me again and I will try to be a little bit more clear. You mean the fact that I had the documents at all?"

At this, the ambassador could not contain himself any longer. "That is my interest," he interjected. "You don't expect me to believe for a minute that you had them for your own entertainment?"

"I didn't say 'entertainment.' I said 'interest,' " Kent corrected him.

Knight returned to the attack. "Do you consider yourself entitled to have them to refresh your memory about their confidentiality?" he asked. When he received no reply, his patience began to wear thin. "You know, you are in an extremely bad situation," he reminded Kent. "If you were English you would be in a very difficult position. You don't impress me by your cocky manner."

"I haven't been making any attempt to be cocky or to impress you," Kent replied. "But I say that the reason is just as I stated."

"You thought they would be useful to you in the future?" Knight asked. "What did you mean, they would be useful?"

"I hadn't any definite plan as to what use I'd make of them," Kent answered. "But they doubtless are of importance as historical documents and throw interesting light on what we are going through."

Kennedy intervened again. "You know, of course, that it is against the law for you to have these documents?"

"I am not aware of that."

"Well, let me assure you that it is," the ambassador continued. "You were not by any chance going to take them with you to Germany when you asked for a transfer there, without our knowledge?"

"No, I couldn't have got them out. I'm not entitled to exemption."

"But I think you will find that in regard to many countries you'd get it," Knight told him.

At this, Kent was silent again. Knight tried a new direction. "Do you consider Anna Wolkoff a loyal British subject?" he asked.

"Well, if you mean that she holds some views that are apparently at variance with some of the ideals possibly of the British government," Kent responded, "that is quite true; but it doesn't mean that she is not a loyal British subject."

Knight pounced on this admission, asking whether a loyal British subject would communicate secretly with the enemy.

Kent tried to back off. "No, but I have absolutely no knowledge of that," he claimed. "This is the first I have heard of it. If you say that she is in communication with the enemy, why of course she is not a loyal British subject; but when you put the question to me this morning I didn't know that."

"But this morning you wouldn't say yes or no," Knight persisted. "A person is either loyal or disloyal."

"If you think that everybody that doesn't approve of what is being done by the country is disloyal, that would . . ."

Knight cut him off abruptly. "Now you are merely trying to talk like a parlor politician, but we are dealing with fundamentals."

Kennedy could tell that Kent did not appreciate the seriousness of the situation. As Kent himself later admitted, he did not for one moment believe that he would ever face a spy trial in London with the possibility of a death sentence at the end of it. To his mind, the worst that could have happened would be deportation to the United States, where the political implications were so explosive that the Roosevelt administration would not have dared prosecute him. This was undoubtedly one reason for his unbearable self-assurance. Kennedy set out to undermine it.

He asked Knight, "If you prove that she is in contact with them she is more or less a spy. If the United States government decides to waive any rights they may have, do I understand that they might very well make Kent part and parcel of that?"

Knight's reply came without hesitation. "Subject to the production of evidence under the law, yes."

But the implied threat appeared to have little effect on Kent; he gave no sign of contrition or hint of cooperation. He still did not attempt to defend his actions, or even to admit that he knew them to have been wrong. Knight decided it was time to move on.

"I think, honestly, that at this stage nothing very useful is to be got by carrying on this conversation," he told Kennedy. The ambassador had no option but to agree. As Knight gathered up those pieces of evidence he needed, Kennedy relieved Kent of his diplomatic passport. Then Detective Inspector Pearson took him away to be formally charged.

· · · ·

While Kent was being questioned in Kennedy's office, Gowen had been busy elsewhere. When they had arrived at the embassy, he had, with the approval of the ambassador, told the telephone switchboard operator that any calls for Kent should be referred to him in room 116, the anteroom to the ambassador's office, where Gowen had his own desk. At the same time, he told the head porter that "as Mr. Kent was doing some work in another room of the embassy," he was to show visitors asking for Kent to waiting room 115 and tell them Kent would see them "as soon as he was free." That would not be for another five and a half years.

During the next day or two, Gowen took a succession of calls, passing himself off as Kent by speaking in a very low voice and tapping the keys of a typewriter alongside the phone to confuse the callers. Each time, he asked for the person's name and telephone number. As soon as the call was finished, he phoned the information to Sir Norman Kendal, the assistant commissioner responsible for the Criminal Investigation Department at Scotland Yard—the third ranking officer in the Metropolitan Police and the most senior detective in Britain—who had now personally taken charge of the police side of the case.

Although Gowen obviously enjoyed entering into the world of cloaks and daggers—it must have been a welcome relief from the tedium of embassy routine—he does seem to have had some qualms. "Of course," he noted, "not all the people who telephoned Kent since his arrest may know what he is up to." Kendal, however, had no such worries. "I always want to be fair," he told Gowen, "but in cases of this kind we cannot take anything for granted—to ascertain who were Kent's friends, and their friends, where they met, and what they did is of utmost importance. So often people who seem to be the most plausible and to enjoy the best reputation are the most dangerous."

There had already been one interesting call, from a woman who gave her number as Bayswater 0757 but refused to leave her name. She had reported, "Mr. Kent's house was raided by the police this morning." After a little while, she called again, still not saying who she was but wanting to see Kent. Gowen told her to come to the embassy, and on her arrival instructed the porter to tell her to wait outside; Kent would see her at one o'clock. She was Irene Danischewsky.

Inspector Pearson told Gowen, "As the woman knows me, I'll walk home with her. I'll tell her that if she keeps interfering with Kent or your embassy, I'll get her into trouble with her husband." The threat must have been effective, for in midafternoon Pearson returned, having searched her flat, presumably with her permission. He said he had found nothing incriminating.

Another caller at the embassy was Mr. E. Sabline, whose card described him as a former Imperial chargé d'affaires in London and president of the Russian Refugee Committee. Gowen sent the uniformed head porter to tell him "Mr. Kent is so sorry but he can't get away and hates to keep you waiting. Will you let him know if you have any message for him, and he will reply at once?" Sabline wrote a note asking for a letter of introduction to someone in the consulate, which Gowen passed on at once, unaware that MI5 suspected that Sabline was controlled by the NKVD. Kendal was delighted and told Gowen it was "most important to collect documentary evidence of this kind, for Mr. Sabline could never deny the authenticity of a message written in his own handwriting and addressed to Kent."

On a more mundane note, one call was from Kent's tailors, Messrs. P. Larsson & Son of 36 Great Pulteney Street, just off Regent Street in the heart of the West End, asking for the return of a pattern book and the payment of an outstanding account for £10.9.0. Of course, there was always the possibility that this was some form of coded message—Larsson & Son do not appear in trade or telephone directories of the time—but the bill was paid by Kent's solicitor on August 2.

Kent's success with the opposite sex was clearly demonstrated. Irene Danischewsky was by no means the only woman in his life; most of the other phone calls over the next two or three days were from females. Patricia Dalglish, of 73 Eaton Square, wanted Kent to meet her "and some friends" for lunch at the Berkeley Hotel's restaurant; Mrs. Samuel Allen, at Sloane 4446, desired Kent to meet her "for a cocktail"; Catherine Ridley, at Fulham 4422, asked Kent to dine with her that evening and again "to meet some friends"; another woman phoned but left no message or number; Catherine Georgesky left a message: "My brother has come home on leave—he is now in this country. I'd like you to meet him. How about this evening? Phone me at Western 3182."

Shortly after Gowen began monitoring Kent's calls, a woman rang and, believing she was speaking to Kent, asked, "Won't you come round for a cocktail this afternoon at about six-thirty?" Gowen answered that he had so many people coming in and out of the room that he would have to be short and could not speak very loudly, but that if he could, he would let her know later or show up at the cocktail party.

"Will it be at the same place?" he asked, trying to get the address.

"Yes," she replied, "right around the corner from your place, at 3 Chesham Street, second floor."

Gowen, now thoroughly immersed in the subterfuges of the clandestine world, was instantly suspicious. Chesham Street was in Belgravia, the grandest district of London. It was about a mile and a half from the embassy, and Kent's flat was a good half mile in the other direction. "Hence," he noted, "the reference to 'right around the corner from your place' is not without significance. Obviously the woman who spoke to me on the phone, thinking that I was Kent, knew full well, as Kent would have known, that 3 Chesham Street is not 'right around the corner' from the embassy or from Kent's house. Therefore it may well be that the message was not a conventional one and that what she really wanted to convey was that she or someone else was ready to meet Kent 'right around the corner' from the embassy."

Gowen reported the telephone conversation first to Kennedy and then to Sir Norman Kendal, who said he was "most happy" to know this, and that he would take immediate action with a view to tapping the telephone at 3 Chesham Street. It did not take Kendal long to establish that the caller was Enid Riddell. A little later, she rang again. This time Gowen, "to be very cautious," did not pretend to be Kent, but told her, "He was here a minute ago but has gone out somewhere. I don't think he'll be back for a while." The woman said she would call later.

That evening at about 9:40, while Gowen was with Kennedy at his London residence, he checked with the embassy and was told there had been a phone call for Kent. He hurried back and waited by his telephone. At 10:45 a man called. "Mr. Kent?" he asked. "Will you come to 3 Chesham Street? If you knock at the door, I will open it."

Gowen rang Scotland Yard and asked that a car be sent to the embassy at once. The officers who had been with him that morning had now gone off duty, but ten minutes later a detective named Moss arrived with a uniformed constable in an unmarked police car. Gowen climbed into the car, and they drove to Chesham Street, pulling up a little way from number 3. Gowen took off his raincoat and gave it to the driver to wear over his uniform. As they approached the house, Moss said he would be glad to cooperate, but added, "At the same time, I have no warrant. I can't go into the house and start anything."

"This looks like a fairly respectable house," Gowen replied. "Surely there will be no harm in ringing the bell. If anyone asks our names I'll mutter something, and you call yourself Spencer."

Gowen rang the front doorbell. A man in his shirtsleeves appeared at the basement service entrance some six to eight feet below street level.

"Who's that?" he called up to them.

"Mr. Kent," Gowen answered.

"Oh, yes. I'll only be a minute. Will you please wait?"

He closed his door, leaving the three men above standing in the utter darkness of the blackout. After a moment, the same man opened the front door. "Mr. Kent?" he called into the gloom, where Gowen was standing back a few feet from the light spilling from the doorway.

"Didn't you know Mr. Kent was coming?" Gowen asked.

"Yes," he responded. "I have something for you."

The man handed him a note.

"Oh, that's very nice," Gowen said, adding boldly, "But is the lady still in?"

"Well, really I would have to phone her to see. She may be in her room." He went into an adjoining room, and Gowen heard a telephone ring in the house. Then the man returned and said the lady must have gone out.

Thanking him, Gowen rejoined the police officers, and together they drove to Scotland Yard, where he took a copy of the note, leaving the original with Detective Constable Moss.

The note was signed "Enid." It said she had something important for him and had waited for him until 9:45. She was most anxious to see Kent, and gave the address of a smart restaurant, La Coquille, with the words "At this address."

Gowen found all this very thrilling, no doubt picturing himself as another FBI agent. "I arranged with Scotland Yard to take immediate action to place Secret Service men on the watch at the restaurant," he wrote in his report, "to tap the phones at 3 Chesham Street, and to keep the house under observation. I then proceeded in the same police car to within about half a block of 3 Chesham Street, and stayed there until about 2 A.M. to keep watch on the house myself. I had planned to take the numbers of any cars that might pull up there, and to find out all I could." With obvious disappointment he concluded, "Nothing happened."

Moss, meanwhile, had arranged for the meeting in the restaurant to be covered by other Special Branch detectives, and next day Inspector Pearson raided the house. He found nothing incriminating, but questioned Enid Riddell, who confessed that she had gone to the restaurant the previous night to meet some friends, one of whom was the Duke del Monte, of the Italian embassy. Tyler Kent had been supposed to join them, and she and del Monte had stayed there until very late, waiting for him.

With this information, Max Knight now had positive evidence linking Kent with del Monte, and thus with the paraphrased Churchill-Roosevelt messages sent from the German embassy in Rome to Berlin.

NINE

A Terrible Blow

THERE WAS CONSTERNATION in Washington when news arrived of Tyler Kent's arrest. The first hint of trouble came at 3:02 P.M. on May 20, when a signal from Kennedy clicked into the State Department's communications center. Marked SE-CRET AND PERSONAL FOR THE SECRETARY, it was decoded imme-diately and taken to the acting secretary of state, Sumner Welles, because Hull was ill. The message read:

Following the receipt on Saturday of information that Tyler Kent associated with a gang of spies working in the interests of Germany and Russia, I today caused his private quarters to be searched, finding there substantial amounts of confidential embassy material, including true readings of messages in most confidential codes; also evidence of his personal connections with the spy group. Minute investigation into all circumstances is being carried out and I consider it essential that Kent be detained by the police authorities. In view of the urgency and importance of this matter, I have indicated to the police that I waive any immunity for Kent regarding such proceedings as may be necessary to develop the facts.

The department was not immediately notified last night inasmuch as the arrest of others, including British subjects, simultaneously with the search of Kent's premises was essential and I wished to leave no possible loophole for Kent's being forewarned.

The department's approval and instructions are urgently requested.

KENNEDY

Welles was appalled by the implications, and no doubt annoyed that such a crisis should break while he was holding the fort for Hull. He immediately summoned Assistant Secretary of State Breckinridge Long to his office and put him in personal charge of the affair.

Long was in a foul mood, which was not improved by his new task. He was already burdened with major problems caused by the latest developments in the war in Europe. Following the Wehrmacht's blitzkrieg through the Low Countries and northern France, thousands of anxious Americans were demanding immediate repatriation. This would have been difficult enough at any time, but the Neutrality Act made it almost impossible.

American ships were forbidden to enter the ports of any belligerent nation, so refugees from continental Europe had to be transported to Italy, Spain, or Portugal before they could be picked up, and those in the United Kingdom had to be ferried across the U-boat–infested Irish Sea in order to be repatriated from Galway, on the west coast of the neutral Irish Republic. The program of evacuating British children to the United States, where they would be tended by temporary foster parents, safe from threats of bombing and invasion, had had to be set aside. And life was further complicated by the disruption of communications with the Balkans and other countries, caused by Ambassador Bullitt's burning of embassy code books and destruction of coding machines in Paris.

With all this to cope with, Long felt he had just wasted four precious hours at the Press Club, listening to speeches by the Belgian ambassador and the Dutch minister, and a further forty-five minutes presenting a copy of the president's book *Looking Forward* to the Merchant Marine Association library. And now he was faced with a potential disaster caused by Kent.

For Long, the most immediate worry was not the contents of the signals Kent had stolen; it was that the department's codes and ciphers had been hopelessly compromised. "It may mean our own communications system is no longer secret," he noted in his diary that night. "It is a very serious matter and we are considering what steps to take, which would involve inspections in our embassies in at least four European capitals."

Washington's first response to the news reflected this concern, with a message dispatched to London at 7:00 P.M.

912
SECRET, TO BE DECIPHERED BY JOHNSON
Your 1276, May 20, 7 P.M.
Insofar as your investigation has proceeded, do you feel that the strip cipher system has been compromised?
Please reply immediately.
Welles for Hull

It was not until an hour later, with no reply having been received, that Welles and Long thought to give an answer to Kennedy's requests:

913
STRICTLY CONFIDENTIAL—FOR THE AMBASSADOR
Your 1276, May 20, 7 P.M.
Upon receipt of your telegram Tyler Kent is dismissed from government service as of this date. Please so inform him. You are therefore authorized to waive immunity for Kent.
Please telegraph department in any code you consider still confidential full details of the results of investigations being made.
Welles for Hull

An hour later, a third signal was flashed across the Atlantic, emphasizing the jitters that were afflicting the shocked officials in Washington:

914
TO BE DECODED BY JOHNSON
Strictly confidential for the ambassador from Welles. With further reference to your 1276, May 20, 7 P.M. If you have not already done, I suggest that a careful check be made of all your code clerks and of their associates and activities outside of the embassy.
Welles for Hull

It was the next day at 1:00 P.M., London time, before a signal from Kennedy confirmed Long's worst fears: copies of true readings of messages sent in the strip cipher had been found among the papers in Kent's possession at his home. The strip cipher system, the department's most secret and secure method of communication, was therefore almost certainly compromised. There was no way of knowing who might now have the means of reading it.

Long was pessimistic. "The disclosure of his activities," he noted in his diary that day, "coupled with known leaks of information which we have been unable to account for but which concerned our correspondence with London, and which appeared at Copenhagen, Berlin, and Bucharest—all have made it apparent that he may have accomplices and confederates."

Long's consternation and concern were matched in London, where Kennedy, desperate to save face, was having the embassy turned upside down to investigate the security position. Twenty-four hours later, on May 22, he was able to cable some reassuring news to Washington: all the code books could be accounted for at all times, and none was missing. He had to admit that Kent had often been left alone in the room, particularly on Sundays and holidays, when only a skeleton staff was on duty, and when round-the-clock duty combined with shortage of staff had meant "a one-clerk shift." In all, Kent had been on duty alone on nine occasions since January 1. The majority of these eight-hour shifts had been during the day, and he had been likely at any time to be interrupted by duty officers and telegraph operators.

Although Kennedy may have been encouraged by these findings, the fact that no code or cipher books were missing could not be entirely reassuring. Clutching at straws, he reported that no staff member could recall seeing Kent take a camera into the embassy. It is, of course, ridiculous to expect that any spy would do so openly, and in any case, in a total of seventy-two hours alone in the room, Kent could easily have copied the code and cipher books, or certainly the most important parts of them, by hand.

In fact, it was not even necessary for Kent to be alone to steal secrets. "I copied very few signals other than the FDR and

Churchill cables," he claimed in an interview for this book. "Most of the documents found in my possession, at 47 Gloucester Place, I took from copies in the file room while my fellow clerk was engaged in the adjacent code room."

As for the hopeful statement that no code or cipher books were missing, Long needed no one to tell him that any cryptanalyst, simply by possessing the true readings of messages that had been intercepted and recorded in their ciphered form, would have been able to work out precisely the codes and ciphers.

When the sixty-seven-page list of the documents recovered from Kent was complete, Kennedy took no chances and sent it to Washington by hand, using his longtime friend and secretary Eddie Moore as a courier. Moore sailed on the S.S. *Roosevelt* and delivered the list to Long; the documents themselves remained locked in the embassy safe.

Long scrutinized the list, and found his worst fears realized:

They are a complete history of our diplomatic correspondence since 1938. It is appalling. Hundreds of copies—true readings—of dispatches, cables, messages. Some months every single message going into and out from the London Embassy were copied and the copies found in his room. It means not only that our codes are cracked . . . but that our every diplomatic maneuver was exposed to Germany and Russia . . .

It is a terrible blow—almost a major catastrophe.

As the days passed, there was no indication that the Germans had, in fact, received American diplomatic codes. Concern over the possibility that Kent had passed State Department codes and ciphers to them, or to the Russians, slowly—though never completely—subsided, but the department's division of communications and records set about revamping them all immediately.

In this respect, Kent had done the State Department a great service, for its code and cipher operations had been in disarray since 1929, when Henry Stimson closed down the American Black Chamber. As secretary of war from 1940 to 1945, Stimson had good cause to regret his earlier decision. So overused and insecure were some Department of State codes that on one occasion a consul leaving his post in Shanghai made his fare-

well speech entirely in the department's standard gray code—
and was understood by everyone present, including the German and Japanese diplomats.

Kent's arrest also alerted the department, at long last, to the
sorry state of security in overseas embassies. Beginning on
June 4, Long held a series of conferences with General Miles of
army intelligence, and FBI chief J. Edgar Hoover. It was as a
result of these meetings that FBI Special Agent Louis Beck,
whose damning report we have referred to, was sent to Moscow, and FBI Inspectors Avery M. Warren and Lawrence C.
Frank were assigned to investigate Alexander Kirk and the
Berlin embassy.

In the short term, this may have been hard on Kent's fellow
clerks; no fewer than eight were dismissed from Moscow as a
consequence of Beck's report, though he somehow missed the
one genuine traitor, Henry Antheil. But Kent's perfidy also
produced lasting benefits for those who survived. Working on
the assumption that Kent's motives had been financial, Long
proposed a general pay increase for all code clerks:

I have come to the conclusion that it is necessary for us to establish a
career service for clerks and pay them higher salaries and to protect
particularly the code clerks. This one incident involved our whole
system of communications, and it just shows how dependent the
Government is upon a comparatively few confidential key positions.

After the interview in Ambassador Kennedy's office, Kent had
been taken through the London afternoon to Cannon Row
police station, adjoining New Scotland Yard, the headquarters
of the Metropolitan Police, directly across the street from the
Houses of Parliament. There, according to his incomplete and
unpublished autobiography, "huge iron gates clanked open
and shut behind the vehicle" and he was escorted to a cell
containing nothing but a toilet and a hard wooden bench built
into the wall and covered with a rough blanket. Supper, he said,
was "a couple of sausages swimming in grease with a handful of
wilted mashed potatoes." Afterward he stretched out on the
bench and slept in his clothes, for the first of more than two
thousand nights of incarceration.

He did not sleep well. "Dawn comes early in England in the

month of May," he wrote, "and soon a pale light filtered through the blacked-out window on one wall of the cell and it was not long before a key crunched in the lock and a surly turnkey left a cup of weak tea and a piece of bread. This might be called a 'breakfast in bed' since the bed-bench were one and the same thing." For entertainment, he had a copy of Anton Chekhov's short stories that had been in his overcoat pocket and that he had been allowed to keep. His watch had been removed, so he had no exact idea of the time, but later in the day he was let out into a courtyard for a half hour's exercise. Although there were several other prisoners in the yard, they were not permitted to speak to one another.

Knight appeared shortly before lunch. Kent described him, erroneously, as "a typical Sandhurst type, with a close-cropped mustache and a stern manner." Knight was not an army officer and had certainly not been to the Royal Military Academy, Sandhurst, though he assumed the rank and uniform of an army captain and was "promoted" to major shortly after arresting Kent. Nor did he ever wear a mustache. But Kent's memory was more accurate when he wrote that Knight was not in military uniform that day, but was "nattily dressed in civilian clothes." He began the interview by presenting Kent with a letter from Kennedy telling him he had been dismissed from the Foreign Service of the United States as of that moment. For this Kent had to sign a receipt, which Knight delivered to Herschel Johnson at the embassy later in the day.

What Knight was most interested in at that time was the source of the three glass negatives. He needed to establish that they were the result of Anna Wolkoff's visit to Eugene Smirnoff's photographic studio on April 13, and what had been done with any prints made from them. Kent was not helpful. He said he had been trying out a camera belonging to a fellow code clerk, Hyman Goldstein, which he was considering purchasing. Goldstein, as Kent well knew, was then en route to a new posting in the Madrid embassy. That evening, Kennedy wired Kent's statement about the camera to Washington and asked that Goldstein be questioned about it on his arrival in Madrid. He also noted that the British authorities were primarily interested in learning whether Kent had communicated with their enemy and wanted to know whether the United States government would object to their prosecuting him.

For Breckinridge Long, in the State Department, the request to contact Madrid highlighted the problems created by Kent's misdeeds, and the department's dependence on clerks in key positions. "For instance," he noted, "we could not telegraph the Embassy in Madrid on this subject without the expectation that the very man who was the subject of the telegram would himself decode the message. And he might have answered it without the knowledge of the Chargé d'Affaires." Long got around the problem by sending a "pilot message" to the chargé, telling him to expect a longer message, which he was to decode, answer, and encipher himself.

The reply, which arrived on Thursday, May 23, said that Goldstein denied ever having lent his camera to anyone. A further check revealed that it used film, not glass plates.

On August 24, 1939, war had become inevitable when Hitler and Stalin announced the signing of their nonaggression pact. That day, Parliament hurriedly passed the Emergency Powers (Defence) Act, giving the government the right to impose a wide range of restrictions on the population if it considered them necessary. One week later, as Hitler invaded Poland, a set of Defence Regulations was issued via an Order in Council, which meant they did not have to pass through Parliament. Kent was arrested under the catch-all Regulation 18B, which gave the home secretary powers to arrest and detain suspects, without trial and for an indefinite period, "if satisfied with respect to any particular person that with a view to preventing him acting in a manner prejudicial to the public safety or the Defence of the Realm it is necessary to do so."

Regulation 18B was always controversial, since it gave the police exceptionally broad powers, and it was regularly under attack in Parliament. By the time of Kent's arrest it had been amended several times. The most important changes were that it could be used only against people "of hostile origin or association" or those who were actively involved in "acts prejudicial to the public safety or the Defence of the Realm." It could no longer be used to arrest people simply on suspicion that they were about to commit an offense.

Knight and his colleagues in MI5 found this understandably frustrating. Amid growing hysteria about spies and fifth-columnists, they found themselves unable to move against members of such extreme right-wing organizations as the British Union of Fascists, the Link, the Anglo-German Fellowship, and, of course, the Right Club.

Both the home secretary, Sir John Anderson, and Major General Sir Vernon Kell, the director of MI5, appeared to be taking a surprisingly tolerant view of these organizations and their leaders. As late as May 18, 1940, the day Knight called on Herschel Johnson to tell him about Kent, Anderson presented a paper to the War Cabinet, saying, "Although the policy of the British Union of Fascists is to oppose the war and to condemn the Government, there is no evidence that they would be likely to assist the enemy." Stating that "their public propaganda strikes a patriotic note," he argued that it would be a mistake to intern leaders like Sir Oswald Mosley, and that the government should hold its hand. In any case, he pointed out, it was difficult to take action when there was no evidence of disloyal activities.

In one swoop, on May 20, Knight was able to demolish Anderson's case: the material found in Tyler Kent's flat provided all the evidence he needed to prove that Captain Ramsay and at least one member of the Right Club were highly dangerous fifth-columnists. Churchill, Anderson, and Chamberlain were quickly informed that Kent had been "in relations" with Anna Wolkoff, and that the Right Club had been involved in pro-German activities and subversive efforts aimed at disorganizing the home front and sabotaging war policy. Knight succeeded in condemning all the extreme right groups by linking them—quite falsely, in most cases—with Ramsay's fanatics.

The immediate result of the arrest of Kent and Anna Wolkoff was a new regulation, 18B(1A), which instantly became law, permitting the arrest of members of "hostile" organizations on suspicion that they were "likely to endanger" public safety, the prosecution of the war, and the defense of the realm.

Churchill flew to France again on May 22, his second visit in a week, for an emergency meeting with France's new premier, Paul Reynaud, and commander-in-chief, General Maxime Weygand, to discuss the possibility of evacuating the British Expeditionary Force through Dunkirk if it proved impossible to break through the German lines and link up with the French on the Somme. But before he left, he asked Chamberlain to chair an immediate meeting of the War Cabinet to approve special new regulations for imprisoning British fascists as well as more enemy aliens. "I will agree to whatever the Cabinet thinks best," he told Chamberlain, adding that "if any doubt existed, the persons in question should be detained without delay."

This suggestion, according to the minutes, "met with general approval," and while Churchill was still airborne on his way to Paris, orders were given for the arrest of Sir Oswald Mosley and more than two hundred of his followers. Mosley was said, quite untruthfully, to have been "in relations" with Captain Ramsay and members of the Right Club. Fearing a possible right-wing plot against the government, the Cabinet directed that action be taken as quickly as possible "against persons known to be members of this organization." With the complete list of names in the red book found in Kent's flat, the roundup of those members considered to be the most dangerous was an easy task. By July, the number of suspected fifth-columnists arrested under 18B from these and other organizations reached a total of 1373, most of whom were released by the spring of 1941.

The detainees included many distinguished citizens, such as Admiral Sir Barry Domvile, a former director of naval intelligence. Among the smaller fish swept up in the net were Anna Wolkoff's parents, who turned out to have been working for the overseas postal censorship, opening and checking mail at Wormwood Scrubs prison, alongside MI5. The admiral was interned for the duration, but his wife was allowed to return to the Tea Room.

On May 23, the effect of Regulation 18B on Kent was reinforced by the more conventional device of a deportation order, number K22673/2, personally signed by Sir John Anderson, "as authorized by the Aliens Restriction Acts of 1914 and 1919." This stated that Kent would not only be deported, at the convenience of the government, but also would never be allowed to return to the United Kingdom. Kent was delighted; he fully expected to be shipped out to America immediately. But the order allowed His Majesty's government to hold him in jail "pending the pleasure of the Home Office"—in other words, as long as they chose. As soon as the order had been served, Kent was moved from the police cell to more permanent lodgings in H.M. Prison, Pentonville, the most central of London's jails.

It was in Pentonville that Knight resumed his interrogation. During the first session in his cell, Kent was forced to admit that his story about Goldstein's lending him a camera was a lie; he thought Goldstein had not yet arrived in Madrid, so the State Department would not have been able to check up on the story. But he stubbornly refused to say whose camera had been used to photograph the Churchill messages, or why.

When questioned about Ramsay and Anna Wolkoff, Kent was evasive. He admitted at first that they had both read the confidential telegrams, but then tried to deny that he had said Ramsay had read them. He also admitted that Anna Wolkoff had been left alone in his rooms at least once for about an hour; he said, vaguely, that this had been about a month before. But he denied that Ramsay had ever been to his rooms, though the MI5 watchers had recorded several visits. On more than one of them Ramsay had been alone, and once when Ramsay had been there on his own the sound of a typewriter had been heard.

When it came to the question of why he had duplicate keys, freshly made in England, to the code and file rooms, Kent surprised Knight by saying quite openly that he had had them cut because "he feared he might be assigned at some time to other work in the embassy, perhaps in the consulate general, and that he wanted to retain the means of access to the file and code rooms."

On the next day, Knight returned to the subject of the glass negatives, and finally squeezed an answer out of Kent, in which he tried to present himself as Anna's cat's-paw. Knight persuaded him to include this in a written statement:

I come to an incident which took place, to the best of my recollection, between 27 March 1940 and 10 April 1940. One day during this period, Anna Wolkoff caught sight of one particular telegram, which I think was a communication from the United States Embassy in London to the State Department in Washington. The document did not seem to me to be very significant, but Anna seemed interested in it. I think it related to shipping matters. She asked if she could borrow it, without saying exactly for what purpose. She said she was interested in the information on it, and I gathered she would abstract something from it. She returned it to me on the following day.

Kent claimed that several days later Anna had handed him a cardboard box containing the three glass negatives, and that was all he knew about them.

This fitted Knight's picture of the case, for, as he told Johnson, he regarded Anna as the "brain in the organization." She was being held in prison two hundred miles away in Manchester, and her interrogation was to be postponed "until the facts have been more completely developed regarding her associates and activities in London." In this respect, the interrogation of Ramsay was proceeding slowly. He had already "trapped himself in several lies," but there could be no doubt about the closeness of his association with Anna.

One of the members of the Right Club who had been arrested, Christabel Nicholson, the wife of Admiral W. S. Nicholson, of Bath, had been found to have in her possession a sealed envelope containing a rough pencil copy of the message from Roosevelt to Churchill transmitted on May 16. Nicholson claimed she had made this from another pencil copy held by Anna.

Enid Riddell, who had invited Kent to dine with her and the Duke del Monte, had also been arrested and was being questioned. Knight told Johnson he was convinced that once he had obtained the full facts from her, they would prove that del Monte was a spy and "probably a channel of communication, through the Italian diplomatic pouch, for information to Germany." Del Monte, of course, was a fully accredited diplomat and could not be arrested; the Italian ambassador was unlikely to follow Kennedy's example and waive his immunity. But Knight said he had little doubt that he would be able to get convictions against Kent, Ramsay, Anna Wolkoff, Christabel Nicholson, and Enid Riddell.

The answer to the all-important question of what had become of the prints made from the glass negatives was found in the decrypted telegram of May 23 from Mackensen in Rome to the German Foreign Office in Berlin. It was quite obvious that the information contained in the telegram came from the stolen Churchill-Roosevelt messages. But the final sentence of Mackensen's telegram gave Knight the vital clue that linked it to the negatives. "I am sending the documentary evidence for this report by the next reliable opportunity," the German ambassador had promised. What else could the "documentary evidence" be but the photographs of Kent's copies of the original messages? Knight's case against Kent and Anna Wolkoff was complete.

When Tyler Kent removed confidential and secret documents from the embassy, he violated his oath of loyalty and became a felon, a common thief with loot that was both interesting and explosive. But when he showed the documents to Anna Wolkoff, Captain Ramsay, and the others, he committed a more serious crime, violating the United States law known as the Yardley Act. According to that law:

Whoever, by virtue of his employment by the United States, shall obtain from another or shall have custody of or access to, any official diplomatic code or any matter prepared in any such code, and shall wilfully, without authorization or competent authority, publish or furnish to another any such code or matter, or any matter which was obtained while in the process of transmission between any foreign government and its diplomatic mission in the United States shall be fined not more than $10,000 or imprisoned not more than ten years, or both.

Since every document Kent had stolen represented a separate offense, he was subject to maximum penalties totaling $19,290,000 and 19,290 years in jail if he were returned to his country and convicted. In spite of this danger, Kent hoped that he would be deported back to the United States. He was even eager to stand trial there, though he believed the U.S. government would never dare put him in court, because the information he might reveal would be political dynamite. Whatever happened, it would be impossible to keep the matter quiet: he would become a celebrity, a hero of the American right, the man who had brought down Roosevelt and kept the nation out of the European war.

"I thought Roosevelt's policy contrary to the best interests of the United States," he claimed. Then, conveniently ignoring that he had been stealing documents continually for six years, went on, "Alarmed by what I read in the dispatches passing through my hands, I began making copies." He agreed he had a loyalty to his ambassador, but declared loftily, "I had a higher loyalty to the people of the United States. I intended to show the documents to the U.S. Senate."

In Washington, however, the administration had no intention of allowing Kent to wreak his mischief. On May 22, Sumner Welles cabled London confirming that Kent's diplomatic immunity had been waived, and stating that Washington had no objection to charges being filed against him for violations of British law. He also warned, with an understatement worthy of the British themselves, "Publicity in connection with such charges might not be helpful under the circumstances." Embassy employees were ordered not to discuss the disappearance of Kent. A blanket of silence was thrown over the entire affair.

Under wartime censorship regulations, the story could be kept out of the press in Britain without a great deal of difficulty. Kennedy was able to report to Hull that he had spoken to Sir Alexander Maxwell, under secretary at the Home Office, who had talked to the chief censor. "They assure me that nothing will be permitted to be printed here or abroad," he signaled. "May I suggest that nothing is given out in the United States from Washington since this case stinks to high heaven."

The clamp-down was so tight that even American reporters in London—some of the best in the business—were unable to uncover any details. The *New York Herald Tribune* for Saturday May 25 carried a brief item stating that an unnamed employee of the American embassy in London was being held by the British authorities. But at a press conference that afternoon, Cordell Hull, back in charge after his illness, denied any knowledge of such an incident. And in London the British authorities, when questioned by American and British newsmen, passed the buck by stating that it was up to the American embassy to make an announcement on the case, "provided they so desired."

Eleven days after the arrest, the Home Office in London

finally issued a one-paragraph statement, approved by Hull and the State Department:

In consequence of action taken by the American Ambassador (Mr. Joseph P. Kennedy) in co-operation with the British authorities, Tyler Kent, a clerk who had been dismissed from the employment of the American government, has been detained by order of the Home Secretary.

The statement was carried on June 1 by the London evening papers, the *Evening Standard,* the *Evening News,* and the *Star,* and next day appeared in American morning papers either from their own London bureaus or from the wire services. Washington news bureaus got a terse "No comment!" from the State Department, which did, however, issue a brief biography of Kent. It mentioned that his mother lived in the United States, but the department refused to give her address.

It was from these news stories that Mrs. Ann Kent, a chubby woman given to wearing hats and gowns of an earlier era, first learned of her son's detention. She got in touch with Hull, who adamantly refused to see her. On June 3, she cabled Ambassador Kennedy through the Western Union office: "I appeal for news of my son Tyler." The cable, received at the Anglo-American Telegraph Company's office at 22 Great Winchester Street, London, was delivered by messenger to the embassy, where it was given to Herschel Johnson. He immediately sent a signal back to Washington:

I have not replied to this telegram and hope the department will make whatever communication to Mrs. Kent that may be necessary and possible. I have informed Scotland Yard of this inquiry and they . . . will ask the governor of the prison to inform Kent that his mother has inquired about him. There is no report that Kent is not physically well.

The State Department, however, made no attempt to reach Mrs. Kent, and on June 7, accompanied by her daughter, also named Ann, she appeared in Hull's outer office, and said she would not leave until he saw her. Hull delegated Breckinridge Long to talk to her.

Long did his best to bring home to her the unique and terrible nature of her son's crime, telling her the whole truth in detail, and adding that "nothing like this has ever happened in American history." According to Long's own account of the conversation, Mrs. Kent showed no emotion, though her daughter shed some tears. "I promised to get a message to the boy sending her love and to ask for a reply to be transmitted to her," he wrote.

When she had gone, Hull cabled Kennedy "to take appropriate steps to ensure that Kent will have competent counsel . . . and that his trial will be fair."

Toward the end of May, Kent was transferred from Pentonville to Brixton Prison in southeast London, a jail holding men awaiting trial and many detainees under Section 18B who had not yet been removed to the Isle of Man. Since this was a remand jail, whose prisoners were still technically innocent of any offense, conditions were then quite bearable. Kent described his life there in his memoirs:

As prisons go, Brixton is a luxury hotel. The detained person wears his own clothes, has access to laundry facilities, restaurant food, books and writing materials, visits from friends and lawyers, etc. It is a far cry from the "penal servitude with hard labor" which, in fact, awaits most of those confined within its walls. This preliminary confinement, at least in the case of Kent, served as a sort of psychological cushion for the penal servitude which finally overtook him. The gradual introduction to prison life is somewhat similar to the difference between entering a pool of cold water gradually or being thrown into it suddenly. There is time for mental and physical adjustment which is really quite beneficial to the prisoner.

Kent's "psychological cushion" was bolstered by his belief that he would not stay in jail very long, and that he would not have to stand trial anywhere. When Knight reminded him that he was entitled to the services of a lawyer, he studiously disregarded the suggestion. On June 11, the prison governor summoned him: "As the officer from the War Office who saw you here on the 28th May informed you, you have a right to consult a solicitor, if you so desire. Since I notice that, unlike many of the 18B prisoners, you have not done so, and since you are not a British subject, I have sent for you to remind you of your right to see a solicitor, so that there shall be no misunderstanding about the matter."

Kent ignored the governor's advice and took no steps to secure legal counsel. But his hopes were ill-founded. That same day, Kennedy received a memorandum from the British authorities confirming that they intended to charge Kent under British law:

Papers dealing with a serious leakage of confidential information from the United States Embassy are today being laid before the Director of Public Prosecutions for his consideration . . . Investigators consider these papers disclose a traitorous and dangerous conspiracy to assist the enemy. The Director of Public Prosecutions is asked to examine the case with a view to preferring serious charges against Miss Anna Wolkoff; Captain Archibald Maule Ramsay, MP; his wife, Mrs. Ramsay; Mrs. Christable [sic] Nicholson; and Tyler Gatewood Kent. All except the last-named are British subjects . . . They will be charged with offences which in substance amount either to espionage on behalf of Germany, or to something very closely akin to it. Investigators feel that in the interests of Great Britain all the defendants should be prosecuted with rigour . . . As the interests of the United States are of a vital nature, they are obliged to ask for assistance in presenting the prosecution's case.

It is . . . essential . . . that a representative of the United States Embassy should attend the trial to give certain formal evidence:

(a) Mr. Kent's position in the Embassy and his dismissal therefrom;

(b) His right, if any, to remove from the Embassy to his private apartment, and there to make copies of, highly confidential documents;

(c) as to certain of the documents purloined and copied by Kent and others . . .

Neither the State Department nor the Foreign Office would be prepared to contemplate . . . public discussion of some of the documents in question . . . However, selected documents . . . could properly be produced in court.

Desired documents are:

(1) Lord Cottenham (War Office) letters on radio detection;

(2) War Office letters signed "G. M. Liddell";

(3) Kent's three photographic negatives and original documents from which the photographs were taken;

(4) Documents dated 9 May relating to the treatment to be given by the Allies to United States shipping;

(5) Cable dated 15 May 1940, 6 p.m., . . . containing a message

from the President of the United States to Mr. Winston Churchill . . .

Proposed defendants believe they are safe from trial and punish-
ment because neither Government dare have these matters discussed
. . . [D]ocuments in question . . . would be produced only behind
locked doors in a cleared court . . . No press man would be present
at the relevant part of the trial. Those who were present would be
most strictly charged not to refer to them subsequently (Official
Secrets Act) . . .

Above information . . . owing to the misconduct of the defendants, is known to several unsatisfactory persons. Criminal proceedings may be instituted within the current week. Early co-operation of
the United States Government would therefore be doubly welcome.

Kent's gamble had failed. He had miscalculated, by forget-
ting or not being aware of a vital difference between the legal
systems of Britain and the United States: in Britain, when matters of state security are involved, trials may be held *in camera,*
behind locked doors, with the press excluded and lawyers and
jurors sworn to secrecy.

In wartime Britain, many spies were arrested and tried in
secret—and only after they were convicted and hanged was the
public informed. Many never came to trial at all, for MI5 preferred, where possible, to turn enemy spies and persuade them
to work for Britain as double agents, feeding false information
to their German spymasters. So successful was the Twenty
Committee responsible for this operation (its name was a private joke, the Roman twenty, XX, being a pun for "double-
cross") that only seventeen captured enemy agents were sent
to trial during the entire war. Fifteen were hanged. One, who
had broken his leg during his parachute landing and could not
stand on the gallows, was tied to a chair and shot by a firing
squad of the Royal Scots Fusiliers. And the remaining one, who
was acquitted of spying, was rearrested as he left the court,
charged with violating the Official Secrets Act, and imprisoned
for the duration.

In such a climate, Tyler Kent stood little chance of achieving
his aims. Had he kept the documents locked away, to be shown
only to members of the Senate back in Washington, as he
claimed was his intention, he might have avoided a British trial
and succeeded in publicizing the messages in the United

States. But Kent did not keep them to himself. He could not resist the opportunity of showing off to his friends, and so laid himself open to prosecution in Britain and a trial *in camera*. No details of what Roosevelt and Churchill were saying to each other would come out. Indeed, the very fact that they were communicating at all would not be released to the public.

Not surprisingly, the U.S. government raised no objections to Kent's being tried in London under the British Official Secrets Act, leaving the possibility of charges in America under the Yardley Act hanging over his head. In Washington, after the brief, one-paragraph statement of June 2 announcing his arrest and detention, the official silence about Kent over the next four years was deafening.

TEN

We Must Protect the Chief

THE ROOSEVELT ADMINISTRATION had good reason to fear Tyler Kent's threatened disclosures. Breckinridge Long's first reaction to Kent's perfidy may have been dismay at the security implications, particularly for American codes and ciphers. But this was quickly overtaken by political considerations, and the realization of the threat to Roosevelt's re-election. "We must take immediate action to protect the chief!" he ordered, and promptly set about doing just that.

With British cooperation, Kent could be silenced—and the British were bound to agree that it would be disastrous at that critical point in history to have Roosevelt replaced as president. But keeping Kent quiet was not the only problem, as Long confided to his diary:

No doubt the Germans will publish another White Book during our political campaign which will have as its purpose the defeat of Roosevelt and the election of a ticket opposed to him and presumably in sympathy with Hitler—an appeasement ticket—an administration to succeed ours which will play ball with Germany or surrender America.

As it happened, the feared white book never appeared, and there were no blasts of triumphant propaganda from Berlin. But the next few months must have been a nerve-racking time for the small circle of people around the president. Information on Kent's actions was limited to a small, tight-knit group: in the State Department, Hull, Welles, Long, Gene Hackworth, the department's legal adviser, and another assistant secretary of state, G. Howland Shaw; in the White House, Roosevelt's closest friend, Harry Hopkins, who had dinner with him on the night of May 22, and Grace Tully, the president's number one secretary; elsewhere, J. Edgar Hoover and General Sherman Miles.

There is no record of when and how Roosevelt himself was told of the affair. The White House appointments book did not list unscheduled meetings with the president, who kept his afternoons open in those hectic days for planning and emergency meetings, for which no names were listed. On May 20, he had no known meetings after his lunch date with his old Dutchess County friend and neighbor, Secretary of the Treasury Henry Morgenthau, Jr. On the next day, he lunched with the U.S. attorney general, Robert H. Jackson, and may well have discussed, among other things, what legal steps could be taken against Kent. On May 22, he saw Sumner Welles at 11:15, several hours before the arrival of Kennedy's signal about the Churchill-Roosevelt messages and the glass negatives. The president would certainly have been informed about this signal immediately after its arrival in the State Department communications center. And there can be no doubt whatever that he would have been fully aware of all the political implications.

For much of his political life, Franklin Delano Roosevelt showed a fine and vigorous disregard for precedent. Until the 1932 Democratic convention, the presidential candidate of each party was officially informed of his nomination some six weeks after the convention. A delegation of the party hierarchy would visit the candidate, who was usually discovered sitting in a rocking chair on his front porch, where he would accept the nomination without indicating that he had had any inkling about it. In 1932, however, Roosevelt not only appeared before the Chicago convention to make his acceptance speech in person, but also flew from Albany to the Windy City, thus becoming the first presidential nominee, and later the first president, to fly in an airplane.

Between the 1932 and 1940 Democratic conventions, he broke many more precedents, both in party politics and in government. But there can be no doubt that in May 1940 he was about to embark on his greatest precedent breaker of all, by running for an unheard-of and highly controversial third term.

Roosevelt made no announcement about his third-term plans, but allowed intimates to suspect he was "available if drafted." Even within the Democratic Party itself, however, he faced substantial opposition, notably from Postmaster General James Farley and John L. Lewis of the United Mine Workers, the nation's most powerful union leader, who were openly against him. So, too, was the vice president, John Nance (Cactus Jack) Garner, one of the men Roosevelt had beaten for the presidential nomination in 1932. Garner was noted for his colorful description of the vice presidency—"It ain't worth a pitcher of warm piss"—but had exploited the position to become the unofficial leader of the opposition in the Senate. Roosevelt, not surprisingly, decided to drop Garner from his ticket, and chose the most liberal member of his Cabinet, Secretary of Agriculture Henry A. Wallace, as his running mate.

The Democratic convention was due to open in Chicago on July 15. Both Farley and Garner announced that they would run against Roosevelt. They were joined by Senator Millard Tydings of Maryland, making a token opposition simply on the grounds that he opposed a third term on principle. There was momentary embarrassment in Boston, when Joseph P. Kennedy, Jr., the ambassador's twenty-five-year-old eldest son, then a Harvard Law School student, pledged to cast his convention ballot for Farley. The Bay State delegation was originally pledged to Farley, but switched some of its votes when pressured by William H. (Onions) Burke, a Roosevelt appointee to the post of collector of customs.

It would have been disastrous for Roosevelt if any one of his Democrat opponents, particularly Farley, had learned that he had been promising help to Britain and even trying to ease out Chamberlain in favor of Churchill, who was disliked by many in Washington for his belligerent stance on naval disarmament in the 1920s and distrusted for his erratic judgment and excessive fondness for alcohol.

It could have been even more disastrous, however, if the traditionally isolationist Republicans had discovered the secret signals. Their convention was due to open in Philadelphia on June 24, a full three weeks before the Democrats', and they would have seized with unbridled delight on evidence pointing to FDR's attempts to aid a sinking Britain. With such ammunition, and against a Democratic Party divided within itself, the GOP might well have pushed Roosevelt out of office and made a reality of Churchill's nightmare vision of America's leaving Britain to her fate. Such a move—which was, of course, precisely what Tyler Kent had hoped to achieve—would not have been unpopular in America in 1940: public opinion polls recorded that a mere 7.7 percent of Americans favored intervention, and a massive 83 percent wanted no part in the European war. They refused to believe that, as Roosevelt was reputed to have said, America's frontier was on the Rhine.

Two days before the Republicans convened, France had signed the surrender document, in the same railway coach used for the 1918 Armistice. The day after, German troops were issued with English phrase books, ready for Hitler's planned invasion of Britain. The last 200,000 British troops, together with 130,000 French soldiers, had been evacuated from Dunkirk three weeks earlier, but all their guns and heavy equipment had been left behind. Now, Britain stood alone and almost unarmed against the Nazis.

Churchill, who had just made the grand historic gesture of offering joint British citizenship to the French, appealed publicly to America "to bring her powerful material aid to the common cause. And thus we shall conquer." In secret, he appealed once more to Roosevelt for the loan of the mothballed First World War destroyers "as a matter of life or death."

He reminded the president that "the fate of the British fleet . . . would be decisive on the future of the United States." A victorious German Navy, joined to the navies of Japan, Italy, and a conquered France, would give Hitler "overwhelming sea power," which would be a threat to American interests. "If we go down," he stated in his message of June 15, "you may have a United States of Europe under the Nazi command far more numerous, far stronger, far better armed than the new [world]."

Roosevelt did not reply. He had his hands full with domestic political matters. He may also have been waiting to see exactly what was going to happen in Britain. In fact, he did not communicate with Churchill for two whole months after the fall of France. It was not until August 13—with the aerial Battle of Britain already beginning to swing in Britain's favor as the RAF inflicted heavy losses on the Luftwaffe—that he cabled the prime minister, offering to lend the destroyers in exchange for concessions in British territories in the western hemisphere.

Roosevelt was well aware of the dangers of a German victory, and believed that America could best be defended by supplying arms to Britain. But to a majority of Americans the collapse of France and the seemingly hopeless position of Britain were good reasons for doing nothing. With Hitler apparently about to complete his conquest, they believed, like Joe Kennedy, that any aid to Britain would be a waste of time, money, and resources. It was suggested that Britain's best course was to surrender: the chairman of the Senate Foreign Relations Committee, Senator Key Pittman of Nevada, proposed that Britain should send its remaining ships to North America and then capitulate. "It is no secret," he said, "that Great Britain is totally unprepared for defense and that nothing the United States has to give can do more than delay the result . . . It is to be hoped that this plan will not be too long delayed by futile encouragement to fight on."

Such an attitude was common to many groups within a broad spectrum of American opinion, both in and out of Congress, unified against Roosevelt under the rubric of isolationism. In 1940, the isolationists posed the greatest threat to his re-election, and therefore had to be dealt with very carefully. Above

all, they had to be denied the sort of ammunition that Kent had
been eager to provide.

The policy of nonintervention had a long and honorable history in the United States, dating from the very beginning of the
Republic. George Washington himself, in his farewell address,
pointed out that "Europe has a set of primary interests which
to us have none or a very remote relation." Jefferson reinforced the view in his famous words "[P]eace, commerce, and
honest friendship with all nations; entangling alliances with
none." And James Monroe, as a corollary to the Monroe Doctrine, stated, "Our policy in regard to Europe, which was
adopted at an early stage of the wars which have so long agi-
tated that quarter of the globe, nevertheless remains the same,
which is, not to interfere in the internal concerns of any of its
powers."

The Spanish-American War in 1898, and the consequent
acquisition by the United States of the Philippines, Guam, and
Puerto Rico as colonies and Cuba as a protectorate, could be
explained away under the Monroe Doctrine, as could interven-
tions in Mexico and the Caribbean. But when the United States
entered the First World War in 1917, and then found itself
entangled in the Europeans' machinations at the Paris Peace
Conference, it seemed to many that the Founding Fathers'
vision was being betrayed.

In Paris, war weariness was added to the old suspicions.
Lloyd George of Britain, Clemenceau of France, and Orlando
of Italy were seen as an evil combine working against the idealistic Woodrow Wilson. The discovery that Wilson, naïve, nar-
row-minded, and inflexible, was incapable of horse trading
with his fellow statesmen only helped to confirm Americans in
their growing determination to withdraw across the Atlantic,
back into the safe world of nonintervention. Isolationism was
born.

Over the next two decades, isolationist sentiment was
strengthened by events in Europe, the Middle East, and Africa,
and by the refusal or inability of the former Allies to repay their
war debts to America. The Great Depression, believed by many
to have been caused by these payment defaults, aided the process even more by turning the focus of Americans inward. And

in the mid-1930s, pacifism boosted the growth of noninterventionist sentiment in general.

American isolationism became an active rather than a passive state at this time largely as a result of the Senate Munitions Committee, chaired by Senator Gerald P. Nye of North Dakota. Vice President Garner's appointment of Nye, a Republican, when the Democrats were the majority party, was one of the worst political blunders in congressional history. The administration did not oppose the committee's examination of the munitions industry, but was shaken when Nye began investigating alleged connections of American bankers with Allied leaders and diplomats during the First World War. The State Department lent classified documents, including diplomatic correspondence, to the committee for the sole purpose of providing background information. Nye immediately released the material to the press. Secretary of State Hull was livid as protests poured in from a dozen countries, particularly from Great Britain, which had specifically refused permission for its correspondence to be made public.

From September 1934 until February 1936, Nye's committee, whose counsel, incidentally, was Alger Hiss, investigated the U.S. armaments industry, Wall Street, and New York bankers, with the maximum possible public exposure. Ignoring all other factors, from the invasion of Belgium and the sinking of the *Lusitania* to unrestricted submarine warfare and the Zimmermann telegram, Nye set out to prove that the United States had been dragged into the Great War solely by the intrigues of financiers like J. P. Morgan and arms makers such as Colt, Winchester, and Remington, who had grown rich on the profits of death.

The reality, which Nye was partially successful in concealing, was somewhat different. Winchester and Remington, along with several other arms and ammunition makers, collapsed after the war. They had spent millions of dollars in expanding their plants to meet the wartime needs of the United States and its associated powers. After the war, drastic retrenchment of facilities was not enough to keep both Remington and Winchester from declaring bankruptcy. Many other munitions companies disappeared altogether.

Nye's biased investigation produced little hard evidence to

support his claims, but the smoke he created led the public to believe there was fire. The accusations were given wide publicity in 1934 through a best-selling book, *Merchants of Death*, by H. C. Engelbrecht and F. C. Hanighen. In May 1935, the popular radio commentator Raymond Gram Swing said on the air, "It is almost a truism that the United States went into the World War in part to save from ruin the bankers who had strained themselves to the utmost to supply Great Britain and France with munitions and credits." And that same year, as Hitler denounced the Versailles Treaty and announced conscription and vast rearmament plans, and Mussolini invaded Ethiopia, Ernest Hemingway weighed in with an impassioned declaration: "Of the hell broth that is brewing in Europe we have no need to drink . . . We were fools to be sucked in once in a European war, and we shall never be sucked in again."

In this climate, pacifist groups were organized throughout the country, many of them attached to churches. The most prominent peace movements included the Women's International League for Peace and Freedom and the Oxford Group, headed by Frank Buchman, an American evangelist who had preached "world-changing through life-changing" at Oxford University in 1921, and who went on to found the controversial Moral Re-Armament movement in 1938.

But pacifism was by no means the only or even the principal source of isolationism. Ethnic origins played a large part as the troubles in Europe polarized more and more around Germany and Britain. Inevitably, the predominant ethnic groups opposing intervention—on the side of Britain against the Nazis—were Americans of German, Italian, and Irish descent. This was reflected in the geographic spread: the main isolationist regions were New England, the Midwest, and Southern California. Cities where isolationist sentiment was strongest included Boston, New York, Philadelphia, Washington, D.C., Chicago, Milwaukee, Indianapolis, Detroit, Minneapolis-St. Paul, Wichita, Houston, Omaha, and Los Angeles. Save for German Americans, most metropolitan isolationists were Catholic; in the Midwest, Catholics were joined by German and Scandinavian Lutherans and fundamentalist Protestants.

On the other side, the strongest pro-British and interventionist sentiment was to be found in the South, where both

residents and members of Congress recalled Britain's aid to
the embattled Confederacy.

Nye's committee did not press for neutrality legislation, but
Nye himself did, rallying support from various quarters, notably from the chairman of the Senate Foreign Relations Committee, Key Pittman. Pittman, the renegade Democratic senator from Nevada, cared only for the silver lobby and was one of
the Senate's more celebrated alcoholics. Under his influence,
the Neutrality Act of 1935 was passed after much wheeling and
dealing. It was updated in 1936 and again in 1937, when its
temporary provisions were made permanent.

Under the terms of the Neutrality Act, the president was
forbidden to sell arms or to lend funds to any belligerent, or to
arm American merchant ships. American citizens were barred
from sailing on the ships of belligerents. In addition to the ban
on arms purchases, nations involved in war that wished to buy
noncontraband goods from the United States were required to
pay in advance and ship the goods themselves; the cash-and-
carry regulations were designed to prevent the running-up of
credit.

Roosevelt was reluctant to sign the act, for it tied his hands
completely. He was required to invoke it as soon as any war
broke out, and was not allowed to discriminate between ag-
gressors and victims. This, Roosevelt realized, would make the
conduct of American diplomacy virtually impossible. But he
was already involved in battles with Congress over appointments to the Supreme Court and needed votes for upcoming
New Deal domestic legislation, so he accepted Hull's recommendation not to make further trouble by vetoing it.

The *New York Herald Tribune* said the legislation should have
been called "an act to preserve the United States from intervention in the War of 1914–18." But the huge isolationist lobby
welcomed it without reservation. As they watched Europe and
Asia moving inexorably down the road to global war, they saw
each step on that road as a further justification of America's
stance.

The new Congress, elected in 1938 and installed in January
1939, was still dominated by the Democrats. It was also still
strongly isolationist. Even in July 1939, despite Roosevelt's

personal intervention, his attempts to repeal the arms' embargo section of the Neutrality Act failed. Congress ignored his request for immediate action and decided to delay consideration until the next session, which was six months away.

When Britain and France declared war on Germany on September 3, Roosevelt went on the air with one of his "fireside chats" to the country. "This nation," he pledged, "will remain a neutral nation, but I cannot ask that every American remain neutral in thought as well. Even a neutral has a right to take account of facts. Even a neutral cannot be asked to close his mind or his conscience." Stressing that the overwhelming masses of the American people wanted peace, and that every effort of the government would be directed toward keeping America out of the war, he concluded with the promise: "As long as it remains within my power to prevent it, there will be no blackout of peace in the United States."

Roosevelt's closing words at least must have pleased the isolationist majority. But they did not have to wait long before they were brutally reminded that in the modern world it is almost impossible for any major nation to remain aloof and untouched by global war. Even while Roosevelt was speaking, Joe Kennedy reported that a German U-boat had sunk the *Athenia,* carrying eleven hundred passengers, including three hundred Americans, and three hundred crew, off the Hebrides. Most of the survivors were taken to Glasgow, where the immediate needs and future transportation of the Americans were handled by Kennedy's second son, John Fitzgerald Kennedy.

Two days later, on September 5, the president obeyed the law by invoking the Neutrality Act. This meant that no arms or other materials of war could be shipped to any belligerent, Allied or Axis, and that no arms—on order, at the docks ready for loading, or aboard ships waiting to sail—could be delivered. It also prevented all American ships from entering any port in a belligerent country, even if they were carrying only passengers or noncontraband cargoes.

On September 11, the day he opened his correspondence with Churchill, the president exercised his prerogative as chief executive and called a special session of Congress for September 21 to reconsider the arms' embargo. This time, with the American public rallying to his support, he was successful. The new Neutrality Act allowed arms and aircraft to be shipped once more, but still, forbade the extension of credit.

As soon as Roosevelt recalled Congress, the isolationists opened up a cannonade that is continued by revisionist historians to this day. They alleged that he behaved dictatorially, was determined to take America into the war, and that he breached America's neutrality by openly favoring Britain and France against Germany. While the first two charges were groundless, there can be no doubt that Roosevelt favored democracy against Nazism. Nor can anyone doubt that he wanted to do all in his power to help the Allies combat Hitler, and found the Neutrality Act an irksome obstacle. But the act was more than that; it gave a potent advantage to Germany, which had been rearming for years, over the democracies, which had been forced to join the race late.

With the coming of war, Britain and France on their own could not hope to manufacture enough arms and aircraft to catch up with the output of Germany's great arsenals, such as the Mauser Werke and Krupp, which had been working flat-out for the past four years. In addition, German production had been strengthened in 1938 and 1939 by Hitler's acquisition first of Austrian manufacturers and then of Czechoslovakia's existing weapons stocks and its arms industry, then the second largest in the world, including the Skoda works, the biggest and most modern in existence.

The plight of the Allies in Europe meant different things to the different sectors of the noninterventionist movement. Those who actively supported Germany wanted the United States to remain isolated and to refrain from arming the Allies; those who longed for peace genuinely feared the cost in lives should America enter the war. The noninterventionists, then, were a disparate group, comprising isolationists, pacifists, anti-Semites and such extreme right-wing organizations as the German American Bund, with its brown-shirted members goose-stepping under swastika banners. The most prominent and powerful native fascists were the Silver Shirts of William Dudley Pelley, publisher of *Liberation* magazine, who was convicted of sedition, his successor the Reverend Gerald L. K. Smith and the Share-Our-Wealth Society, and, of course, the Ku Klux Klan.

The isolationist viewpoint was fostered by large and influential sections of the press, especially the newspapers of William Randolph Hearst, with more than fifty metropolitan dailies, plus the *Chicago Tribune* of Colonel Robert McCormick, and the *Washington Times-Herald* and *New York Daily News* belonging to McCormick's cousins Eleanor (Cissy) Patterson and Joseph Medill Patterson, respectively.

The figurehead of the most virulent anti-Allied aid groups throughout the United States was Colonel Charles Augustus Lindbergh. Lindbergh, though the world's most famous flier, was politically naïve. He had fallen under Hitler's spell at the Berlin Olympics in 1936, and had accepted Germany's highest decoration from him in October 1938, shortly after the Nazis had marched into the Sudetenland and only three weeks before they unleashed the horrors of Kristallnacht.

But the person heading the single most influential isolationist hate campaign against Roosevelt was the radio priest Father Charles E. Coughlin. A man of immense charisma, Coughlin started broadcasting from Detroit in 1926. At first, he confined his Sunday afternoon programs to religion, but soon shifted to politics and economics. His program became one of the five most popular radio shows in the country, but in late 1931 CBS canceled his broadcasts because of his attacks on bankers and financiers. During the Depression, however, such attacks were understandably popular, and Coughlin was soon able to create his own national radio network. A poll of listeners by a Philadelphia station revealed that while the music program with which CBS had replaced Coughlin had an audience in the city of 11,000, nearly 200,000 tuned in to the radio priest.

Coughlin's National Union for Social Justice received an average of 80,000 letters each week. After certain hard-hitting broadcasts his mail reached 500,000 letters, many containing money. His weekly magazine, *Social Justice,* had a circulation of 200,000 and an estimated readership of a million.

Coughlin had supported Roosevelt during his governorship of New York and in the early days of the presidency, but he switched to attack during 1935, and continued on this line until he went off the air toward the end of the war. The administration, hampered by the difficulty of rebutting a priest, largely ignored him. Soon it became obvious that he had moved from populism to fascism, and the administration was able to score against him by arguing against other groups with similar philosophies.

After Hitler's unprovoked attacks on neutral Denmark, Norway, and the Low Countries in April and May 1940, it was obvious to everyone that he was not to be trusted. His blitzkriegs against the British and French armies began at last to alert many Americans to the danger he posed to world order. Although public sentiment remained overwhelmingly against direct American involvement in the war, many citizens felt the need to do everything short of entering the war to help the British and French.

In May, the bipartisan Committee to Defend America by Aiding the Allies was formed by one of the country's best known newspaper editors, William Allen White of the *Emporia* (Kansas) *Gazette,* a leading moral force in the Republican Party. Chapters were soon set up across the nation, with many eminent people as members. One of these, Douglas Fairbanks, Jr., used his fame as a movie star to warn of the dangers of isolationism. When he talked to Roosevelt about the task, the president told him: "I have to be like the captain in front of his troops. If I get too far ahead in expressing my own sympathies and opinion, then I'll lose the people behind." He concluded that he could be only a little way ahead, and that it was the job of Fairbanks and his fellows to push public opinion.

The isolationists, however, were not prepared to give Fairbanks and his friends an easy ride. Shortly after the creation of the Committee to Defend, they formed their own organization, the America First Committee, with the aim of keeping America out of the war. Like the Committee to Defend, America First set up chapters in every state and in thousands of communities. Under the chairmanship of General Robert Wood, chairman of the board of Sears, Roebuck, and with Lindbergh as its figurehead, it attracted many leading industrialists, educators, and public figures. Membership soon soared to 850,000 active supporters, covering an amazing range of interests, from proto-Nazis and fascists to big businessmen and churchmen, socialists, even Communist Party members, to mothers fearful of their sons' being sent to fight.

Outside America First, the isolationist cause was actively promoted by many pro-Nazi industries, including General Motors, Ford, Du Pont, and the Rockefellers' Chase National Bank, which had heavy investments in and relationships with German industry. Such companies were eager not to lose their lucrative business with Hitler, and were prepared to go to almost any lengths to protect it. Both Standard Oil of New Jersey and Texaco, for example, continued to supply petroleum products to Germany, circumventing the Neutrality Act by transshipping through nonbelligerent ports.

Standard Oil, in fact, had earlier formed a cartel with I. G. Farben, the giant Nazi chemical corporation, and refused to develop hundred-octane aviation fuel for the U.S. Army because it was not allowed to share its research secrets with the Germans. The cartel arrangement gave the German company exclusive world rights to manufacture artificial rubber, a deal that was to cause both Britain and America manifold problems during the war. When the Japanese occupied Malaya and the Dutch East Indies, and German U-boats began taking a heavy toll of shipping from Brazil and Liberia, the Allies' supplies of natural rubber were reduced to a perilously tiny trickle. It took more than a year to build an artificial rubber factory in America.

Such industrialists poured substantial funds into the Republican Party's campaign to unseat Roosevelt. So, indirectly, did the German embassy, which was doing everything it could to sway American public opinion. This included giving Republican senators under-the-table payments to finance fifty isolationist congressmen to attend the convention, "so that they may work on the delegates in favor of an isolationist foreign policy."

German Foreign Office documents also noted that the Democratic Party, too, received its share of attention and German money. The German legation in Mexico City reported that a pro-German oil executive, who was largely responsible for transshipping petroleum products through neutral ports, had donated about $160,000 to the Pennsylvania Democratic organization to promote the candidacy, in the primary, of a man opposed to Joe Guffey, an anti-German senator, and also to buy Pennsylvania delegates to vote against Roosevelt at the July convention in Chicago. But the $160,000 was wasted; Guffey was re-elected, and Roosevelt carried the Pennsylvania delegation.

More money from the Reich's $200 million budget for overseas propaganda and subversion went to getting the message into print. Hearst's *New York Journal-American* and his other newspapers published a sympathetic interview with Hitler, conducted by Karl von Wiegand, a Hearst correspondent who was on the secret payroll of Goebbels's Ministry of Propaganda and Public Enlightenment. On June 27, Dr. Hans Thomsen, the chargé d'affaires in Washington, cabled Berlin:

The English translation of the Führer interview appeared today in No. 27 of the embassy bulletin *Facts in Review*, in an edition of 100,000. I was able through a confidential agent to induce the isolationist Representative Thorkelson to have the interview inserted in the *Congressional Record* of June 22. This assures the Führer interview once more the widest distribution.

Thorkelson of Montana was rated by John Gunther in his *Inside U.S.A.* as the worst anti-Semite ever to sit in Congress.

From the same propaganda budget, the Germans financed a full-page advertisement in the *New York Times*, headed "Keep America Out of the War!"

In fact, Roosevelt was determined, as he regularly proclaimed in public, to do everything in his power to achieve exactly that aim. But he was equally determined to back up his belief that it could best be done by supporting Britain and heeding Churchill's pleas. "Give us the tools, and we will finish the job," the British prime minister was to tell him in a famous world broadcast on February 9, 1941. By then, most Americans accepted that American aid was a vital part of the free world's fight against Hitler. But in the summer of 1940 the idea was still greeted with suspicion. Roosevelt's actions and intentions could very easily be twisted by his opponents to condemn him as a warmonger and even as a potential dictator. Such men would seize on Tyler Kent's information as political manna

from heaven once the presidential election campaign began to
roll.

On Thursday, August 1, 1940, a bright, sunny day in London,
Tyler Kent was driven across London from Brixton Prison to
Bow Street police station in Covent Garden, across the street
from the Royal Opera House. Bow Street has a special place in
the history of jurisprudence, for it was there, in 1748, that the
famous novelist Henry Fielding, who was a justice of the peace,
organized eight constables from the City of Westminster into
the Bow Street Patrol. Eighty-one years later, the Bow Street
Runners, as they had become known, with their red waistcoats
and blue cutaway coats, formed the basis of the world's first
metropolitan police force, officially established on June 6,
1829, by the home secretary, Sir Robert Peel.

On the site of Fielding's house, amid the clatter and bustle of
market porters dashing about the pavements outside, hauling
barrows laden with fruit and vegetables and balancing towers
of circular wicker baskets on their heads, Kent saw Anna
Wolkoff again for the first time since Saturday, May 18. Anna
had been brought down from Manchester for the hearing, and
was lodged in the women's prison at Holloway. She was described in a three-paragraph Associated Press story as "a beautiful Russian dressmaker said to have family connections with a
high officer in the czarist regime."

After they had been fingerprinted and photographed, Kent
and Wolkoff were taken into the adjoining magistrates' court,
where they were both charged with several violations of the
Official Secrets Act. Kent was also charged with larceny, and
Wolkoff with violations of the Defence Regulations. When
asked whether he wished to make a statement, Kent replied,
"Not at this time." They were both remanded in custody and
returned to their cells. The press, which had not been allowed
into the hearing, was given only the general charges and not
the specific allegations.

For the first time, Kent was forced to take his situation seriously. He had been visited in Brixton the previous day by
Consul General John Erhardt, who had told him he was to
appear in court and suggested that he be represented by a
lawyer. "Up to this point," Kent said in an interview in 1988, "I

fully expected to be deported and not tried. I decided it was now time to obtain legal counsel."

The State Department and the embassy were in an anomalous position. As the injured parties, their prime object, apart from concealing the Churchill-Roosevelt correspondence, was a speedy and secret trial for Kent in a British court. With the available evidence and Kent's admissions, conviction was a certainty. At the same time, however, as a "distressed American in a foreign country," Kent was entitled to their support, and neither the British nor the American authorities wanted him to have any reason to complain that he had been denied a fair trial or deprived of proper and competent legal counsel.

Throughout the month of August, the embassy busied itself with making sure Kent had the best possible representation. The New York law firm of Breed, Abbott and Morgan occasionally handled State Department business. Their London representative, Gilbert F. Kennedy, an American and a social agent of the Department of Justice, instructed a reputable London solicitor, F. Graham Maw, to act for Kent. On August 9, Ambassador Kennedy cabled Cordell Hull:

Lawyers point out the well-known fact that the briefing of leading counsel in the country is a very expensive matter. They appreciate that Kent's family is not possessed of any considerable means, but estimate at this stage that solicitors, expenses, and counsel fees for the preliminary hearings at the magistrate's court would amount to a minimum of $400 to $500. Expenses of the trial itself would be considerable but if the solicitor is not instructed to brief leading counsel these expenses could be kept to a minimum. Ordinarily, cost of defense with a leading counsel and solicitors, in a case of this type, would amount to anywhere from $1500 to $2000. If this is absolutely beyond the scope of Kent's family, Mr. Maw and Breed, Abbott & Morgan will make every endeavor to obtain best defense and will approach a prominent counsel with a view to obtaining his services on a small or nominal basis.

I should add that the firm of Breed, Abbott & Morgan is not appearing in this case at all.

Kent had $2000 in his Washington account with Riggs National Bank. Maw, through Kent's mother, arranged for this to be transferred to his firm's account in the United Kingdom. He then briefed one of the country's most eminent king's counsel, Maurice Healy, to represent Kent in the high court.

On Tuesday, August 27, Kent and Wolkoff appeared before the Bow Street magistrates again, and were committed for trial at the Central Criminal Court, the Old Bailey. The trials were scheduled to start on Wednesday, October 23, thirteen days before the presidential election in the United States.

By the end of August, the presidential campaign was beginning to heat up. Roosevelt had trounced his opponents at the Democratic convention. The Republicans had nominated a New York attorney and businessman who came from Midwestern German stock, Wendell Willkie. Willkie, a renegade Democrat, had been an outspoken opponent of the New Deal. As head of a giant electricity company, he had been particularly opposed to the Tennessee Valley Authority. He was an attractive and intelligent man with an appealing personality, and was a strong candidate posing a genuine threat to the Democrats. His selection seems to have been the final factor that determined Roosevelt to run for a third term.

In fact, despite his German roots, Willkie sympathized with Britain, and personally supported the policy of providing all help short of war. But the Republican Party was still dominated by the isolationists, and as he began to fall behind Roosevelt in the polls, he succumbed to party pressure to attack the president on his attitude to the war. He implied that Roosevelt had made secret deals with Britain, warning, "If you re-elect him you may expect war in April 1941."

Roosevelt's response was the pledge, later much criticized, to America's fathers and mothers: "Your boys are not going to be sent to any foreign wars." Before then, however, on September 2, he had announced the deal he had made with Churchill to trade the fifty old Navy destroyers for eight bases on British territories in the western hemisphere. He had used his powers as commander-in-chief to bypass Congress and issue an executive order, thus provoking outraged cries of "Dictator!" There was a powerful backlash, but it did have some popular backing. Even though the majority of Americans were still solidly against entering the war, they were gradually coming around to the idea of giving Britain every possible support short of fighting.

When the first of the destroyers arrived in Britain on September 28, British hearts were warmed by the care with which American shipyard workers had fitted them out. There were bars of soap and clean towels, fully stocked bars in messes and wardrooms—unlike those of the U.S. Navy, Royal Navy ships have never been "dry"—and even toys left for the children of the British sailors. There was one exception to the generally immaculate state of the ships: on walks and bulkheads everywhere messages had been scrawled in chalk, exhorting their new crews to "Sock 'em to Hell!" and "Kill the Bastards!"

Such sentiment was fostered by the reports of American war correspondents in London, led by CBS's bureau chief, the redoubtable Ed Murrow. As the Battle of Britain raged, and the skies rained death and destruction night after night, Murrow and his fellow commentators broadcast live reports of the action directly into American homes. For their listeners, the three thousand miles between the two nations disappeared as they listened to the sounds of gunfire and exploding bombs and the wail of the air-raid sirens. Listening to Murrow, they felt they were sharing the experience of an embattled people, often in the most direct and personal way. On September 11, for instance, his deep voice was heard all over the United States, whispering, "The air raid is still on. I shall speak rather softly because three or four people are sleeping on mattresses on the floor of this studio." The impact of such reporting was tremendous, exciting huge waves of sympathy among American listeners.

Other reports from London at that time, however, struck a decidedly sour note. On September 27, Kennedy signaled to the State Department:

I was delighted to see that the President said he was not going to enter the war, because to enter this war, imagining for a minute that the English have anything to offer in the line of leadership or productive capacity in industry that could be of the slightest value to us, would be a complete misapprehension . . . It breaks my heart to draw these conclusions about a people that I sincerely hoped might be victorious, but I cannot get myself to the point where I believe they can be of any assistance to the cause in which they are involved.

Apologists for Kennedy claim that he was simply doing his job and trying to give an objective rather than an overoptimistic view. As the distinguished Harvard economist and longtime friend of the Kennedy family John Kenneth Galbraith put it:

To be fair to Kennedy it should be understood that anyone reporting on Britain after the fall of France who didn't say there was little hope would be doing a bad job of reporting. In purely rational terms, Kennedy's dim assessment of British prospects was correct. Yet this was one of those rare occasions in history when romantic and heroic optimists managed to be right. Why? Because Hitler didn't realize his full strength after Dunkirk. Because he turned on the Soviet Union first before finishing Britain off. Because Churchill's rallying of the intrinsic strength of the British was remarkable. And, of course, because the U.S. finally got involved.

Galbraith is correct in pointing out just how heavily the odds were stacked against Britain in June 1940. But he is as wrong as Kennedy was in blaming Hitler's lack of confidence, or his turning on the Soviet Union, for his failure to finish Britain off. The truth is that Hitler did not finish Britain off because he could not. In September 1940, the young British Spitfire and Hurricane pilots inflicted a crushing defeat on the Luftwaffe, forcing Hitler to abandon his invasion plans. With the RAF in control of the skies over the Channel, he dared not launch his armada of troop-carrying barges. As for the productive capacity of British industry, so derided by Kennedy, it managed almost to double its output of warplanes in 1940, turning out nearly 50 percent more than the Germans—and, incidentally, about 150 percent more than the Americans over the same period. But the British still desperately needed all the help they could get, and it was fortunate for them that Roosevelt was receiving other counsel besides Kennedy's doom-laden pronouncements.

By October, the Battle of Britain had been won, but the Battle of the Atlantic was still heating up. So, too, was the battle for America. Painfully aware that the war was moving ever closer to the United States, Roosevelt broke yet another precedent by signing the Selective Service Act, conscripting men for the armed services in peacetime for the first time ever. His defense plans called for a massive armaments program, including the building of fifty thousand military aircraft a year, which incidentally was responsible for transforming and revitalizing American industry, providing hundreds of thousands of new jobs.

Roosevelt was immediately branded a warmonger by Willkie and the isolationists. The campaign became daily more bitter, as Republican speakers insinuated that he had made a secret commitment with Britain to go to war. No one, however, spoke of the American code clerk awaiting trial in London, or of the signals he had stolen. The secrets, like Kent himself, were safely locked away.

Throughout the campaign, Kennedy was forced to stay in London, growing bitter and frustrated. For he, too, was effectively silenced. Although he may have agreed with Kent's stated motives for stealing the documents—and indeed he was also collecting copies of signals for his own purposes—as ambassador he was outraged at actions that he regarded as disloyal to himself. The chief of mission is ultimately responsible for overseeing security precautions, so Kennedy found Kent's treachery a deep personal embarrassment. In any case, he was first and foremost a patriotic American, albeit at times a misguided one. Kent was regarded as a spy for the Germans and possibly the Soviets. In Kennedy's eyes, therefore, he was a traitor as well as a thief.

It has been suggested that Churchill allowed Kent to go on stealing documents without informing the ambassador in order to cause Kennedy the maximum amount of embarrassment and to ensure his removal from the London post. There is no evidence whatever for such a view, nor even for Churchill's being aware of Kent's existence or activities until May 18. It is certainly unlikely that either Churchill or the Foreign Office was exactly heartbroken by Kennedy's embarrassment, but the real bonus was that Kennedy was unable to make use of the information himself to charge Roosevelt publicly with warmongering or collusion with Churchill or any other impropriety.

Kennedy may well have hoped that Roosevelt would feel indebted to him for helping keep his contacts with Churchill secret from his opponents in the Democratic Party, as well as isolationists elsewhere. He may have hoped that this would further his own presidential ambitions, which were being regularly promoted in the American press, particularly by Henry Luce's *Time* and *Life* magazines. There can be no doubt that he was bitterly disappointed by Roosevelt's opting to run for a third term, destroying his own chances, at least for 1940.

Disappointment combined with resentment at two real or imagined slights. Earlier that year the president had sent Sumner Welles on a fact-finding mission to Berlin, partly at Kennedy's suggestion. But Welles had also visited Britain to survey morale in the United Kingdom, and had not consulted him. A further and deeper resentment came in July, when Roosevelt sent Colonel William Donovan as a special envoy to Britain to assess the situation, again without consulting the ambassador.

Donovan, a First World War hero and prominent Wall Street lawyer, was a staunch Republican. But he was also a convinced and outspoken interventionist, whose views were diametrically opposed to Kennedy's. Roosevelt gave him his full personal authority and a letter of credit for $10,000. By arrangement with the newspaper publisher Colonel Frank Knox—one of Theodore Roosevelt's Rough Riders during the 1898 war with Spain and shortly to be appointed Franklin Roosevelt's secretary of the Navy—Donovan traveled under cover as a special correspondent for Knox's *Chicago Daily News*. Knox's genuine chief European correspondent, Edgar Ansel Mowrer, accompanied Donovan, and actually wrote the series of four articles on the war in Europe that appeared under their joint names.

During a three-week stay in London, Donovan totally ignored Kennedy and the embassy, but was given the plushest of red carpet treatments by the British. Every door was open to him. He was granted an audience by King George VI; he conferred with Churchill and other leading politicians, with army, navy, and air force chiefs, and with most intelligence chiefs, who willingly gave him every bit of advice he needed to set up an American intelligence organization, which became the OSS and ultimately the CIA. When he returned to New York on a British Imperial Airways flying boat on August 4, he delivered a glowingly optimistic report to Roosevelt. William Stephenson, head of British Security Coordination in New York, who had been instrumental in arranging the trip, cabled MI6: "Donovan believes you will have within a few days very favourable news, and thinks he has restored confidence as to Britain's determination and ability to resist." The "very favourable news" was Roosevelt's offer of a deal on the destroyers, in direct opposition to Kennedy's advice.

The combination of disappointment, frustration, and anger proved too much for Kennedy. He decided to return home, resign, and make a last-minute radio speech attacking Roosevelt—unless, in the meantime, Roosevelt chose to offer him a top-level Cabinet post.

ELEVEN

Rex *versus* Tyler Kent

TYLER KENT'S TRIAL opened on Wednesday, October 23, in courtroom number one at the Old Bailey, the world's most famous criminal court, scene of countless famous trials. Kent was driven from Brixton in a black prison van, arriving just after 9:00 A.M. in the inner courtyard of the solid, gray stone building with the exhortation carved above the entrance: "Defend the children of the poor and punish the wrongdoer." The Old Bailey's familiar dome, echoing that of nearby St. Paul's Cathedral, was topped by the golden figure of blindfolded Justice.

Anna Wolkoff arrived shortly afterward. They were placed in separate, white-tiled cells in the basement until eleven, when they were taken up the short flight of steps that led directly into the dock in the center of the carved wood-paneled courtroom, facing the judge.

Sitting in his high-backed chair beneath the royal coat of arms and the upturned sword of justice on the wall, his table decorated with a single red rose, was Mr. Justice Tucker, resplendent in red robes with white facings, and white wig. Malcolm Muggeridge, there as an official observer for MI6, remembered him as "a strange, remote, barely human figure; glasses on beaked nose, layers of wig and folds of cloth about his withered person, fingers tapping, or scribbling down a word or two." In fact, at the age of fifty-two, Sir Frederick Tucker was the youngest justice on the King's Bench.

On the judge's right, facing inward from their box, sat the members of the jury. At their desks in the well of the court sat the various counsel in their black gowns, white bands at their throats and short horsehair wigs perched on top of their heads. Kent's counsel, Maurice Healy, was assisted by Mr. F. R. Hollins. Anna Wolkoff was represented by Mr. C. G. L. Du Cann, a member of a distinguished legal family. For the Crown, the prosecuting counsel was the solicitor general, Sir William Jowitt (later the Earl Jowitt), a Labour member of Parliament in Churchill's coalition government, assisted by Mr. C. B. McClure.

It was Jowitt who opened the proceedings, after the clerk of the court had read out the ten counts of the indictments against Kent and Anna, by making an application that the whole case be heard *in camera*. Healy and Du Cann raised no objections.

"Very well then," the judge ruled. "Throughout the whole of this trial nobody must be present except those who are particularly connected with the prosecution and the defense."

The court was then cleared of all spectators, including the press, though the official observers for MI5 and MI6, including Malcolm Muggeridge, were allowed to stay. Large sheets of brown wrapping paper were pasted over the courtroom windows and on the glass panels in the doors. The clerk then began to ask Kent and Wolkoff for their pleas, but before he could finish, Maurice Healy was on his feet.

"If I may interrupt the learned clerk," he began, "I desire in this case, on behalf of the prisoner Kent, to challenge the jurisdiction of the court to try him at all."

"Very well," the judge replied, not in the least put out. "We will take the plea of the other defendant."

Anna was charged on three counts: that on or about April 9, 1940, she obtained from Tyler Kent, "for a purpose prejudicial to the safety or interests of the state," two copies of telegrams, "documents which might be useful to an enemy"; that she recorded those documents, again "for a purpose prejudicial"; and thirdly, that on April 9, "with intent to assist an enemy, did an act which was likely to assist an enemy and to prejudice the public safety, the defence of the realm, and the efficient prosecution of the war, in that she, by secret means, attempted to send a letter in code addressed to one Joyce, known as Lord Haw-Haw, in Berlin."

She pleaded not guilty to all three charges.

The next day and a half were taken up with the argument about the validity of the court's jurisdiction over Kent. Healy put up a valiant effort, with a learned dissertation on why he believed the waiver of Kent's immunity was improper. The result was of great legal importance, since it concerned the nature and effect of diplomatic privilege, under which any person in the diplomatic corps of a foreign country is immune from the jurisdiction of the courts of the country in which he or she is serving. Jowitt himself later explained the central point:

Was Kent's diplomatic privilege the privilege of his Ambassador, which covered each employee as a mere incident of the Ambassador's privilege; or was it a privilege which belonged personally and individually to each member of the Embassy staff? If the former, it was plainly possible for the Ambassador to waive the privilege; if the latter, the privilege could only be waived by the individual member concerned. The trial Judge heard arguments on this question, and decided that the privilege belonged to the Ambassador, and that if the Ambassador decided to withdraw it from one of his servants, that servant no longer possessed any privilege and could therefore be tried in our courts for any infringement of our law of which he was accused.

Healy demanded that the Crown produce documentation of the waiver of Kent's immunity. Jowitt called Franklin Gowen, who said he could not produce the cable from Hull, since it also included "very, very secret" information. Jowitt then called Max Knight, who testified that he had personally delivered to Kent in prison a letter from Ambassador Kennedy discharging him from the Foreign Service. Kent's case was destroyed: it was ruled that his discharge automatically ended his diplomatic immunity. He had to stand trial in Britain.

At Du Cann's request, it was decided that Kent and Anna should be tried separately. Anna was taken away, and the charges against Kent were put to him. There were seven counts in all, four of obtaining "for a purpose prejudicial to the safety or interests of the State" documents "which might be directly or indirectly useful to an enemy," one communicating them to Anna Wolkoff, and two of stealing documents "being the property of His Excellency the American Ambassador."

Kent pleaded not guilty to all the charges, and the trial proper got under way. Muggeridge found it fascinating. "I became quite absorbed in the case," he recalled later, "snatching a quick snack at a pub opposite the Old Bailey in order to be back in court in time to miss none of the proceedings. The fact that every now and then the sirens sounded, and one and all—Judge, Learned Counsel, prisoners, witnesses—repaired to the underground cellars to await the All Clear, only added to the drama. Outside, such sound and fury; inside, the Judge with his wheezy dispassionateness, doodling or listening with closed eyes to interminable cross-examinations."

Jowitt opened the case for the prosecution with a detailed description of the indictments. Dealing with the Churchill-Roosevelt messages of January 29 and February 28, he reminded the jury that these were highly confidential documents. "My instructions are not to reveal, or not to reveal unless it is necessary, who the writers of these documents were . . . It is perhaps not difficult to guess, and if the responsibility is mine I would rather it remained a matter of guess than make it a certainty." It was obvious from the documents, he said, "that somebody who was, in January of 1940, a high authority in the Admiralty, is writing to someone in the United States."

After describing how Kent gave the documents to Anna Wolkoff, who had them photographed, Jowitt went on, "It is probable, as I will show you by the evidence, that they were conveyed to the Italian military attaché in this country, and of course they may have been conveyed to other places."

The other two documents being offered in evidence were

letters from Guy Liddell to Herschel Johnson, concerning the Soviet agent Armand Labis.

"Owing to the fact that we are happily on good terms with the citizens of the United States and their government," Jowitt told the jury, "our secret service has been able to avail itself of the help of their secret service . . . These documents are documents in which we are making inquiries about the Russian secret service and as far as this document shows we are interested in certain people who were probably in the secret service of Russia and who were operating in America. We are asking the American secret service to make inquiries about these people and to see what we could get out of them. If, for instance, that information is conveyed to the Russians you may be pretty certain that any inquiries made by the American secret service would be thwarted, and if it were conveyed to the Russians it might also get to other foreign powers and prove a great source of embarrassment, if it were known that this sort of relationship existed between our secret service and the American secret service."

Jowitt read out the letters, and went on to explain the meaning of the Official Secrets Act. He then handed over to his junior, C. B. McClure, examination of the Crown witnesses. First on the stand was Max Knight, who testified to the raid on Kent's flat, the discovery there of the 1929 documents, including the four that had been presented in evidence, the duplicate keys to the code room, Kent's correspondence with Alexander Kirk in Berlin, and the three glass negatives. Under cross-examination by Healy, he told of the rise of a fascist party and of the Right Club, and explained in detail about the keys.

Max Knight's testimony alone would probably have been enough to convict Kent, but the Crown was taking no chances, and called a string of other witnesses to solidify its case. Captain William Derek Stephens of the Royal Navy, deputy director of naval intelligence, testified that the signals might indeed be useful to the enemy. Under cross-examination he agreed that they might also be of use to "anybody taking an interest in American politics."

Guy Liddell, described as a "civil assistant on the general staff of the War Office," identified both the original and Kent's copies of the two letters written by himself. When asked whether the information in the letters might be useful to an enemy, he replied that it certainly would. In cross-examination, Healy asked him whether the letters might also be useful to somebody in America who wanted to raise the question of foreign agents. Liddell agreed they might be.

Franklin Gowen was recalled to testify that the stolen documents were secret, and that Kent had "no right or reason to copy them or to have copies made." He also testified that one of the signals "To the President from Former Naval Person" found in Kent's flat was not an original carbon copy but another one obviously made by Kent, presumably for nefarious purposes. Gowen further testified that Kent "had no right whatsoever to have duplicate keys made for any purpose whatsoever."

After a police photographic specialist had given technical evidence on the glass negatives, the photographer Eugene Smirnoff was called. He testified that on Saturday, April 13, 1940, Anna Wolkoff had brought him three sheets of documents to be photographed. Mrs. Smirnoff had given her a cup of tea while she waited for the plates to dry; then she had put them into her handbag, together with the original documents, and left. He said that later she brought some documents in German to be photographed. When she did not return for them—she was probably in jail by then—he destroyed them.

There could be no doubt that Kent had stolen the documents produced in evidence, though the charge relating to the Churchill-Roosevelt message of January 29 was dropped on a technicality, since he had merely made his own copy of it and had not physically taken away the document itself. There could be no doubt, either, that he had shown them to Anna Wolkoff and Captain Ramsay. But the Official Secrets Act of 1911 not only required proof of obtaining documents or information and communicating them to someone else; it also needed proof that the purpose was "prejudicial to the safety or interests of the State." Proving purpose is always difficult, but in 1920 the act had been amended to provide that such a purpose could be inferred if it were shown that the accused had "been in communication with or attempted to communicate with a foreign agent." And a "foreign agent" was defined as anyone who could be reasonably suspected of having committed such a prejudicial act.

Since Tyler Kent maintained that he had "collected" the documents for his own interest, the prosecution had to prove that Anna Wolkoff was a "foreign agent" as defined in the act. So, although Anna was not herself on trial at that moment, and was not even in court, Jowitt instructed McClure to examine two of Knight's agents from the Right Club, the Belgian girl Helene de Munck and Marjorie Mackie.

Helene described her role in the Right Club, and then told of the letter she had carried to Brussels via Anna, questioning the loyalty of a member there and asking for a report on "our work in Belgium." Healy cross-examined briefly, pointing out to the jury that the latest charge against Kent was on February 28, but it was not until April 9 that Anna had asked de Munck to take the letter to Belgium.

"Of course," he concluded, "the moment she asked you to take a message abroad for her, it was clear to you that at least she was a suspicious person or a person to be suspected of seeking to get in touch with Germany."

De Munck agreed, and stood down. Marjorie Mackie was then called. She testified that the Right Club was very anti-Semitic and that she had seen Kent with Anna Wolkoff at the Russian Tea Room, adding that she had introduced Joan Miller to Anna there.

"Did Anna Wolkoff ever mention to you the name of Captain Liddell?" McClure asked.

"Yes."

"In what connection was that?"

"Some radio detectors from [J. Edgar] Hoover. She said she had seen Captain Liddell's signature on a document which had to do with radio detectors," Marjorie Mackie replied, thus tying Kent to Wolkoff by the showing of the letter, which was properly the property of the Crown.

To complete the proof of Anna's connection with Kent and her pro-German attitude, Detective Sergeant Harold Sutling of the Special Branch, who had searched Anna's flat at the time of her arrest, described two documents he had found there. The first was a copy of her report to Ramsay of her visit to Germany in the summer of 1939. McClure read aloud part of it: "On the

Kent immediately after his arrest by the Metropolitan Police/Scotland Yard.

Secretary of State Cordell Hull ordered the lifting of Kent's diplomatic immunity and sacked him immediately after.

Under Secretary of State Sumner Welles was the first State Department officer in Washington to learn of Kent's treachery.

J. Edgar Hoover. Between 1940 and 1963, the FBI conducted several investigations into Tyler Kent's background and activities. He also ordered an investigation into the lax security in the Moscow embassy. As a result, eight employees were fired.

Montana Historical Society

Burton K. Wheeler (D., Montana).

Minnesota Historical Society

Henrik Shipstead (R., Minnesota).

South Dakota Historical Society

Gerald P. Nye (R., South Dakota).

Anti-Roosevelt isolationists in the U.S. Senate who vigorously led a floor fight for release of Kent from his British prison.

Hoboken, New Jersey, December 4, 1945. Tyler Kent steps ashore after nearly six years in British prisons. He is watched by a Hoboken police sergeant. More than forty reporters, photographers, and newsreel cameramen greeted him with a barrage of questions.

Kent's mother, who made an emotional but factually inaccurate fight for her son's freedom.

Seven months after his return to the United States, Kent married Clara Hyatt, a multimillionaire divorcée, shown here in a 1968 passport photo.

Kent at the height of his opulent lifestyle in the late 1950s. Ironically, he was to die nearly a pauper in Kerrville, Texas, on November 20, 1988.

Clara bought Kent an eighty-acre estate in Satsuma, Florida, complete with guest houses, swimming pool, tennis court, and this "English-style" cottage, designed by Kent.

One of Kent's earlier and smaller yachts, photographed in Annapolis.

Tyler Kent's high life on the high seas. Kent (seated, fifth from left) took frequent cruises aboard British luxury liners. Mrs. Kent is not at the table.

17th of July I met General Frank, the right-hand man of
Henlein, whom I was to have met, but he was suddenly called
to Berchtesgaden. Frank and I talked for two and a half hours,
and it was then that I learned of the forthcoming German-
Soviet pact and all it would imply. It is too long to describe the
interview in this letter but one day I will give you all the details."

McClure then turned to the second document. He described
it as "a letter to Miss Wolkoff signed Tyler Kent. 'I am enclosing a few Chesterfields which I promised you. It's not very
much,' and so on. 'I am driving down to the South Coast . . .'
Then at the end there are some words in some foreign language. Also, after the signature, in brackets, the words Anatoli
Vassilovich."

The prosecution had effectively proved that Anna Wolkoff
was a foreign agent as defined in the Official Secrets Act, and
that Kent had been in communication with her. Now, it was
time to open the defense, for which there was only one witness
—Tyler Kent himself.

Kent took the stand after lunch on Tuesday, October 29,
wearing a gray flannel suit, white shirt, and blue tie. To Malcolm Muggeridge he looked like "one of those intensely gentlemanly Americans who wear well-cut tailor-made suits, with
waistcoat and watch-chain, drink wine instead of highballs, and
easily become furiously indignant. They always strike me as
being somehow a little mad." His testimony, under examination by Maurice Healy, lasted throughout the afternoon and
the following morning. "I knew," he said in his 1988 interview,
"that I would be found guilty. I hoped to offer mitigating
motives and circumstances which would keep my forthcoming
sentence minimal."

Healy led Kent through a recital of his family history, educa-
tion, and his State Department assignments, and questioned
him about his anti-Semitic feelings and his attitude toward
Germany. Kent freely admitted that he had strong anti-Semitic
views. He also said that during several visits to Germany he had
formed the impression that the economic and financial methods of the Hitler regime were good.

Having admitted to being anti-Semitic and pro-Nazi, Kent
did not take long to display his amazing arrogance. He claimed

that while serving in Moscow he had disagreed with his ambassador's approach to foreign affairs, and had begun taking copies of official documents and keeping them for his own use. He thought the American ambassadors both in Warsaw and Paris were too involved in the policies of the countries they were accredited to, and that their attitude increased the risk of the United States becoming involved in the European war. His view, he explained, was that American ambassadors should give no advice to the governments of foreign countries. He said the idea was maturing in his mind of bringing the circumstances to the attention of American senators, and that he would need documents to support his allegations. He had, he said, burned all the papers he had accumulated in Moscow before being transferred to London, but admitted that he had started making copies of documents again as soon as he started work in Britain.

Kent agreed that he was in sympathy with the anti-Semitic views of Anna Wolkoff and Captain Ramsay, and that he had thought it right to let them see the documents he had collected, stressing that neither of them was in any way concerned with any foreign government.

He said he believed that as a code clerk he had conflicting loyalties, on the one hand to the embassy and on the other to the American people. It was in obedience to his duty to the people that he had taken documents in order to study them, since he felt he might have to show them to persons in prominent positions in public life in the United States. He wanted to make sure that the United States gave no help to any country outside the American continent.

Opening his cross-examination, Sir William Jowitt homed in on the question of Kent's duty to the embassy, "a duty of the highest confidence," as he put it.

"Correspondence could not go on between an ambassador in one country and his government at home unless he could rely on the fact that his message were kept secret. That is right, is it not?" he demanded.

"It is more than that," Kent replied. "It requires qualification."

"What qualification do you wish to give it?"

"Correspondence by Americans in foreign affairs is not secret correspondence."

"I am not dealing with foreign affairs," Sir William countered. "I am dealing with messages. Do you wish the jury to
understand that these messages sent in code from the American ambassador in London to his government, or from his
government . . . are not to be kept secret?"

"They are to be kept secret from foreign powers, yes. That is
the main object of using codes," Kent responded.

"When you say foreign powers, do you mean that any American is entitled to know them?" Jowitt asked, incredulously.

"That is a moot question of course . . ."

"You realize that it is a bit difficult, perhaps, to keep a secret
if 130 million people know it?"

"Yes," Kent agreed. "But it is also a question of the extent
the American government is protected by the Constitution and
the American practice to engage in these matters."

Jowitt was not going to let Kent off the hook now. "Would
you feel yourself entitled to reveal a communication to one of
your own compatriots at the dinner table, a person who had
nothing whatsoever to do with the embassy, stating what had
been put into code and what had been translated that day?"

"To an American subject, yes," Kent told him, unperturbed.
"I should not have hesitated to reveal any of these things to an
elected representative of America, Canada, or France."

"With regard to America," Jowitt went on, "you wanted
them to give no sort of help or encouragement to this country
or her allies?"

"Not to any European or any country outside the western
hemisphere," Kent replied firmly.

Leaving aside that any secret information given to 130 million Americans would automatically be available to the rest of
the world through the press, Sir William said he thought it odd
that if Kent wanted only Americans to know about the messages, he had made them available to at least four others, all
British subjects. Kent's feeble reply was that he trusted them.
Sir William turned to one of the Churchill-Roosevelt messages
and asked why Kent had shown it to Anna Wolkoff.

"When I first met Captain Ramsay in the month of March,"
Kent replied, "we began to discuss various political questions

referring to the background of the war, chiefly. During the course of those conversations I found that Captain Ramsay was ignorant or misinformed on certain points that dealt with the origin of the war. Those conversations took place in the presence of Anna Wolkoff in Captain Ramsay's residence. I therefore invited Captain Ramsay and Anna Wolkoff—who was acting practically as his political secretary—to come over to my place and look at certain documents which illustrated certain points relating to the background of the European situation, going back several years. During the examination of those documents, and the reading of some of them, this document also came into Captain Ramsay's hands and to his attention."

"If it be true that you were giving documents to Captain Ramsay to enlighten him as to the true origin of the war," Jowitt asked, "this much is plain—that this document has no possible bearing on the origin of the war, and this document has no bearing on the Jews?"

"No," Kent admitted.

"And it has no bearing on Freemasons?"

"Apparently not."

"Then I ask you again: Why did you give this document to Anna Wolkoff?"

"May I continue with what I was saying?"

"By all means."

"During the process of showing Captain Ramsay these documents," Kent continued, still totally ignoring the question about Anna, "I did not select them all; I gave him a group to look through himself. At the time, they were not sorted according to the subject matter, or according to the country of origin, and so forth. He therefore, quite naturally, saw this document amongst others which did have a bearing on the discussions which were going on between myself and Captain Ramsay."

Jowitt apparently gave up trying to pin Kent down about Anna and the photographed documents, and settled for the answer about Ramsay. "Is it your evidence that, being desirous of enlightening Captain Ramsay as to the origin of the war, you gave him carte blanche to read through all the documents?"

"To read through most of them, probably, not all."

"But as far as you were concerned, you left him free to roam at large through the whole lot?" Jowitt persisted.

"That is more or less true," Kent admitted.

Changing tack, Sir William introduced the correspondence between Kent and Alexander Kirk, the chargé d'affaires in Berlin, about a possible transfer. If he had been transferred, Sir William asked, was he contemplating turning over to the Germans the documents he had acquired in London? Kent did not deny or confirm this, saying merely that the question was hypothetical. He claimed, under questioning, that he was more interested in the governments of Germany and the Soviet Union than he was in that of Britain.

Jowitt finished his cross-examination. Maurice Healy conducted a brief re-examination to confirm Kent's statement that he had been interested only in informing Ramsay, and that the latter had seen the Churchill-Roosevelt documents only by accident. But the judge was not satisfied.

"You have told us your reasons for obtaining this document," he said to Kent, "and I want to ask you a question or two about your reasons for passing on the information contained in the document. You say that Anna Wolkoff was merely an intermediary or go-between?"

"Yes, in my opinion," Kent replied.

"And that the real person to whom the contents of these documents were to be communicated was Captain Ramsay?"

"That is so."

"You said in your statement that the three of you—that is, Anna Wolkoff, Captain Ramsay, and yourself—struck up a friendship more or less as a result of a general community of outlook regarding political views. Is that right?"

"Yes," Kent agreed, "that is the way in which it could be described."

"Would you agree that the revealing of the contents of the documents was a big step, going a great deal further than merely taking them from the embassy for the purpose which you have described?"

"Yes, but it did not strike me as so at the time, although it does now."

"You say your justification for taking them was to enlighten the American people; but if that was so, why were you communicating them to a British subject in this country, because a

British subject would not be interested in them from that aspect?"

"No."

"Captain Ramsay was not interested in the propriety of the conduct of the American ambassadors in Europe?"

"No."

"Or of America becoming involved in a war by reason of those matters?"

"No."

"Then what was the aspect of the matter contained in those documents which interested Captain Ramsay sufficiently to cause him to want to have copies of them?"

"I do not know actually that he did want to take copies."

"Or sufficient reason for his secretary to want to borrow them?"

"The first reason for showing him the documents was purely of an historical nature," Kent reiterated. "Then, with regard to these two specific documents, it was a question of the propriety of the correspondence which was going on from the British point of view."

"What could be questioned in the propriety of the correspondence from the British point of view?"

"The fact that it was not being conducted through the Foreign Office."

"A mere matter of procedure," Mr. Justice Tucker concluded scathingly. "Not of substance?"

"Yes," Kent agreed, "a matter of procedure."

Having managed to extract an oblique and unwilling admission that there was a political motive, the judge had only one more point to clear up.

"You have told us about Captain Ramsay's views with regard to the origin of the war and your common community of outlook," he went on. "But, apart from his attitude to the Jews, what did you gather was Captain Ramsay's political outlook—by which I mean his outlook in connection with the war?"

"To put it in general terms, he thought that the war could well have been avoided."

"And once started, what about it then?"

"That nothing could be done about it."

After Jowitt had addressed the jury for the prosecution, Maurice Healy made his closing speech. According to Jowitt, "He stated with his customary charm and eloquence, with occasional flashes of wit, all that could be said on behalf of Tyler Kent, his client."

In his summing up, Mr. Justice Tucker reminded the jury of the unique position of Kent, and warned them that they had to consider the case "very, very carefully and in as dispassionate a way as you can.

"You may think," he told them, "having regard to his cross-examination—and I do not desire to mince my language about this—you may hold extremely strong views with regard to his conduct, on his own showing, towards his embassy. You may think that it displays a shocking disregard for every principle of decency and honor and loyalty, and so forth. But Mr. Healy is right when he says that it is not what you are trying him for in this case . . . [A]s far as the Official Secrets Act is concerned, you are not trying him for being disloyal to the ambassador or being guilty of shocking breaches of confidence . . .

"It is suggested for the prosecution that you could not possibly accept his own story as being the real and true explanation of his motives for doing what he admits he did do. It is said that on his own showing it displays such a remarkable and extraordinary attitude, and such a disloyal attitude, that you cannot possibly believe it as being a reasonable explanation, and that accordingly you should be driven to take the view of the facts which the prosecution invites you to take, namely, that these things were done for a purpose prejudicial to the interests of this country, and not for the reasons he has given. That is the only bearing upon this case which any adverse opinion you may have formed with regard to his conduct has, because he is not being tried for that."

On Anna Wolkoff, the judge carefully explained to the jury that she was not being tried before them, but would have a separate trial of her own. The only thing that was of interest to them was whether or not she was a foreign agent within the definition of act, and whether Kent had been in communication with her. Concluding his summing up, he directed the jury on the relevant law, and at 3:35 P.M. they retired. It took only twenty-four minutes for them to return with verdicts of guilty on all six counts.

Mr. Justice Tucker announced that he would defer sentencing until after Anna Wolkoff's trial. He discharged the jury and adjourned the court. Kent was taken back to Brixton Prison to wait until a verdict had been passed on Anna.

Anna Wolkoff's trial began the following morning. The transcript will not be available until the year 2015, though copies of the transcript of Tyler Kent's trial may be found in the United States National Archives, as well as in Kent's own papers. But there are at least two sources of information on Anna's trial: Lord Jowitt's book, *Some Were Spies,* based on the transcripts with official approval, and the memoirs and memory of Malcolm Muggeridge, who, when interviewed for this work, was probably the only living person who was there.

In addition to two charges under the Official Secrets Act, covering the documents she had photographed, Anna also faced the even more serious charge under the Defence Regulations of passing a letter in code to Lord Haw-Haw in Berlin, "an act which was likely to assist the enemy." She pleaded not guilty to them all, maintaining that she was only against the Jews, and not against the war. Supporting this claim, her father told the court that she felt the family misfortunes more keenly than he did; he explained this by saying he was old. He said that she blamed all their misfortunes, and indeed the downfall of the Russian Empire, on the Jews and the communists.

As character witnesses, Anna called many old friends. "At one point," Malcolm Muggeridge recalled, "a whole contingent of internees under Regulation 18B were summoned from the Isle of Man . . . distraught women in battered fur coats, blond hair whitening and disheveled, make-up running; men in tweed jackets to their knees, leather-patched, frayed club ties, suede shoes; Sir Oswald Mosely himself, bearded at this time, his suit crumpled, speaking with the vibrant voice of a wronged man who asked only to be allowed to join his regiment in the battle line to fight for King and Country."

Captain Ramsay, of course, gave evidence on Anna's behalf, though whether this was an advantage or a disadvantage is open to question. Muggeridge recalled a letter of his being read out, in which he referred to "those two lovely ships," the *Scharnhorst* and *Gneisenau,* German battle cruisers that sank the

British armed merchantman *Rawalpindi* on November 23, 1939, and how sad it would be if anything happened to them. "This," said Muggeridge, "brought a prodding finger" from Sir William Jowitt, who asked if this was any way to speak of two enemy warships. "With the benighted innocence of the crazed," Muggeridge continued, "Ramsay said that when he wrote the letter it still seemed possible that the war, though declared, would never get going; in which case the loss of the ships would have been a pity."

German ships seem to have held a fascination for Anna's friends. Jowitt records that one woman friend—unnamed by him but possibly Christabel Nicholson—had written to Anna on December 18, 1939, about the battle of the River Plate, which had ended the day before with the sinking of the German pocket battleship *Graf Spee*. "Yesterday," the letter said, "was a day of black despair. Such an end to that beautiful ship, and how one wished she could have accounted for at least one good shot into the *Hood*. The sneers and rejoicing all round were painful in the extreme."

Muggeridge summed up the irony of the situation with his usual pungency: "Ramsay and the others were a woebegone procession indeed, as, one after the other, they held up a Bible and swore to tell the truth, the whole truth, and nothing but the truth, while outside their erstwhile heroes and putative allies tried to blow the Old Bailey, along with the rest of London town, including them, to smithereens."

Anna freely admitted her extreme anti-Semitism, saying it had been bred into her, as into all Russian aristocrats, from birth. She also admitted that she had been responsible for the sticky-back campaign, but claimed that after her brother, Gabriel, had pleaded with their father to persuade her to stop it, she had gone to the authorities to ask whether they had any objection to the campaign, and they had, she said, given her a noncommittal answer.

The evidence against Anna that had been presented at Kent's trial was repeated, and this time Joan Miller joined Helene de Munck and Marjorie Mackie as Max Knight's star witnesses. She told the court that Anna had said that when the Germans were in control of Britain she, Anna, would be the Julius Streicher and that Joan would occupy a post on the staff of the local Himmler. Anna denied this, but admitted that she had told Joan she had been responsible for the Italians protesting about the special concessions being made by Britain to American shipping. She qualified this, however, by claiming that it had been a lie, made up to impress Joan, who she had thought might be a communist spy.

When it came to the letter to Lord Haw-Haw, however, she tried to deny everything, implying that the whole thing had been a plant. Her story was that a young naval officer friend had introduced her to a man who had asked if she would be prepared to do "something that would really help in the cause of anti-Semitism." She said she answered that she would do anything to injure Jewry.

"Have you ever sent anything to the Continent through a diplomatic bag?" the man is supposed to have continued, to which Anna said she replied, "Well, if it's very important I might be able to get it sent." The man then took out of his pocket an envelope addressed to "Herr W. B. Joyce, Rundfunkhaus, Berlin," and handed it to her. When she asked what the contents of the letter were, he told her, "Oh, some good anti-Jewish stuff, I believe. Can you send it?"

This, said Anna, was the letter she had given to Helene de Munck, who had told her she had access to the Romanian diplomatic bag. She also said that her naval friend had given her a reassuring account of the mystery man, who had said he was a friend of William Joyce's, but that when she had mentioned him to Captain Ramsay—without saying anything about the letter—Ramsay had warned her against him, saying the man had several aliases and that she should have nothing to do with him. Despite this, she had given the letter to Helene.

Anna's claims were utterly demolished when Helene described how she had retrieved the letter the next morning for Anna to add a postscript. At this, Anna changed her story, claiming that she had been "indulging in a gigantic game of bluff." Suspecting that the mystery man had been trying to plant a message on her, she had, in turn, determined to plant it on Helene, since she had never believed the Belgian girl's claim that she could get letters delivered to Germany through the Romanian embassy.

On the question of the glass negatives found in Kent's flat, she claimed that she had given the prints to Kent—but, revealingly, she did not call him to corroborate this. And as to the packet she and Joan Miller had posted through the Duke del Monte's door, this had been part of a trap she was helping del Monte to set. He suspected someone in his household of stealing a press summary, and had asked her to get a copy of a similar summary from the American embassy, through her friend Tyler Kent, so that he could see if that, too, got stolen.

Anna's claim that the letter to Joyce had been planted on her does have the whiff of an MI5 "dirty trick" at a time when Knight had been desperate to wrap up the case, but she had destroyed her credibility by adding the postscript herself, in front of a witness. Her far-fetched excuse for the visit to del Monte's house at the dead of night could not have helped her case, either. In the event, the jury took only a few minutes to find her guilty on all three charges.

On Thursday, November 7, Kent was brought back into court for sentencing. When asked if he had anything to say, he complained bitterly that he had been tried on the basis of four documents "from a group of over five hundred other documents" [sic] that were in his possession, and therefore had been taken out of context.

"The jury has been asked to determine so subjective a thing as my intent with regard to these four documents," he said, "and they have had no opportunity of seeing the four documents in their proper light, namely, against the background of the total sum of documents in my possession."

The embassy, he said, had prevented him from producing these other documents, which were essential to his defense in determining motive. They had also denied his counsel access to a file of his personal correspondence, which contained papers that he also considered essential to his defense. The only paper from this file that had been introduced in evidence was his letter to Kirk in Berlin, "and much insinuation was based upon it." He said there were other letters, written at earlier dates, "which in court would have enabled me to refute the propositions of the prosecution."

He also complained that he had not been able to introduce a letter from the director of public prosecutions saying there was no intention of claiming that he was in any way connected with, or had any knowledge of, Anna Wolkoff's alleged communication with Germany. And yet, he said, "the jury has listened for the better part of three days to evidence concerning this matter, and that has undoubtedly influenced their minds."

He had, he claimed, been convicted of a felony "on the basis of partial and one-sided evidence, and that I have been convicted of an offense which I did not intentionally commit . . . Your Lordship, I submit that I have not committed a felony, because I had no felonious intent. I have committed a gross indiscretion, possibly a misdemeanor, but I submit that felonious intent is a prerequisite to the commission of a felony.

"In closing, I should like to submit to Your Lordship that I am a loyal citizen of the United States of America, in spite of the allegations to the contrary by the prosecution in this case."

The judge heard him out courteously, then asked whether Kent would like him to read the letter from the director of public prosecutions. Kent said he would, and a copy was handed to the judge. After reading it, he announced that he would pass sentence in open court. The court was declared open, and press men poured in, eager to hear and see what little they were allowed. The *Daily Express* reporter seemed to have been a little disappointed. "The spectators did not find Anna Wolkoff, dressed in fox furs, a beautiful spy. She is 37, with dark and greying hair, with a lined and pale face. Tyler Kent was handsome enough, though, with well-cut clothes and an extravagant air."

Kent was sentenced to seven years' penal servitude on each of the Official Secrets charges, and twelve months' imprisonment on the larceny charge; all the sentences were to run concurrently. Anna Wolkoff was sentenced to ten years for attempting to assist the enemy, and five years for each of the Official Secrets charges, the sentences, again, to run concurrently. They were led downstairs separately and driven to their respective prisons. Anna was soon moved to prison on the Isle of Man, where she remained until she was released, in 1947. Kent gave notice of appeal, and stayed in Brixton until this was heard.

The press found there was little they could say about the trial, and generally had to content themselves with the bare fact of the sentences. From London, Frank R. Kelley reported to the *New York Herald Tribune:*

After the longest and most secret trial heard in London's famous criminal court, the Old Bailey, since the spy cases of the World War, Tyler G. Kent, 29-year-old American citizen and former clerk at the American Embassy here, was today sentenced to seven years' penal servitude for offenses under the Official Secrets Act.

The London story, passed through the strict wartime censorship, was followed by one originating in New York and thus not subject to censorship. The lead read:

The British Government, it was learned in New York yesterday, has been in the habit of giving to the American Embassy at London important secret documents for transmission to Washington. Airplane and gun plans and much highly confidential information on supplies and prospects were passed on by the Embassy.

Then came the revelation that had been long feared both by the administration in Washington and by Whitehall. It came not from the expected German sources, however, but from a source either in the British-American community or within the administration:

A raid on his [Kent's] apartment revealed suitcases full of documents. Among them was a communication between Prime Minister Winston Churchill and President Roosevelt which had been handed to the Embassy that morning.

Fortunately for Roosevelt, no damage control was necessary; the only signal between him and Churchill mentioned in the story was sent ten days after Churchill became prime minister, and thus there was no impropriety in their communicating directly with each other. The *Herald Tribune*'s unknown source was clearly unaware of the previous signals.

In any case, however, whatever exposé there might have been was too late for the Republicans: two days before the press was allowed into court to hear Kent sentenced, Roosevelt had been re-elected for a third term.

Kennedy had left London during Kent's trial, arriving in New York after his first transatlantic flight, on the *Dixie Clipper* flying boat, on Sunday, October 27. He was met by his wife, Rose—

and a command from the president to have dinner at the White House that evening. Roosevelt had sent a private plane to fly the Kennedys to Washington, and on the flight Joe told Rose of his plans to attack Roosevelt. Rose was appalled and told her husband how much he owed to Roosevelt; her recent wonderful stay in England, and the great honor Kennedy had enjoyed of being the first Catholic American ambassador to St. James's, were due entirely to Roosevelt.

Over predinner drinks, Kennedy lashed out at the president for bypassing his ambassadorial authority with his special envoys, Welles and Donovan. There are two versions of what happened next. In one, the president surprisingly agreed with Kennedy, blaming the machinations and the bureaucracy of the State Department, then asked him whether he would make a nationwide radio speech on Tuesday night supporting Roosevelt. Kennedy said he would make the speech, on condition that he wrote it himself, that no one would see it until he spoke, and that he paid the $20,000 broadcast fee himself.

The other version of events comes from the late President Lyndon B. Johnson, who said that at their meeting Roosevelt had "thrown the red meat on the floor," telling Kennedy he had confirmed intelligence reports that the ambassador had been associating with a German propagandist, a Dr. Westphal, and with pro-German industrialists such as James Mooney of General Motors. In essence, according to Johnson, Roosevelt was saying, "Give me public support or I'll throw you to the public as a pro-German bastard." The blackmail worked, and Kennedy stepped into line with his Tuesday night radio speech.

Either way, the ambassador's agreement brought much relief to Roosevelt, who had suffered through Kennedy's personal attacks. He needed his support now, since most of the nation's Irish population—a substantial proportion of America's twenty-five million Catholics—were turning against him for helping Britain, a serious crime in the eyes of many Irishmen who would have enjoyed seeing the British defeated by Hitler.

To the dismay of the Republicans, who had hoped Kennedy would attack Roosevelt, he gave the president his all-out support in the broadcast. However, he refused to appear with Roosevelt when he made his last major speech of the campaign at Boston's Fenway Park, home of the Boston Red Sox, on Saturday, November 2. And on the Wednesday following Roosevelt's triumphant return to the White House by twenty-seven million Americans, he submitted his resignation. Roosevelt accepted it, with the provision that it should not be made public until he had chosen a replacement. This was to take three months, before the announcement of the appointment of New Hampshire Governor John G. Winant, a Republican who was destined to become one of America's best-loved representatives in London of all time.

But Kennedy was not quite done. On the Saturday following his resignation, at Boston's Ritz-Carlton hotel, he gave an interview to two newsmen from St. Louis and to Louis Lyons, who had been a *Boston Globe* reporter since 1919. In his shirtsleeves, with his suspenders hanging down, and eating apple pie, Kennedy talked. Because he understood the ninety-minute interview to be off the record, he spent most of the time blasting the British.

The St. Louis newsmen, true to their earlier agreement, did not use the material from the interview. Lyons, however, was unaware that it was supposed to be off the record. His story, written as a feature, appeared on the front page of Sunday's *Globe*. Rated as one of the ten top news stories of the year, it was immediately picked up by the wire services—Associated Press, United Press, International News Service, and Reuters—and the following day appeared in every English-language newspaper throughout the world. KENNEDY QUOTED AS SAYING THE BRITISH ARE THROUGH, the *Washington Post* headlined. DEMOCRACY DIES IF US ENTERS THE WAR—KENNEDY, blazoned the *Washington Times-Herald*.

Political cartoonists had a field day. John McCutcheon of the *Chicago Tribune* syndicate, probably the most distinguished American cartoonist in the field, showed Kennedy saying: "Democracy is finished in England. It may be here. I'm willing to spend all I've got to keep us out of war. There's no sense our getting in. We'd just be holding the bag. Help Britain but avoid war." McCutcheon's Roosevelt was saying: "America is proud of its share in maintaining the era of democracy in the World War. Democracy will be saved."

British journalists, of course, had their say, too. A. J. Cummings, a distinguished political columnist on the Liberal *News Chronicle*, wrote:

It is all to the good . . . [T]he British people now know just where Kennedy stands. His suspicion that his standing in London is gone is justified. While he was here his suave monotonous style, his nice over-photographed children and his hail-fellow-well-met manner concealed a hard-boiled businessman's eagerness to do a professional business deal with the dictators and he deceived many decent English people.

In the *Daily Mail*, George Murray addressed the former ambassador in an open letter:

You have said thing about us that we regret to hear . . . [T]hey are things which in time, I think, you will regret having said . . . Perhaps you were always a defeatist and never owned to it in public . . . We can forgive wrongheadedness but not bad faith.

Kennedy immediately denied the statements and said the interview had been off the record. But the damage was done—and there was more to follow. Three days later he went to California, where he addressed a conclave of his old friends and associates in the motion picture industry. It was a private meeting, but in "Washington Merry-Go-Round," a widely syndicated column, Robert Allen—later to be General Patton's assistant intelligence officer—and Drew Pearson revealed that he had said Hollywood producers should stop making films that were offensive to the dictators. A British intelligence report said Kennedy had told the producers they should not protest as Jews because Jewish outcries would make the world believe that this was a Jewish war.

After leaving Hollywood, Kennedy traveled east to Hyde Park, where the president and Mrs. Roosevelt were celebrating Thanksgiving. There is no record of exactly what passed between them, but Kennedy had been with the president for only a few minutes when Roosevelt asked him to leave the room. Mrs. Roosevelt later said she had never seen her husband so angry. The president rarely swore, but that day he shouted: "I never want to see that son of a bitch again as long as I live. Take his resignation and get him out of here!"

Mrs. Roosevelt protested that Kennedy was a weekend guest, and there would be other guests for lunch. But FDR replied, "Give him a sandwich and get him out of here!"

Kennedy's hopes of a Cabinet-level post were in ashes, as was his entire political career. He would never again hold public office.

TWELVE

This Unspeakable Blackguard

KENT'S APPEAL against his conviction was heard on February 5, 1940, in the ornate red brick Victorian buildings of the Royal Courts of Justice in the Strand, by the Lord Chief Justice, Viscount Caldecote of Bristol, with Mr. Justice Humphries and Mr. Justice Singleton. Sir William Jowitt appeared once more for the Crown, but Kent chose to conduct his own case, partly, no doubt for reasons of expense, but also because of his low opinion of all the British apart from Captain Ramsay. He dispensed with the services of both his counsel, Maurice Healy, and his solicitor, F. Graham Maw, considering Maw to be a tool of the American embassy and Healy an incompetent drunk, charges that were totally without foundation.

Kent gave as his primary grounds:

1. That the Official Secrets Acts of 1911 and 1920 do not apply to acts done by a diplomatic agent while employed as such.

2. That the judge was wrong in law in holding that I was not entitled to diplomatic privilege.

3. That I was not guilty of larceny in law.

4. That the judge misdirected the jury in law and in fact.

5. That material documents necessary for my defense were not produced.

He fared no better without his lawyers than he had done with them. The court ruled against him on all counts, and he was transferred from Brixton to Camp Hill Prison on the Isle of Wight to serve out his sentence. As a protest against the dismissal of his appeal, he went on a two-week hunger strike. It is not clear whether this was before he left Brixton or after he arrived at Camp Hill; we do know, however, that he spent some time in the infirmary at Camp Hill soon after his arrival there.

Since the records of his imprisonment are still considered an Official Secret, we can only surmise that the hunger strike was an attempt to get his case referred to the House of Lords, the ultimate court of appeals in Britain. If so, it failed. He was at Camp Hill for the next four and three-quarter years working as a farm laborer. For the rest of his sentence he remained a model prisoner—as did Anna Wolkoff, who found an outlet for her domineering character by taking charge of the prison gardens on the Isle of Man and bossing the other prisoners who worked under her direction.

Of the other plotters arrested at the same time as Kent and Anna Wolkoff, only Christabel Nicholson was ever charged. She was held in Holloway Prison until her trial, *in camera*, at the Old Bailey early in 1941, when she was found innocent of all charges. However, as she left court number one, she was re-arrested under Regulation 18B, and returned to Holloway, where she was detained for three years. Neither Enid Riddell nor Ismay Ramsay was ever charged.

Captain Ramsay was never charged or tried, either, but was held in Brixton under 18B following his arrest on the steps of his Onslow Square house as he returned from two weeks in Scotland on the morning of May 23, 1940. Ramsay claimed that, as a member of Parliament, he was immune from arrest, and on August 24 he appeared before the Committee on Parliamentary Privilege to argue his case.

The Home Office had drawn up a two-page summary of the reasons for his internment, dated June 24. Presumably written by Max Knight, it made damning reading, detailing how the Right Club, while ostensibly directing its activities against Jews, Freemasons, and communists, was in reality "designed secretly to spread subversive and defeatist views among the civil population of Great Britain, to obstruct the war effort of Great Britain, and thus to endanger public safety and the defence of the Realm."

It said Ramsay had kept the names of members strictly secret in order to prevent the real aims of the club from becoming known, and that he had "stated that he had taken steps to mislead the Police and the Intelligence Branch of the War Office as to the real activities of the Organization." He had "frequently expressed sympathy with the policy and aims of the German Government; and at times expressed his desire to cooperate with the German Government in the conquest and subsequent Government of Great Britain."

He had, the Home Office report claimed, tried to introduce members of the Right Club into the Foreign Office, the censorship, the intelligence branch of the War Office, and government departments in order to further his aims. And he had "associated and made use of persons known to him to be active in opposition to the interests of Great Britain," among them Anna Wolkoff and Tyler Kent.

"In particular," the report went on, "with knowledge that Kent had abstracted important documents, the property of the Embassy and of the United States of America, he visited Kent's flat at 47, Gloucester Place, where many of the said documents were kept, and inspected them for his own purposes. He further deposited with the said Kent the secret register of the members of the Right Club, of which Organization Kent had become an important member, in order to try and keep the nature of the Organization secret." Finally, he had "permitted and authorized" his wife to act for him in making use of such people as Kent, Wolkoff, and Christabel Nicholson.

None of these allegations had been proved in a court of law, of course, but they were enough to convince the parliamentary committee that Ramsay should be locked up. They were also, it seems, enough to persuade the committee to rule that parliamentary privilege did not protect MPs from arrest and imprisonment. Ramsay was returned to Brixton Prison, where, although unconvicted, he stayed for a total of four years, four months, and three days. He refused, however, to resign his seat. With no conviction against him, there were no grounds for disqualifying him, so he remained an MP, but for the whole of that time his constituents—who had been trying unsuccessfully to get rid of him since 1938—had no representation in the House of Commons. Ramsay did make one public appearance during those years, however: in July 1941, he was the plaintiff in a libel action against the *New York Times,* initiated in February. This arose out of the articles written by Edgar Ansel Mowrer and Colonel William J. Donovan as a cover for Donovan's visit to Britain in July 1940.

The four articles had appeared in every reputable newspaper in the United States. They were preceded by a brief introduction from Secretary of the Navy Colonel Frank Knox:

At my request Colonel William J. Donovan went to London. In London he was met by veteran foreign correspondent Edgar Mowrer, who had just reached London following the French debacle.

These two men, on behalf of the United States, made the most thoroughgoing survey of German "Fifth Column" methods used in weakening resistance of possible enemies and undermining the morale of countries they proposed to attack.

The results of this careful study, made with every official source made available to these two men, is to be found in the series of articles which follow. They are designed to make America fully conscious of methods used by the totalitarian powers, so that if or when such methods are used here they will instantly be recognized for what they are and their effects nullified.

I regard defense against possible enemy propaganda as second only to defense against enemy armaments.

FRANK KNOX
Secretary of the Navy

After publication of four articles, from August 20 to August 24, the *New York Times* published its own summary, based on a long cable sent from its London correspondent and managing director, Raymond Daniell. One paragraph in the story read:

A car from Brixton Prison drew up last week at the British House of Commons. Waiting was the Serjeant-at-Arms . . . He took from police custody of Captain Archibald Henry Maule Ramsay, M.P., World War veteran of the Coldstream Guards. The captain, arrested last May under Defense Regulations, has been brought to Westminster to argue that his detention violated traditional parliamentary rights of immunity . . . Before the war he was strongly anti-Communist, anti-Semitic and pro-Hitler. Though no specific charges were made against him on his arrest—Defense Regulations allow that—informed American sources said that he had sent to the German Legation in Dublin treasonable information given him by Tyler Kent, clerk in the American embassy in London.

It may be that the "informed American sources" were, in fact, Ambassador Kennedy. But wherever the information came from, Ramsay seized on it with great indignation. In February 1941, he issued a writ for libel against the *New York Times*.

Ramsay's timing was particularly good—or bad, depending from which side it was viewed. The Battle of the Atlantic and the blitz were raging more fiercely than ever, and Britain's dollar reserves were all but exhausted. Roosevelt and his people were in the middle of delicate horse trading with Congress over the passage of the controversial Lend-Lease legislation, which would provide Britain with desperately needed supplies to be returned or paid for later. Isolationists and noninterventionists, who made up a higher proportion of Congress than of the population at large, were opposing it bitterly, fighting every inch of the way. Many Americans were deeply suspicious of Britain; they found it hard to believe that a nation which still ruled the world's greatest empire could really be on the verge of bankruptcy.

The interventionists argued that helping Britain was the only realistic way of defending America; the bill was astutely titled "An Act to Promote the Defense of the United States." Isolationists, on the other hand, claimed it would give the president far too much power—the "dictator" argument again—and would suck America into the war. The debate, both in and out of Congress, was acrimonious: one of the bill's leading proponents, Senator Claude Pepper, was even burned in effigy outside the Senate by a group of women proclaiming that he was trying to murder their sons.

In the thick of this battle, news of Ramsay's move against the *New York Times* was decidedly unwelcome to the administration. Unlike the criminal trials at the Old Bailey, the libel action was a civil suit, which would be heard in open court. Ramsay might take the opportunity to divulge the secret of the Roosevelt-Churchill correspondence, and thus provide the president's opponents with devastating new ammunition, which could scupper Lend-Lease and end the vital aid to Britain.

Churchill later described Lend-Lease as "the most unsordid act in the history of any nation." At the time, however, although duly grateful for the lifeline that Roosevelt had thrown him, he was very conscious of its high cost. As with the loan of the fifty old destroyers, American philanthropy was tempered with a series of hard-nosed business deals. All the British gold reserves stored in South Africa were picked up by an American destroyer and delivered to Washington; a major British-owned company in the United States, American Viscose, was compulsorily sold at a knock-down price to a consortium of American bankers, who promptly resold it at a considerable profit to themselves; and so on.

At one point, Churchill drafted an angry telegram to Roosevelt, saying, "It is not fitting that any nation should put itself wholly in the hands of another, least of all a nation which is fighting under increasingly severe conditions for what is proclaimed to be a cause of general concern." But he thought better of it, and the telegram was never sent. After the war, he wrote that "certain things were done which seemed harsh and painful to us." But at the time they were essential—without them, Roosevelt could never have persuaded Congress to agree—and in the end they worked.

Between February 7, 1941, and the court hearing in July, more than twenty signals about the Ramsay case flashed between the American embassy in London and the State Department in Washington. It was only during the first month that Lend-Lease was in danger; the act was signed by Roosevelt on

March 11 and Averell Harriman was soon sent across the Atlantic to take charge of the London end. But during that month, it was essential to keep the lid firmly closed on what could prove to be a Pandora's box.

On February 8, the *New York Times*'s Washington bureau chief, Delbert Clark, delivered by hand to Assistant Secretary of State Long a telegram he had just received from his managing editor in New York asking for a transcript of the Tyler Kent trial to be made available to the paper's London lawyers. The State Department consulted the British government, which refused to release any part of the transcript, pointing out to Herschel Johnson in London that "under Section 16, Criminal Appeal Code 1907, a transcript may be furnished only to an interested party . . . [T]he *New York Times* does not . . . fall into the category of an interested party . . . If these rules were not, as they seem to the public prosecutor, conclusive, the question would still arise . . . whether the transcript could be shown since the case was heard in camera." No doubt to the great relief of the State Department, the director of public prosecutions told Johnson, "It would require an act of Parliament and not even the Home Secretary could waive the restriction."

The *New York Times* had no option but to accept this refusal, but then asked that Secretary Gowen be allowed to appear as a witness for the defense. The State Department simply said no.

The case was heard in the High Court during the last week of July before Mr. Justice Atkinson of the King's Bench Division, without a jury. It lasted six days, during which Ramsay's testimony was published daily, a continuous diatribe against Jews and communists. He equated Jews either with communism or with a cabal of international bankers, and lauded Hitler—who had invaded the Soviet Union five weeks earlier, on June 22—as the world's most staunch anticommunist.

The judge was not impressed. Although he ruled that the *New York Times*'s plea of innocent dissemination had failed, he delivered a scathing indictment of Ramsay. "I believe that his claim to loyalty is false," he said. "I am convinced that Hitler would call Captain Ramsay a friend. He was disloyal in heart and soul to our king, our government, and our people."

"The thief Tyler Kent" figured large in Mr. Justice Atkinson's summary. After giving an account of the Right Club, and of the trials of Kent and Anna Wolkoff and the sentences they received—without going into any details of the contents of the confidential documents Kent was "abstracting (to use a word which would not offend Captain Ramsay)"—he went on:

When Anna Wolkoff found out what Kent was doing she took him to Captain Ramsay. Would she have brought him to anyone to whom she could not bring him safely? Within a week Captain Ramsay was visiting Kent and reading documents which he was quite sure had been wrongfully taken from the American Embassy . . .

He deposited the Right Club book in a locker in Kent's room, he said for safety from burglars. It came out later that the attraction was that that room would have the benefit of diplomatic privilege. I have yet to learn that burglars pay any respect to diplomatic privilege, but the police, of course, do.

Ramsay, the judge said, had enrolled Kent in the Right Club for a reason:

Knowing that the confidential documents had been wickedly stolen or abstracted from the American Embassy, he took advantage of that crime, and I am satisfied he took advantage of it to secure something which he could use to further his views. He was seeking something which he knew neither our Government nor the American Embassy would willingly disclose—something which would help him to convert people intent on victory to appeasement and preservation of Nazism.

Although he found in favor of Ramsay, Mr. Justice Atkinson concluded that no jury would have given him damage of more than a farthing—then Britain's smallest coin, worth a quarter of a penny—and therefore judgment would be entered for that amount in each of the actions against the New York Times Company and the New York Times Company Limited, of London, making a grand total of one halfpenny.

Reporting on the result of the case, Herschel Johnson told Washington that London newspapers all congratulated the *New York Times* on its courageous defense, expressed wholehearted agreement with the award, and said that Ramsay's own evidence justified his continuing detention. He added that a few days later Ramsay's constituency association asked him to resign his seat as their member of Parliament.

Ramsay doggedly refused to stand down, however, and continued to fight on. In August 1942 he circularized fellow MPs with a twelve-page statement listing the charges made against him and his replies to those charges, which consisted largely of a condensed repetition of the anti-Jewish, anticommunist, and pro-Hitler tirades made during the court hearing. Far from swaying the members to his support, the statement served only to harden their determination that he should stay behind bars as long as possible.

Feelings in Parliament against Ramsay did not diminish with time. On the morning of September 26, 1944, when Herbert Morrison, the pugnacious cockney who had taken over from Sir John Anderson as home secretary and minister of home security in September 1940, announced to the House that Ramsay was no longer considered to be a security risk and would be released from prison later that day, there was uproar. The former Clydeside docker Willie Gallacher, Britain's sole communist MP—and one of the best liked and most respected individuals in the House of Commons—immediately launched an attack on Morrison.

"I want to ask the home secretary this," he demanded. "If the mothers of this country, whose lads are being sacrificed now, are to be informed by him that their sacrifices have enabled him to release this unspeakable blackguard?"

To call any other member a blackguard is strictly against the rules of parliamentary behavior. The speaker demanded that Gallacher withdraw the remark. Gallacher refused. The speaker, bound by standing orders, ordered him to leave the House for the remainder of the day's sitting. Gallacher left as other members leaped to his defense. Emanuel Shinwell, a fellow Scot and a leading Labour MP, reminded the House that Captain Ramsay "had not been incarcerated for his innocence." Tom Driberg, formerly an MI5 agent who had worked for Max Knight, told members that Gallacher's son had been killed in action a few weeks earlier, and that this could explain his use of unparliamentary language.

No one thought to mention that Ramsay, too, had lost his eldest son, killed in action in 1943. But Morrison defended his action in releasing him and assured members that there would

be no mass release of those still detained under Regulation
18B. The speaker concluded the debate by sympathizing with
Gallacher, but adhering to his ruling that he must withdraw for
the day.

The following morning at 10:30, Ramsay resumed his seat in
the chamber of the House of Lords—the Commons had moved
there after their own chamber was destroyed in a huge air raid
on May 11, 1941, when 550 German aircraft dropped thousands of tons of high-explosive bombs and 100,000 incendiar-
ies, killing 1400 Londoners during that one night. Throughout
the remaining months of the Parliament, until Churchill's coalition government resigned on May 23, 1945, to clear the way
for a return to normal party politics, he was treated with distant
civility but no affability. It was hardly surprising that his local
party refused to select him as its candidate. But in any case the
seat went to Labour as part of its landslide victory on July 5,
which swept Churchill and the Conservatives out of office.

Following the Ramsay libel action against the *New York Times* in
July 1941, the reverberations of the Tyler Kent affair had faded
to insignificance on both sides of the Atlantic. There had been
a brief flurry on November 11, 1941, when two left-wing members of Parliament, Richard Stokes of the Labour Party and
John McGovern, a former plumber, of the minuscule Independent Labour Party, tried to mount an attack on Churchill based
on the stolen signals. Stokes claimed that Churchill had evaded
censorship by sending telegrams to Roosevelt, and should
have been prosecuted. McGovern followed up by charging that
the messages had been sent "behind the back of the then prime
minister." Herbert Morrison declined to answer either question, and there the matter ended.

McGovern had already put his question on October 16,
1941. It was presumably notification of this, plus advance notice of Stokes's question, that led Roosevelt to ask Cordell Hull
on Saturday, November 8, for copies of his telegrams to Churchill dated March 5 and May 16, 1940. No doubt the president
wanted to be prepared for any flak that might result from
reports of the questions. Hull had the two signals delivered to
the White House the following Monday, November 10. On the
next day, Roosevelt wrote him a memo setting out his defense:

. . . These messages, together with others, might well be called the precursors of two subsequent logical developments. First, the sale for cash to Great Britain, at the time of and subsequent to Dunkirk, of various Army and Navy equipment which we considered at that time either surplusage or out of date—such as field guns which so greatly helped Britain to build up its defense against probable invasion in July, August and September, 1940.

These messages were also precursors of the arrangement for the sale of the fifty American destroyers in exchange for the eight naval bases which extend American defense areas a long distance to seaward and northward and southward.

In the event, no justification was needed, for the attack never developed. The only major American newspaper to carry the story, and then merely as a single-column item on page 5, with a small picture of Kent, was the antiadministration *Washington Times-Herald.* The story began:

COMMONS AIRS
CHURCHILL CABLES
TO ROOSEVELT
Messages Exchanged
Behind Chamberlain's
Back, M.P. Charges

Questions in the British House of Commons yesterday regarding Winston Churchill's cablegrams to President Roosevelt behind the back of Prime Minister Chamberlain brought into open a subject of much whispering in official circles here . . .

This attempt to stir up a little anti-Roosevelt mud was doomed to failure. Although there were reported discussions among isolationist groups calling for an investigation, the wheels of Congress rotated very slowly. They were still barely moving twenty-five days later when the Japanese attacked Pearl Harbor and even the most die-hard isolationists found themselves with no choice but to go along, at least for the time being, with the tide of patriotic fervor sweeping the nation. No more questions were posed in public print until June 1944, the year of the next presidential election.

Kent was not entirely forgotten during those years, however. Ann Kent learned of the Roosevelt-Churchill messages for the first time from the *Times-Herald* news story, and immediately launched a campaign for her son's release, which she pursued relentlessly until his return to the United States in November 1945. Her initial efforts to interest congressmen in his case floundered with Pearl Harbor, but she continued to bombard right-wing senators and representatives with letters and petitions. As the years passed, her claims grew ever wilder, ever further from reality.

Immediately after the *Times-Herald* story appeared, she made three major charges, which would ultimately become a rallying cry for the anti-Roosevelt elements in Congress and the nation. These were: that Roosevelt and Churchill had plotted behind the backs of Congress and the American people to drag the United States into the war against Germany and Italy; that they had plotted to oust Chamberlain and replace him with the first lord of the Admiralty; and that Roosevelt had violated U.S. criminal statutes by making secret U.S. codes available to a foreigner, that is, Churchill.

In time, she added more charges, all without foundation in fact. The most startling, and the one that gained the most widespread attention, was the allegation that one early signal from Churchill said: "I am half American and the natural person to work with you. It is evident that we see eye to eye. Were I to become prime minister of Britain we could control the world." According to Ann Kent, Tyler had been imprisoned in Britain without due process of law for threatening to do his patriotic duty by disclosing this correspondence—"several hundred telegrams"—to the Congress.

Displaying an ignorance of the law that was both woeful and willful, she alleged that Tyler had been illegally stripped of his diplomatic immunity and improperly discharged from his State Department position, and that in any case the British had no right to arrest, try, convict, and imprison an American citizen.

Another of her allegations that was given wide publicity was that Stalin had secured copies of the Roosevelt-Churchill correspondence and would use them to blackmail the two leaders at their various wartime meetings. Ironically, given our current knowledge of Kent's NKVD connections, it is entirely possible that Stalin received copies of the signals through him. Ann Kent would have been devastated to learn that he had passed them over willingly. The possibility of their use for blackmail against anyone but Kent himself, however, remains pure fantasy.

Kent, in fact, both resented and was embarrassed by his mother's campaign on his behalf; he denied Churchill's alleged statement about ruling the world as soon as he heard about it. But disowning his mother was nothing new for him: he had been embarrassed by her, and by her obsession with his welfare, since early childhood. As one example, he had not appreciated her having him transferred from the Kent School in Connecticut to St. Albans in Washington so that she could see him more often.

It was not unusual for a boy of that age and era to be embarrassed by obvious attention from a parent, but Kent even then was preoccupied with appearances. Always well tailored himself, he was equally interested in seeing women looking smart. There can be little doubt that when his mother visited him in school or college, he compared her dowdy clothes with the classic Peck & Peck uniforms of gray flannel or tweed suits, or gray flannel skirts with cashmere sweaters and a single strand of pearls, worn by the mothers of his classmates, most of whom were graduates of such Seven Sisters colleges as Smith, Mount Holyoke, Radcliffe, and Wellesley. Mrs. Kent, in contrast, wore dresses, hats, and coats that were years out of date, and looked more like a grandmother than the parent of a prep school student.

Later, following his father's death in 1936, Kent snobbishly resented that his mother supplemented her small pension by running her Washington home at 2112 Wyoming Avenue, N.W., as a rooming house for government clerks. During his eleven years abroad, even when he was not in prison, he rarely corresponded with her, and after his return to America in 1945 and his marriage in 1946, he rarely wrote to or visited her, nor did he welcome her visits to his home.

During the early months of his incarceration, Kent was in an extremely depressed state of mind. For some time his mother was not allowed to write to him, and his only contact with the outside world came through Irene Danischewsky and Graham Maw; the latter seems not to have taken offense at being dropped from the appeal. Although Maw visited Kent only once, he took a fatherly interest in him, storing his clothes, books, and personal effects in his office during the whole term of his imprisonment; they were delivered to the ship the morning Kent finally sailed for America.

Irene Danischewsky made the eighty-five-mile rail-and-ferry trip from London to the Isle of Wight at least once and often twice monthly from the spring of 1941 until Kent's release, with the exception of a period of some months immediately preceding D-day, June 6, 1944, when all ports on the south coast were closed to civilians not connected with the invasion. This demonstrated considerable devotion at a time when rail travel in Britain was often difficult and uncomfortable. Her husband, fortunately, was away from home for most of this time, serving with Orde Wingate's Chindits, behind Japanese lines in the jungles of Burma.

Danischewsky had to obtain Home Office permission for her visits, which always seems to have been forthcoming. On one occasion, she and Maw planned to visit Kent together; permission was granted for her but refused to the lawyer. Such leniency strengthens the supposition that her visits were allowed or even arranged by the Home Office in return for her debriefing by MI5, presumably by Max Knight.

The possible aid by the Home Office does not mean she was not genuinely fond of Kent. She kept him supplied with cigarettes and other small luxuries, and provided him with books, often in foreign languages for use in the night classes he held to teach other prisoners. She also wrote regularly to Mrs. Kent in Washington—far more regularly and at much greater length than Kent himself ever did. Prison regulations allowed him to send two letters a month. At least one of these always went to Irene, with an occasional one to Maw. But poor Ann Kent received very few.

At his death, Kent's correspondence files contained nearly a thousand letters written and received between 1941 and 1988; he kept everything, methodically stored in cabinets. There are no fewer than seventeen letters from Irene Danischewsky to Mrs. Kent, some of them twenty pages long, but only six from Kent to his mother. In her letters, Irene reiterated her determination to "help Tyler in every possible way." She reported that he was always tanned and healthy-looking from his outdoor work on the farm, and that he was eating well, since his job entitled him to extra rations. The one food package Mrs. Kent shipped to him was confiscated by the authorities.

When he did write to his mother, Kent kept his letters brief. In one note, his first to her in more than a year, he said it would be short because he had to go out to teach some of his fellow inmates the game of baseball. In another, objecting to her campaign on his behalf—she kept him informed in her letters and cables, and regularly sent clippings from newspapers—he warned her "not to get hysterical."

As the time for Kent's release approached, Maw suggested to Irene that she let Mrs. Kent know that it might be better if her son did not return immediately to the United States, but waited until the authorities there were more amenable. He filed a petition with the home secretary for the vacating of the 1940 deportation order on Kent, but the request was unsuccessful.

Kent agreed with Maw's thinking. He had good reason to do so. "Throughout my prison term," he said in an interview for this book, "I always considered the possibility that once I landed in the United States, I would be arrested and charged with violating the Yardley Act. That was something I wished to avoid." When the petition on the deportation order failed, he asked to be sent to some country other than the United States, preferably Argentina. But this, too, was denied him.

Mrs. Kent had her own ideas, which in retrospect seem quite bizarre. "If I were in Tyler's position," she wrote in a letter to Irene Danischewsky on September 28, 1944, "I would try to become a British subject if possible. I believe in the days to come that the English part of the Anglo-Saxon people will 'find itself' before the American part. I may be wrong, but I cannot see anything for Tyler over here in the predictable future. Please get this idea of mine to him—it is, of course, only an idea, but one worth thinking about, I am sure."

Tyler's objections to his mother's efforts on his behalf had little effect on her activities during his imprisonment. Mrs. Kent continued to pursue her campaign with all her strength. In the fall of 1942, she hired a former Baltimore radio station reporter, Ian Ross MacFarlane, to go to England and interview her son in prison. He was Kent's only visitor apart from Irene Danischewsky and Graham Maw.

On his return, MacFarlane informed her that Tyler "no longer felt kindly toward Captain Ramsay." This came as something of a shock to Mrs. Kent, who had always made a great deal of Kent's friendship with Ramsay. "The fact that I always linked Tyler with a *man* and a Member of Parliament as well," she told Danischewsky in a tactless letter, "served the purpose intended to counteract the disgusting smear campaign carried on in our newspapers of linking Tyler, not with *one* but with many disreputable women. It has been one of the most disgusting cases of cruel sensationalism that I have ever read or heard of. I am writing to you thus frankly because I think the time has come to be open on all sides—and because I think you will understand."

MacFarlane's interview with Kent was never made public, but his journey was responsible for the recruitment of another supporter to the cause, who would himself become part of the mythology surrounding the Kent affair. As he was returning to Washington, MacFarlane's plane was grounded in Halifax, Nova Scotia, by adverse weather conditions. While waiting at the airfield, he bought four cups of coffee for a fellow passenger who admitted he was broke. The penniless passenger was John Bryan Owen, grandson of William Jennings Bryan, the three-time Democratic presidential nominee and secretary of state under Woodrow Wilson, popularly known to Americans of his day as the Great Commoner. Young Owen's mother, Ruth Bryan Owen, was a prominent Democrat; she was one of the first women elected to Congress (1929–1933) and the first woman ever to hold a ministerial post in the U.S. Foreign Service when she served as minister to Denmark from 1933 to 1936. His half sister was the daughter-in-law of New York governor Herbert H. Lehman.

The weather over Halifax did not clear, and the passengers continued their journey to New York by ship. During the voyage, MacFarlane discussed the Kent case at some length with Owen, who had himself been deported from Britain under Regulation 18B. Owen was deeply interested, and declared, "I am going to make my life's work the exposure of the Kent case."

When the ship docked, MacFarlane took a train for Washington to report to Mrs. Kent, and Owen went to his flat at 23 West 9 Street, New York, and began doing what he could to rally support for Kent. A few weeks later, at 3:10 A.M. on January 3, 1943, a neighbor called the police after hearing "a loud thud" from Owen's flat. Owen was found lying on the floor, "with bruises on his head and blood on his face." Dr. William Carr of St. Vincent's Hospital arrived on the scene and pronounced him dead. Detective John Maguire regarded the death as suspicious, because of the blood and bruises, but the assistant medical examiner, Dr. Milton Halperin, recorded it as being from natural causes and "gestation of the viscera." The body was claimed from the morgue by his half sister.

An aura of mystery surrounded Owen's death right from the start. Halperin's report was given prominence by the *New York Times* and the *Herald Tribune.* But the *New York Journal-American,* one of Hearst's publications, quoted the police on the cause of death as "an extremely large dose of veronal," and listed Owen as a suicide.

The difference between the medical examiner's report and the autopsy findings may be explained by the character of the aggressive, publicity-seeking Halperin, who later served for more than a quarter century as New York's most noted or notorious medical examiner. He was known to be far from immune to political considerations, and though there is no trace of evidence that pressure was applied by the Lehman family, Halperin may have believed that his action in suppressing the real cause of death would be looked on by them with favor. Whatever the reason behind it, the discrepancy was enough to provide Ann Kent with fuel for her claim that Owen had been murdered because he was investigating her son's case and that there had been an official cover-up to protect Roosevelt.

The suspicion surrounding Owen's death was perfect fodder for the scandalmongers. Although the case disappeared from the newspapers for eighteen months, the rumors continued to circulate. On July 19, 1944, the day before Roosevelt was nominated in Chicago for his fourth term, Upton Close, a popular NBC radio commentator stationed on the West Coast, went on the air asking whether Owen's "mysterious" death was linked to Kent's imprisonment.

Close, who was ultimately fired because of his highly vocal profascist views, misstated several facts of the case. Whether this was deliberate or an error is not known, but he said Mrs. Kent had sent MacFarlane to England to bring back Owen, "a close associate of Ramsay, to the United States to tell her what he knew of Tyler's imprisonment." The contents of Close's Hollywood broadcast were carried across the nation by the wire services and were widely reported in print. Even today, there are Kent supporters who subscribe to the myth of the murder of John Bryan Owen.

THIRTEEN

The Myths Exploded

BY THE TIME of the 1944 Democratic convention, Tyler Kent had become a hot issue once more in the United States, and his imprisonment a weapon to be used against Roosevelt by his enemies in both main parties. The case had surfaced again in London, in a House of Commons debate on June 16—ten days after the Allied landings in Normandy—when John McGovern returned to the attack after a gap of three and a half years.

The Commons debate was about Regulation 18B, which many MPs, together with an increasing number of newspapers, felt should be rescinded now that there was no longer any danger of a German invasion of Britain. Most of the detainees had already been released, but a few, including Captain Ramsay, were still locked up in jails and internment camps. Linking the detention of Ramsay with the conviction of Tyler Kent, McGovern asked whether the reason for Ramsay's continued imprisonment was the fear that he might make sensational disclosures about prewar negotiations between Churchill and Roosevelt.

I have been told that Captain Ramsay is not in because he is a fascist [he said to the Commons], but because Tyler Kent took copies of letters from a diplomatic bag between the prime minister and the president of the United States. The prime minister was soliciting military aid in the event this country was going to war and preparations were made and promises given by the president of the United States through the diplomatic bag.

I am told that while the present prime minister was first lord of the Admiralty under the late Neville Chamberlain he was still carrying on this campaign behind the back of his prime minister, engaging in the exchange of letters through the diplomatic bag in order to find out the strength of American support and whether America could be relied upon to come into the war.

It is said that if Ramsay was released, it would be extremely dangerous and difficult for him to be going around substantiating these things and stating that they are true, and therefore that he is being held because the prime minister does not want him to be liberated.

McGovern, a socialist, was careful to dissociate himself from Ramsay's views. "I discussed things with the honorable and gallant Member for Peebles and Southern Midlothian," he said, "and my own conclusion is that he should be detained in a mental institution rather than in some criminal place of detention."

Reports of the debate were immediately flashed across the Atlantic by the wire services from London, and were seized upon with glee by the anti-Roosevelt press. Inevitably, the *Washington Times-Herald* was in the forefront, running the story prominently under the headline COMMONS TOLD FDR PLEDGED AID BEFORE WAR—MP SAYS CHURCHILL GOT PROMISE. The opening sentence was unequivocal: "President Roosevelt promised Prime Minister Churchill before Britain entered the war that America would come to her aid."

On the morning of June 19, the Senate dining room was abuzz with clusters of senators discussing the implications of the Roosevelt-Churchill correspondence. All were agreed that, with the Democratic convention less than five weeks away, the news from London would provide necessary ammunition for

Roosevelt's opponents in both parties. Following the successful landings in Normandy, they clearly could not fault his conduct of the war. Their main strategy, therefore, was to smear him with the charge that he had known in advance about the Japanese attack on Pearl Harbor but had done nothing about it —indeed, had even deliberately provoked the Japanese into attacking in order to get America into the war against Hitler.

The leaders of the "FDR lied us into war" campaign were many of the congressmen who had spearheaded the isolationist movement in the days before Pearl Harbor: Senators Burton K. Wheeler (D.-Montana), Gerald Nye (R.-North Dakota), Ralph Owen Brewster (R.-Maine), and Henrick Shipstead (R.-Minnesota), and Representative Hamilton Fish, Jr. (R.-New York). They had a powerful ally in the chairman of the Senate Naval Affairs Committee, a Democrat from Massachusetts.

Shipstead and Wheeler were chosen to launch the attack on June 19, and the Democrats fittingly selected the chairman of the Senate Foreign Affairs Committee, Tom Connally of Texas, to rebut the charges. Waving a copy of the *Times-Herald,* Shipstead opened the offensive. The debate in Parliament, he claimed, was "of such a grave character that it reflects upon the integrity not only of the government of the United States, but also, to some extent, upon the integrity of the government of Great Britain." He was, he said, amazed that the British censor had passed the report, "but because the British censor has passed it, I assume that it has the imprimatur of the British government. We hear much gossip, and many stories have been peddled around for years, and no one has said anything about them; but because a foreign government has officially taken cognizance of it, it seems to me to be the duty of the Congress of the United States also to take cognizance of it, since it reflects upon the integrity of our own government."

Shipstead then proceeded to read out the report in full to ensure that it was included in the record. As he reached the end, Wheeler intervened, and for several minutes the two senators fed each other lines and cues, playing out a double act that would not have been out of place in vaudeville.

Brimming with righteous indignation, Wheeler recounted how Mrs. Kent had come to see him sometime before, and had told him of her son's arrest and imprisonment. "I was unable to believe," he declaimed, "that an American boy connected with the American embassy could be tried in a secret British court, under the protocol and under the laws of the United States. So I wrote a letter to Secretary Hull, asking him how it was that an American boy could be tried in a secret British court for stealing, or embezzling, or getting hold of papers which went through the American embassy. I received no answer to that letter. Because of the fact that Mr. Joseph P. Kennedy was at that time American ambassador to Great Britain, I sent him a copy of the letter."

Although he had received no replies, he went on, the State Department had sent an official to explain what had happened. The explanation had not satisfied him. He could not uphold Kent in what he did, but he still failed to understand how an American citizen could be tried in a British secret court. "What would happen," he asked, "if we should arrest a member of the British embassy here and endeavor to try him in an American secret court? Of course, the British government would immediately protest, and we would not try him in a secret or a public court."

"He would be sent back to England to be tried under the laws of England," Shipstead chimed in.

"He would be sent back to be tried in England," Wheeler echoed. He then went on to allege that Churchill had been illegally allowed to use American codes because he did not dare to seek Chamberlain's consent to use British codes "to send the kind of message which was sent."

All told, Wheeler and Shipstead produced nothing but a farrago of demagogic nonsense with little basis in fact and none in law. Connally had no difficulty in demolishing their arguments, pointing out that Kent had indeed violated British law. "If we had desired," he said, "we could have invoked diplomatic immunity in this case and perhaps prevented his prosecution in the British courts. But here was a conspiracy. One prong of it was a boy working for the American embassy; another prong was a member of the British Parliament, and a third prong was a person from Russia. All of them were engaged in enterprises which under the British law were inimical to the safety of the British realm . . .

"Mr. President [of the Senate], this war is not helped, it is not aided, its successful prosecution is not furthered, its cause not advanced by things of this sort—picking up a newspaper somewhere and reading that John Smith said that Bill Jones told him that the Widow McCafferty told him that Mr. Roosevelt told Churchill before he was even prime minister that we were going to help him militarily. I do not know whether Mr. Churchill invoked the president's aid. Everyone in this chamber knows that Mr. Roosevelt could not send a soldier, he could not send a dollar of military supplies to Mr. Churchill or his government or any other government until the Congress of the United States authorized such action."

Connally finished with a rousing call for unity until the end of the war, and an end to "sabotage . . . this sniping and shooting behind the lines." But in spite of this appeal, and of his comprehensive demolition of Wheeler's and Shipstead's arguments, other senators continued the barrage. The following day the anti-Roosevelt press, particularly the Hearst, Patterson, and McCormick papers, took it up and launched an attack that continued long past the president's electoral victory in November and even past his death, on April 12, 1945.

As the opening of the Democratic presidential convention approached, the attacks grew ever fiercer from columnists and commentators such as Upton Close and Walter Trohan, Washington bureau chief of the *Chicago Tribune*. And fighting right alongside them was a small, dumpy figure in outmoded clothes and a grandmotherly hat. As the thousand-plus delegates arrived at the convention hall, each was handed a flier titled "My Appeal for Fairness—Petition for Justice on Behalf of a Loyal American Against Whom Injustice Continues, by Mrs. Ann H. P. Kent, founder, organizer, president, and treasurer of the Justice for Tyler Kent Committee.

Mrs. Kent seems to have made little or no impression on the delegates, who proceeded to nominate President Roosevelt for an unprecedented fourth term. Vice President Henry Agard Wallace was dumped in favor of a racket-busting legislator from Missouri, Senator Harry S. Truman. Undaunted, she wrote letters to both the president and Mrs. Roosevelt and to Secretary Hull. None of them replied.

With little more than a hundred days to the presidential

election, Mrs. Kent composed her own account of her son's case and sent more than four thousand copies to newspapers of all sizes across the nation, from major dailies to back-country weeklies, many of which published her "plea for justice." Typical of many of the outrageous and ill-informed claims arising from her campaign was this extract from the June–July 1944 edition of Gerald L. K. Smith's America First paper:

Tyler Kent is in a British prison. He was a code expert in the American Embassy in London. It has been brought out on the floor of Parliament that Kent had exposed a secret deal made by Churchill and Roosevelt before the war and before even Churchill became Prime Minister. The story is almost too hot to touch. It is too sensational to discuss. There may be a Senate investigation. If facts can support rumors, the truth concerning Tyler Kent might bring the political careers of Roosevelt and Churchill to an abrupt end.

Mr. Kent's mother lives in Washington. She is saying some very alarming things. I shall watch this case carefully and inform you as soon as more facts are available.

Snide insinuations like this inevitably had their effect on a large section of the American public. In addition to undermining Roosevelt's position, they also threatened Anglo-American relations at a time when cooperation was vital to the combined war effort, particularly in France.

The most effective way to calm the hysteria and restore balance, of course, would have been to reveal the truth of what had happened, and what had actually passed between Roosevelt and Churchill in 1939 and 1940.

Lord Halifax, the British ambassador in Washington since December 1940—when Churchill, having finally lost patience with his foreign secretary's continuing advocacy of a negotiated peace had removed him from London—suggested this to the Foreign Office as early as June 25. He said anything that could be made public without prejudicing security would do much to clear the air. "Otherwise," he said, "there is considerable danger that the issue of alleged collusion between the President and Mr. Churchill behind the backs of Congress and the people to make American entrance into the war inescapable will be injected into election issues to our detriment and will continue to cloud pages of journalists and historians long after."

The American government had come to much the same conclusion, and after a great deal of cautious consideration on both sides of the ocean, the State Department in Washington issued a 2500-word statement to the press on September 2, wisely choosing a Saturday for the release, to take advantage of the Sunday newspapers' extra pages and larger circulation.

Most of the report was taken up with a detailed factual summary of Kent's activities, and of his arrest and trial. The administration's sense of outrage showed through only in the justification given for the waiving of Kent's diplomatic immunity. Pointing out that "the police also established that some of the papers found had been transmitted to an agent of a foreign power," the statement went on:

An examination of the documents found in his room indicated that Kent had begun classifying the material by subject, but this work was far from completed. They covered practically every subject on which the Embassy was carrying on correspondence with the Department of State. As may be supposed, they included copies of telegrams embodying information collected by the Embassy which otherwise would not have been permitted to leave Great Britain without censorship. As may be likewise supposed, they contained information which would have been useful to Germany and which Great Britain would not have permitted to reach Germany. It is of interest to note, in this connection, that Kent had, during his service in London, written to the Chargé d'Affaires of the American Embassy in Berlin asking his assistance in arranging for his (Kent's) transfer to Berlin . . .

Regardless of the purpose for which Kent had taken this material from the Embassy, he had done so without authorization, in violation of the most elementary principles governing the rules for the preservation of the secrecy of the Government's correspondence. By his own showing he had, while occupying a very special position of confidence within the Embassy, displayed a shocking disregard for every principle of decency and honor so far as his obligation towards the United States was concerned. The removal of so large a number of documents from the Embassy premises compromised the whole confidential communications system of the United States, bringing into question the security of the secret ciphers . . .

In reviewing the Kent case it is important to bear in mind the circumstances surrounding it. At the time of Kent's arrest and trial

Great Britain was at war and the United States was not. The case involved a group of people suspected of subversive activities. The evidence relating to individuals of the group was inextricably mixed, and the activities of no single suspect could be separated from the activities of the others. The interest of Great Britain in such a case, at a time when it was fighting for its existence, was therefore pre-eminent. Deep as was the concern of the Government of the United States over a betrayal of trust by one of its employees, it is hardly conceivable that it would have been justified in asking the Government of Great Britain to waive jurisdiction over an American citizen in the circumstances described. Kent was within the jurisdiction of the British courts, and all the evidence, witnesses, et cetera, were available to the British courts . . . The question whether the United States will prefer additional charges against Kent will be decided after his release from imprisonment in Great Britain and he again comes under the jurisdiction of our courts.

Two days after the statement was released to the press, Joseph Kennedy gave an interview by telephone from his summer home on Cape Cod to Thomas Chase of the Boston bureau of the Associated Press. This was largely a summary of the State Department's press release, but on some matters his memory was faulty, and he made several overstatements, which have inevitably become part of the mythology surrounding the case.

Kennedy claimed that because Kent had compromised the "secret codes," there had been a blackout of all communications in Europe for six weeks. In fact, the ambassador himself had continued using the codes at that time. He also speculated that Italy had deliberately stayed out of the war until June 10, 1940, because Germany considered its role as a channel for communications to be more valuable than its military assistance. There is, of course, no evidence to support such a contention. But it all helped to emphasize Kent's perfidy. And just in case there could have been any doubt left in anyone's mind, Kennedy concluded the interview with the dramatic statement: "If this country had been at war, I would have recommended that he be sent home and shot."

When Kent heard from his mother about Kennedy's statement, he tried to sue the former ambassador for libel. The British authorities refused permission, saying, "Prisoners in this country are not ordinarily allowed to institute legal proceedings during the currency of their sentence, and we see no ground for making an exception in this case."

Reaction to the statements from the State Department and Kennedy was both immediate and continuing. Many anti-Roosevelt congressmen, while continuing their campaign against the president, distanced themselves from Tyler Kent and Mrs. Kent's misinformation service. Thousands of mothers who had believed Kent to be a victim of injustice withdrew their support. The Tyler Kent case was effectively derailed as a campaign issue. Mrs. Kent, however, refused to give in. She was receiving financial backing from several sources, especially from Charles Parsons, an eccentric right-wing extremist who had inherited a fortune of millions of dollars, and who paid for printing, mailing, and many other needs. There is evidence, too, that Colonel McCormick of the *Chicago Tribune*, who owned the radio station WGN (World's Greatest Newspaper), supported her not only editorially but also financially, though by the end of the year he was describing Kent as "a bad egg."

In Detroit, Don Mahone Harlan, a prestigious attorney who was frequently retained by Henry Ford, an anti-Semite and a Roosevelt hater, provided Mrs. Kent with legal services. On September 11, 1944, he filed with the U.S. Supreme Court a petition for a writ of mandamus based on Article III, Section 2, of the Constitution.

Harlan must have known that the issuing of the writ was highly unlikely: Kent had been convicted, and the conviction sustained under appeal, under the due process of English law. But it was an opportunity to belabor Roosevelt and to create mischief. The Supreme Court promptly threw out the motion, without comment, on October 16, declining to listen to oral arguments and thus denying Harlan and Mrs. Kent a platform.

McCormick's newspaper did what it could to make a story, claiming in a report by its Washington correspondent, Willard Edwards, that the court had stifled "discussion of charges that Kent was railroaded to prison to conceal behind the scenes dickering between Roosevelt and Churchill before the latter became prime minister.

Mrs. Ann H. P. Kent [the article went on], mother of the prisoner, has made such allegations in her four-year campaign to clear her son. She said Kent had been handed a coded cable from Churchill to Mr. Roosevelt in October 1939 which said in part, 'Were I to become prime minister, we could control the world' . . .

Democratic leaders admitted privately the publicity of court proceedings . . . might have proved politically damaging to Mr. Roosevelt in his neck-and-neck race with Gov. Dewey.

The nine justices of the Supreme Court, seven of whom received their appointments from the President, trooped to the White House this evening to pay their respects to Mr. Roosevelt. The visit is an annual affair.

Such innuendoes and smear tactics were ineffective, however, in halting Roosevelt's victory over Thomas E. Dewey. In November he was re-elected to a historic fourth term. With the election settled, the losers had no further use for their martyr in Camp Hill Prison. Nothing more was heard in Congress about Kent until after Roosevelt's death, when Harlan tried to file a suit against the U.S. government on Kent's behalf for arrears of salary and travel expenses for his return to the United States, on the grounds that he had been wrongfully dismissed in 1940. There was no possibility whatever of the suit's succeeding, but Harlan and Mrs. Kent saw this as another effort to establish Tyler Kent as an isolationist hero. It was also an opportunity to blacken the memory of the president who had just died, after thirteen years in office.

President Franklin Delano Roosevelt died in Warm Springs, Georgia, at 4:35 P.M. Central War Time, on April 12, 1945. Five days later, Churchill, in an emotion-racked voice, paid tribute to his fallen comrade before a packed House of Commons in London. During his speech, the prime minister made public reference for the first time to his correspondence with Roosevelt before as well as after Pearl Harbor:

My friendship with the great man to whose work and fame we pay tribute today began and ripened during the war. I had met him only for a few minutes, after the close of the last war, and as soon as I went to the Admiralty in September 1939 he telegraphed me [in fact, the first message was a letter], inviting me to correspond with him direct on naval or other matters if at any time I felt inclined. Having obtained the permission of the prime minister, I did so . . .

When I became prime minister and the war broke out in all its hideous fury, when our own life and survival hung in the balance, I was already in a position to telegraph the president on terms of association which had become intimate and, to me, most agreeable. This continued throughout all the ups and downs of the world struggle until Thursday last when I received my last message from him. I may mention that this correspondence which, of course, greatly increased after the United States' entry into the war, comprised to and fro, between us, over 1700 messages. Many of these were lengthy messages, and the majority dealt with those more difficult points which come to be discussed upon the level between heads of governments only after official solutions had been reached at another stage . . .

Roosevelt's critics in the United States were quick to take note of Churchill's confirmation that the correspondence had begun long before December 1941. They looked forward eagerly to seeing the signals, particularly those from the Kent period. They were to have a long wait. It was another thirty years before that part of the correspondence was released.

The delay inevitably served to feed their suspicions. There were loud shrieks of "Cover-up!" from many quarters. The slurs against Roosevelt became ever more accepted items of political mythology. Over the years, these grew out of all proportion: it was even alleged that from the beginning of the war in Europe until Kent's arrest, the two leaders had exchanged more than two thousand signals, an average of eight signals a day for 252 days, which would have left neither of them much time for running a country! Kent himself claimed a figure of between 125 and 150, though in 1973 he reduced this to between twenty-five and fifty.

Kent contributed to the obfuscation with further inventions of his own, stating that he had been required to encode and decode "many long letters," and that after an initial delay of a few weeks, the frequency of the messages increased until sometimes "there were several in one day." He charged, again totally without foundation, that Roosevelt and Churchill discussed Lend-Lease during that time, though the idea was not even conceived of until late in 1940.

In fact, there was no sinister intent in delaying publication: the thirty-year hold was entirely in keeping with international protocol on diplomatic correspondence, though Churchill himself had included some of the messages in his history of the war, the first two volumes of which were published in 1948 and 1949. Although the United States normally operated by a fifteen-year rule, in Britain the usual period before publication of government records was thirty years, and the American government simply followed standard practice in harmonizing with the other partner.

It was March 1971 when the State Department notified the Roosevelt Library that the Kent-era correspondence, now declassified, could be released. Historians were astounded to discover that, after all the hullabaloo over the signals stolen by Kent, only one telegram from Roosevelt and five from Churchill had been found in his possession when he was arrested. Over the entire period between September 11, 1939, and May 20, 1940, Roosevelt had sent three letters and one telegram; Churchill had sent two letters and nine telegrams. Kent had not had access to the letters. We do not know why he did not steal Churchill's other four telegrams; he may have regarded them as of no interest, but it is also possible that he gave his copies to someone unknown.

As more and more of the signals were released and made public—culminating in the publication by Princeton University Press in 1985 of the monumental *Churchill and Roosevelt: The Complete Correspondence, 1939–45*, edited by Warren Kimball, professor of history at Rutgers—the wild charges made against Roosevelt were finally exploded.

There was nothing whatever to substantiate the isolationists' main accusation, that Roosevelt and Churchill had conspired to bring the United States into the war. Indeed, it can be seen quite clearly that, though the British prime minister was ardently wooing the president with his "educational" signals on naval battles and other affairs, the president remained unmoved by his blandishments.

Churchill made no bones about his hope of drawing America into the war. In his eyes, Britain was fighting not for its own interests but for the survival of democracy, not for territorial or political gain but for the very principles of freedom and justice, and he believed it was therefore America's war, too. His son, Randolph, later recounted a discussion with his father on the morning of May 18, 1940, in the face of impending disaster in France:

I went up to my father's bedroom. He was standing in front of his basin and was shaving with his old-fashioned Valet razor [a self-stropping safety razor]. He had a tough beard, and as usual was hacking away.

"Sit down, dear boy, and read the papers while I finish shaving." I did as told. After two or three minutes of hacking away, he half turned and said: "I think I can see my way through." He resumed his shaving. I was astounded, and said: "Do you mean that we can avoid defeat (which seemed credible) or beat the bastards (which seemed incredible)?"

He flung his Valet razor into the basin, swung around, and said:— "Of course I mean we can beat them."

Me: "Well, I'm all for it, but I don't see how you can do it."

By this time he had dried and sponged his face and, turning round to me, said with great intensity:—"I shall drag the United States in."

Naturally, Churchill never said this directly to Roosevelt. But the president was far too astute not to be aware of what was at stake, and was determined to avoid any direct involvement in the war for as long as possible. The president's responses to Churchill's pleas for the fifty aged destroyers also show conclusively that he was in no way inveigled into prematurely aiding Britain's war effort.

Roosevelt's signal of May 16 explained that only Congress could approve the sale of the ships, and Churchill's reply showed that he understood and accepted the situation. The president knew that at the time there was no hope of Congress's approving such a move. It was only when American public opinion began to shift in Britain's favor during the Battle of Britain that he began actively seeking a way to make it possible.

In late August 1940, Attorney General Robert H. Jackson, later a Supreme Court justice, ventured the legal opinion that the president, as commander-in-chief of the U.S. armed forces, could legally sell the destroyers without congressional approval. Secretary Hull commented that in such a case, the president "should be able to satisfy Congress that, in return for the destroyers, we were obtaining facilities at bases which would clearly give us greater security than would retention of the fifty destroyers." Only then did Roosevelt decide to move. When the deal was concluded, on September 3, he announced it to Congress in terms that should have left little doubt that it was more to the advantage of America than of Britain.

"This is the most important action in the reinforcement of our national defense," he told Congress, "that has been taken since the Louisiana Purchase. Then, as now, considerations of safety from overseas attack were fundamental."

The isolationists' second charge, that Roosevelt and Churchill conspired to oust Neville Chamberlain as prime minister, could not be backed up by a single word in any of the messages. In any case, Churchill announced publicly, in his oration on Roosevelt's death, that he had obtained Chamberlain's approval before replying to the president's first message, and this is borne out by War Cabinet minutes showing that the Cabinet had indeed been consulted.

The third charge, that the president violated the U.S. criminal code by making "secret codes" available to a foreigner, that is, Churchill, cannot be refuted by an examination of the signals themselves. However, letters were sent "in clear," meaning that no codes were involved, and instructions and other documentation accompanying the telegrams clearly indicate that Churchill did not have access to U.S. codes and ciphers. His messages to and from Roosevelt were encoded or decoded in the U.S. embassy in London—often, of course, by Kent in the early months.

Any message from Churchill was delivered by hand to the embassy, in clear. A message received by the embassy for Churchill from Washington was decoded, typed out in clear, and placed in an envelope bearing the prime minister's name. This in turn was placed in another envelope, addressed to Major Desmond Morton or John Colville. The Admiralty was alerted, and a British officer collected the message and delivered it by hand. At no time did Churchill, or any member of his staff, see a message in code.

Of course, those who charged that Roosevelt was breaking the law in this respect seem to have been unaware that as commander-in-chief he would have had the right to share codes with Churchill, or with anyone he chose, if he deemed such a revelation to be in the best interests of his country's security.

All the charges made against Roosevelt in connection with his correspondence with Churchill and the Tyler Kent case can therefore be dismissed as baseless fabrications. In perspective, they can be seen as nothing more than hollow echoes from a time when many Americans still believed they could remain insulated from the troubles of the rest of the world; a time when the United States was hesitating on the brink of accepting —for the second time—the responsibilities of a major power.

FOURTEEN

Going Home

ON SEPTEMBER 23, 1945, Irene Danischewsky took a late train from Portsmouth for the ninety-minute journey back to London. She had waited all day on the wind-lashed quay at Newport, on the Isle of Wight, in the hope of a brief meeting with Kent, or even a quick glimpse of him as he boarded the ferry to the mainland at the end of his sentence in Camp Hill. But the closed van that carried him from the jail offered no sight of the prisoners within, and she returned to London alone and disconsolate.

Kent's seven-year sentence had been remitted by slightly more than two years, following the standard British practice of a one-third remission for good behavior. He was not released, however, but merely transferred back to Brixton to await deportation under the order of May 23, 1940. Almost immediately after his arrival there, he was visited by a minor official from the embassy, who registered him under the Selective Service System for the draft, which remained in force for some time after the end of the war. He would receive his classification notice some months after he returned home but was never drafted.

Typically, Kent did not submit quietly to his deportation from Britain. He repeated his earlier request to be sent to Argentina, or possibly Eire, rather than to the United States, and when this failed he demanded first-class passage, claiming it as his right. Mrs. Kent joined in, besieging the State Department, the London embassy, the British Home Office, and finally Prime Minister Clement Attlee, demanding to be allowed to make private arrangements for Kent's journey. At one point, she even arranged to charter an airplane to fly him home; presumably her rich supporters would have borne the cost. But the authorities on both sides of the Atlantic wanted to be certain he could not divert to some other country. They were adamant that Kent's journey remain firmly under their control, and that unless he chose to pay the difference, he would travel third class.

The first ship chosen to carry Kent back across the ocean proved to be unsuitable for some reason that is not recorded. By the time a second passage had been arranged, on the recently built 8000-ton passenger freighter *Silver Oak,* Britain was in the grip of a national dock strike. It was seven weeks before Kent could be moved. During that time he continued to make waves, claiming that he had been held in prison longer than his sentence. Ignoring that his remission and release under license were entirely discretionary, he even instructed the long-suffering Graham Maw to issue a writ of habeas corpus.

Kent also caused a flurry in both the Home Office and Foreign Office by requesting a copy of the official transcript of his trial, which was being kept strictly secret. The Home Office was worried that Kent would publish all or part of the transcript once he returned to the United States, and in doing so reveal the identities of MI5 agents and officers, especially Marjorie Mackie, who had not previously been named. The matter was referred to both Attlee and Churchill, and was settled by a meeting at the highest level with representatives from MI5 and the Foreign Office. It was pointed out that with or without the transcript Kent would undoubtedly publicize the entire affair once he was back in America, so it would be futile to withhold it. In any case, Marjorie Mackie had since retired from the Security Service. Although it was agreed that a transcript should be provided, in 1963 Kent had still not received it.

Eventually, the dock strike ended and the *Silver Oak* was ready to depart from London. On the morning of Wednesday, November 21, Kent was driven to the ship in a police car, boarding in time to join the forty-six other passengers for lunch, his first meal in freedom for more than five and a half years.

After a stormy voyage of thirteen days, the ship docked at pier 3 in Hoboken, New Jersey, on the morning of Tuesday, December 4. Kent, traveling on a temporary passport issued by the embassy in London, was passed swiftly through immigration and customs, to be greeted by his mother, who clutched him tearfully to her bosom. Flanked by two men she had hired from the Shields Detective Agency as protection for Tyler, they emerged to face more than forty reporters, photographers, and cameramen representing all the New York City dailies, all the major American and British newspapers with New York correspondents, *Time, Life, Newsweek,* the Associated Press, United Press, International News Service, the BBC and American radio networks, and the major film newsreels.

Kent's statement was brief—to the evident disappointment of many reporters—but he characteristically held out the promise of significant revelations to come. Headlines in the New York papers show the line he took:

KENT HERE, SAYS HE CAN HELP
ANSWER PEARL HARBOR RIDDLE
New York World-Telegram

TYLER KENT ARRIVES, GETS CHANCE
TO TELL ALL AND THEN DOESN'T
New York Herald Tribune

KENT HOME FROM CELL, CHARGES
KENNEDY LIED
New York Times

KENT RETURNS HOME,
DEFENDS ACTION
New York Journal-American

Kent's hint that he could help solve the so-called Pearl Harbor mystery was, of course, yet another of his wild claims. A joint congressional hearing was under way at the time: its testimony would fill thirty-nine volumes. When Alben Barkley, a Democratic Senator from Kentucky, and later vice president during Truman's full term, asked Kent to substantiate his statement, he replied that he had no real facts but could testify to Roosevelt's attempt to take the United States into the war.

Kent's reticence with the press on his arrival may have been partly due to his mother's having previously suggested to Consolidated Features Syndicate, a supplier of features to daily newspapers throughout America, that they commission a series of articles from him. Very shortly after his return he signed a contract to write a total of twenty thousand words, for which he received an advance payment of $1000.

But the threat of prosecution by the U.S. government under the Yardley Act was still hanging over him. On February 25, 1946, he wrote to Secretary of State James F. Byrnes, requesting "formal assurance that the Department of State will entertain no objection" to publication by him of "a series of syndicated newspaper articles of my experiences abroad from 1934 onwards, the circumstances of my prosecution by a British court and of the contents of official messages with which I was familiar at the time of my arrest." The material he proposed to publish, he said, consisted of "such miscellaneous matter as is well within the purview of our traditional concepts of free speech and reasoned personal opinion."

Byrnes replied on March 7 that, without seeing what Kent proposed to write, he could give no such assurances, and that "the publication will have to proceed at the risk of yourself and the syndicate." Kent immediately asked his editor to cancel the contract. We do not know whether he ever returned the $1000 advance. But he did complain for several years afterward that he had been muzzled by the State Department. He claimed he had been forbidden to make a personal statement, and even persuaded Ernie Adamson, onetime chief investigator for the

House Un-American Activities Committee, to question Byrnes about this, in 1951.

Kent may have lost money by canceling his contract with Consolidated Features, but he soon found a much more lucrative and permanent source of finance, one that would support him for the rest of his life. At a party soon after his arrival in Washington, he met forty-eight-year-old Clara Hyatt. Clara was the former wife of A. Dana Hodgson, the Foreign Service officer who had traveled to Russia in 1934 in the same party as Kent to become U.S. visa officer in Riga. Clara had divorced Hodgson in 1933, "because of his womanizing," and had reverted to her maiden name. Perhaps his having known her former husband attracted Kent to Clara. But what probably attracted him even more to a woman thirteen years his senior was her great wealth.

Clara Hyatt, who was then supervising the running of her large dairy farm in Frederick, Maryland, was a major heir to a family fortune derived from the manufacture of Carter's Little Liver Pills, one of the most successful products in the history of patent medicines throughout the world. Her mother was a Carter; her father came from an old Maryland family, founders of the town of Hyattsville. Kent did not waste any time on a long courtship.

"I met Tyler at a party during the spring of 1946," Clara told the authors of this book, "and we were married in Juarez, Mexico, the Fourth of July weekend that year. Tyler never discussed with me his years in London. A very private person, he kept most of his thoughts to himself."

Clara's son, A. Dana Hodgson, Jr., had no illusions about Kent's motives. "He married my mother for her money," he said at an interview in 1989 at his McLean, Virginia, apartment. "He never did an honest day's work in the forty-two years of their marriage. He played gentleman farmer, owned yachts, read, and wrote letters. I invested my mother's fortune—a million dollars plus—in several solid portfolios. The interest would have kept both Kent and my mother in comfortable fashion. He persuaded Mother to let him handle her financial affairs and then charged her ten thousand dollars a year for the privilege of dissipating her fortune."

The fortune lasted nearly thirty years, providing a bonanza for Kent, as he enjoyed the high life with fine houses, a succession of yachts, and, of course, the finest tailored clothes from London. His one regret was that he was unable to travel to Bond Street or Savile Row for fittings, but he provided a London tailor with his measurements for suits, jackets, trousers, and shirts, and sent patterns of his feet to have his shoes—which he always referred to as "boots"—custom-made by an exclusive London bootmaker. He was also able to build a library of several thousand volumes, mostly of anti-Semitic, anti-Negro, and anti-FDR books.

For the first five years of marriage, Kent seemed content with life on his wife's Maryland "estate." But five years was the longest he had ever spent in any one place, including prison, and by 1951 he was hankering for a move. He bought and refitted his first yacht at Annapolis, then sold the Maryland property and moved to Fort Lauderdale, Florida, where he made plans for a two-year cruise through the West Indies.

Before he left, however, Edward Flynn, the United States attorney for Baltimore, asked the FBI to investigate Kent to determine whether he should register as an agent of a foreign power. There had already been brief FBI investigations into his background in 1941 and 1944, but after MI5 and the CIA had reclassified him, there was a suspicion that he might still be working for the Soviet Union. This led to a more extensive check into his time in Moscow and London. Unfortunately, much of the information concerning those years remains blacked out in both Washington and London; the final decision, however, was that if he had been a Soviet agent, he was one no longer, but had become simply a playboy, married to a wealthy woman, whose main interest was yachting. Doubts clearly remained, though: between 1952 and 1963 there were to be six more FBI investigations, all ending inconclusively.

From 1951, the Kents spent most of their time cruising out of Fort Lauderdale or Miami, until, in 1957, Kent used Clara's money to buy about eighty acres of land with a 1600-foot waterfront on the St. Johns River in Satsuma, near Palatka,

Putnam County, in northeastern Florida. There he built an English-style "country cottage," with a swimming pool, tennis court, guest house, and other outbuildings, including a large boathouse to hold his latest yacht, a forty-six-foot cruiser with a flying bridge.

Despite the guest house, Kent did not care to socialize. Carefully guarding his privacy, as he had done since his return to America, he always used his initials, T. G. Kent, rather than his full name, which might be recognized. He named his estate Hermit's Cove, and his writing paper was headed with a line drawing of a monk reading in a cell. Generally, he preferred the company of his cats to that of humans, and kept most of his contact with people, apart from the usual amenities of neighbors, to correspondence: he was a voluminous writer; carbon copies of all his own letters were meticulously arranged in jam-packed filing cabinets.

Kent's only intimate was George Deatheridge, one of the nation's most virulent racists. A self-taught engineer who accumulated a comfortable fortune from selling mail-order courses in civil engineering, Deatheridge was the organizer and director of the Knights of the White Camellia, an anti-Negro organization espousing policies far to the right of the Ku Klux Klan. Deatheridge had attained national notoriety during the war when he was charged with sedition, but the presiding judge died during the trial and the prosecution was never resumed.

Two years after settling in Satsuma, no doubt with the encouragement of Deatheridge, Kent began a new phase of his career as a right-wing propagandist. In 1959, he purchased the *Putnam County Weekly Sun,* a newspaper published in the nearby county seat of Palatka. In place of the local news carried by most weekly papers, the new proprietor immediately began devoting most of the space to attacks on the deceased President Roosevelt, Negroes, and Jews. He also tried to gain a foothold in local politics, but failed in his bid to win the Democratic nomination for county commissioner, a power post in Florida government.

When John F. Kennedy was elected president, Kent ran a full-page house advertisement in his paper, reading:

The American People
Have Just Elected Their
First Communist President
JOHN F. KENNEDY

He also carried on an extensive correspondence with a John Birch Society director, Revilo P. Oliver ("Revilo" is Oliver written backward), who stunned members of the Warren Commission investigating Kennedy's assassination by announcing: "I know who killed President Kennedy. He was killed by his former communist comrades because he was turning American."

Nathan Perlmutter learned of Kent's hate sheet in 1961, and immediately set in train a course of events that was to bring about Kent's second downfall. Perlmutter was the executive director of the Florida unit of the Anti Defamation League of B'Nai B'rith, the Jewish organization whose primary function is to combat anti-Semitism, particularly in the press. In mid-March he contacted Stephen Trumbull, the star investigative reporter of the *Miami Herald*, and showed him clippings of anti-Semitic and anti-Negro stories from the *Putnam County Weekly Sun*. He told Trumbull that the *Sun*'s publisher, T. G. Kent, was probably the same Tyler Gatewood Kent who had been imprisoned in Britain during the war for stealing secret U.S. documents and passing them to agents of Nazi Germany.

Perlmutter's tip-off had the makings of a juicy story, and Trumbull went to work on it at once, delving in the *Herald*'s files. He also phoned David Gerald Kraslow, Washington correspondent for the *Herald* and other papers in the Knight group, and enlisted his cooperation. Kraslow contacted two friends in the Justice Department, John Siegenthaler, a future editor of the *Nashville Tennessean*, and Edwin O. Guthman, formerly of the *Seattle Times* and 1950 winner of the Pulitzer Prize for national reporting.

Siegenthaler and Guthman, listed as "administrative assistants to the attorney general," had worked with Robert F. Kennedy since he had recruited them as investigators for his Senate committee on labor racketeering in 1956. Both men had worked on the battle lines of the civil rights movement in

Alabama and elsewhere in the South. They had seen blacks beaten, firehosed, attacked by police dogs, and subjected to other inhumane treatment. They were only too glad to assist Kraslow. They got him access to the State Department's copy of Kent's official trial transcript and other documents, and arranged for him to meet Attorney General Kennedy, who in turn arranged a telephone interview with Ambassador Joseph Kennedy, which proved to be essentially a summary of his 1944 statement about Kent.

Kraslow and Trumbull wrote their story together; Laurence Leslie Thompson, a reporter on the *Herald* for fifteen years, was assigned to interview Kent by telephone. The results appeared on the front pages of the *Miami Herald,* the *St. Petersburg Times,* and other Knight newspapers throughout the country The *Herald* headline read:

HE HELPED NAZIS,
NOW PEDDLES HATE
IN FLORIDA PAPER

The story continued inside with a five-column heading:

SPY CASE FIGURE RUNS HATE SHEET

The text was accompanied by a head-and-shoulders photograph of Kent, a map of Florida indicating the location of Palatka and Satsuma, and an effective montage of several headlines from Kent's paper. The story was picked up by the wire services and carried throughout the world.

Kent, naturally, was incensed. On April 11 he announced that he was suing the *Miami Herald* and the *St. Petersburg Times*—though it was not until nearly two years later, on April 6, 1963, that he filed suit for $50,000 each from the *Herald,* the *Times,* and Ambassador Kennedy, claiming that he had been libeled by the allegations that he had helped the Nazis and that his newspaper was racist. It was another year before the case was settled.

By April 1962, even Clara's money could not continue to prop up the *Putnam County Weekly Sun,* and Kent was forced to close it down. No doubt hoping to receive substantial compensation when the libel case finally came to court, he blamed his "enemies" for influencing advertisers to withdraw their support. A more likely reason was given in a sworn deposition from the publisher of the *Palatka Daily News*, Arthur Burns, who testified that Kent had the local reputation of being "contumacious and controversial." There were no buyers prepared to take the paper off his hands, so the Kents' losses were substantial. However, with typical insouciance Kent promptly took Clara off on a trip to Ireland and Europe. A request to the British home secretary to be allowed to visit England went unanswered.

The main reason for Kent's delay in filing suit was the involved process of obtaining a copy of the official trial transcript from the Home Office in London. Kent believed, wrongly as it turned out, that the transcript would prove he had never been a Nazi agent. However, when he asked the State Department for a copy of this and other documents which he considered relevant to his case, the department decided that it would be unfair to provide them to him without providing the same documents to Kennedy, which created complications with the British government reminiscent of *The New York Times*'s efforts to obtain a copy for its defense against Captain Ramsay's libel charges. At the same time, someone high up in the department—it may well have been Secretary of State Dean Rusk himself—approved a request from Kennedy that Franklin C. Gowen be allowed to give evidence on what happened when Kent was arrested.

All three defendants asked the court for a summary judgment, which meant that a judge sitting alone would deliver a verdict after reviewing the evidence. This negated Kent's request for a jury trial. Once again, he had been denied the glory of a public appearance in court. Instead, each defendant and his witnesses gave sworn depositions, on which they were examined, cross-examined, and re-examined. On March 23, 1964, Sixth Circuit Court Judge C. Richard Leavengood dismissed the case against the *Herald* and the *Times* and issued a summary judgment in their favor. His ruling, which occupied four legal pages, was based in large part on Kent's official trial transcript, and on the State Department's 2500-word statement of September 2, 1944. The evidence that Kent believed would substantiate his claims had been used against him.

The judge noted that "Joseph P. Kennedy, father of the

assassinated President John F. Kennedy, was also named as an original defendant to the suit, but has since received a summary judgment in his favor by order of this court." Judge Leavengood had ruled that more than three years had passed since Kennedy's alleged libel, and that in any case the suit should have been brought for slander—defamation by the spoken word—rather than for libel. He indicated, however, that his verdict would have been the same in either case.

Had there been a trial, Ambassador Kennedy would not have been able to testify, since he had suffered a stroke on December 19, 1961, which left him totally paralyzed on his right side and bereft of the power of speech. It may have been partly because of this that his attorneys and staff indulged in what may be described as an unusual delaying tactic.

Early in the proceedings, Kennedy's attorney, Neal Rutledge of Milledge, Rutledge and Milledge, Miami, denied that the ambassador had ever been served with a mail notice of the impending suit. His contention was supported by an affidavit sworn to by Diana First, Kennedy's personal secretary, in which she stated that it was her task to open and deal with all mail addressed to him and that she had "never opened" a notice of suit from Kent or his attorneys. The secretary was perfectly truthful in her statement. The authors have in their possession an envelope and its contents, sent by Kent to "Mr. Joseph P. Kennedy, 1095 North Ocean Boulevard, Palm Beach, Florida." The envelope carries the U.S. Postal Service sticker "Certified Mail, number 741601," and is rubber-stamped with the instruction "Return Receipt Requested." Written in ink is *REFUSED* and the words "Return to Sender."

But it was Kent whose behavior was most questionable after the verdicts. He did nothing to rectify the myth, accepted and fostered by several historians sympathetic to him and his cause, that his suits against the newspapers and Kennedy had been settled out of court in his favor. And some weeks after Judge Leavengood had issued his summary judgments in favor of the newspapers, he deliberately added to the confusion by writing to his longtime friend and admirer Dr. Harry Elmer Barnes, the revisionist historian, claiming that because of a Supreme Court decision in another case, *New York Times* versus Sullivan, on

March 9, he had been "compelled to withdraw" his two libel suits.

"I, together with my lawyer, have read the decision line by line and word for word," he wrote. "It states that: 'where public men are concerned and matters of public concern are involved, anyone claiming to be defamed by communication must show actual malice' or go remediless. Three judges file minority opinions concurring with the majority by stating that the decision does not go far enough. They claim that all libel laws with respect to public affairs and public men should be abolished."

Kent's social standing in Putnam County plummeted after the revelations of his past. He was forced to resign as commodore of the local power boat squadron. But what probably hurt Kent more was that he had to sell his yacht: after the expense of the libel actions, and the failure of the newspaper, the Kents' finances were much reduced. Not long afterward, he sold Hermit's Cove—the asking price was $100,000, though at recent real estate prices the property might have raised well over a million—and moved with the long-suffering Clara to Nogales, Arizona, close to the Mexican border. In the early 1970s, they crossed the border to live in an apartment in Jocotepec, Jalisco, where Kent embarked on a plan to boost Clara's dwindling fortune through currency speculation. The gamble failed, disastrously, when the bottom fell out of the peso market. With their hitherto comfortable income cut to a pittance, Kent was frequently reduced to appealing for "loans" from his stepson, who was not always inclined to oblige with a handout.

The remaining fifteen or so years of Kent's life were spent in a steady decline, during which, according to A. Dana Hodgson, Jr., he subjected Clara to continuing verbal abuse. Clara herself makes no complaint, but clearly there was very little communication between them. "After he gave up his last yacht in 1964," she says, "he devoted his time to reading and writing. A very private person, he kept most of his thoughts to himself."

In 1982, another turn in the downward spiral of Kent's life took him and Clara away from Mexico to a trailer, which Kent referred to as his "mobile home," in Mission, Texas. Kent said that they had moved to the dusty, isolated small town near the

Rio Grande because Clara needed to live at a lower elevation for the sake of her health. However, the wind-driven desolation of the place, a far cry indeed from the grand homes they had once owned in Maryland and Florida, soon proved too much for Kent. In the mid-eighties he and Clara moved to Kerrville, seat of Kerr County in the pleasant hill country of southwest central Texas, some fifty-five miles northwest of San Antonio on Interstate 10. A town of about fifteen thousand inhabitants, situated along the Guadaloupe River, Kerrville is a popular retirement community for former military personnel who enjoy hunting and fishing.

The Kent trailer, built of vertical wood siding, is situated in a park some miles west of the town. It is located on a corner lot and has a shade tree, a sizable lawn, and an aluminum garage filled with about forty large packing cases of Kent's books. Inside, it has a kitchen-dining area comparable in size to that in many small suburban homes, and a far more spacious living room than is normally found in trailers, with Mexican paintings on the walls and comfortable furniture, relics of more prosperous years. The Kents had separate bedrooms: Clara's comfortable and airy, Tyler's cramped and cell-like. His quarters, to the rear of the kitchen, are entered through a long hallway lined from floor to ceiling with bookcases. His small study, also lined with books and filing cabinets, houses a desk and a large closet filled with expensive suits and jackets. Tyler Kent never lost his taste for good clothes.

The suits are still there, hanging neatly from their rail, a monument to the vanity of a man born with many advantages, all of which he wasted because of the flaws inherent in his character. At the time of this writing, Clara is there, too. A cheerful, pleasant woman, still feisty at ninety-four, she is much liked by her neighbors, who are happy to take care of her errands and other needs.

By the time he moved to Kerrville, Kent had—with one possible exception—outlived all the other principal characters connected with his case. Roosevelt and Churchill, of course, were both long dead. Ambassador Kennedy, after eight years of stricken silence, died in 1969. So, too, did Anna Wolkoff. She had been released from prison in 1947. Shortly afterward, her father died and the Russian Tea Room closed its doors. Shunned by the White Russian community in London and by her former society clients, she eked out a tacky existence as a free-lance seamstress, living in a tiny attic flat in a bohemian lodging house in Chelsea owned by a friend, Felix Hope-Nicholson. Never a physically attractive woman, Anna grew obese, and had no known male lovers. In 1969, she accepted an invitation from a friend to take a motoring holiday in Spain. She was killed there in a car accident.

Captain Ramsay, separated from his wife, continued his racist activities after the war, publishing at his own expense an anti-Semitic diatribe, *The Nameless War*, in 1953. He kept up his social life, regularly attending such events as the Eton-Harrow cricket match at Lords and celebrating the opening of the grouse-shooting season in Scotland on August 12 each year until his death, on March 11, 1956. His friend Christabel Nicholson died in the summer of 1974, at the age of eighty-five.

Of the hunters who tracked and captured Kent, Max Knight, long weakened by heart disease, died of pneumonia on January 26, 1968. The Kent case had proved to be the final highlight of his career in MI5. He spent much of the remainder of his time in the service trying vainly to convince those at the top that it had been penetrated by at least one communist mole. His warnings went unheeded, and he switched his interest to his other great passion in life, natural history. He began a broadcasting career in 1946, and swiftly became famous as a radio naturalist and author. A memorial service in St. James's Church, Piccadilly, on February 20, 1968, was attended by several hundred devoted friends and admirers of the man who had become known to millions of BBC listeners as Uncle Max. No one at the church or in any of his many laudatory obituaries mentioned his thirty-two years with MI5, or his successes with the Woolwich Arsenal spies and the case of Tyler Kent.

Joan Miller, Knight's beautiful assistant, died in June 1984, at the age of sixty-six, at her home on the island of Malta. After three sexually frustrated years of living with Knight, she had left him in 1943, contracted an unsuccessful marriage to a naval officer, and romped through the rest of the war with a series of assorted lovers. For more than twenty years she was a prominent member of London café society, seen constantly at all the best places—Cowes, Henley, Ascot, Antibes on the French Riviera, the top hotels and night clubs, and at hundreds of country weekends. A younger member of the same social set described her as a snob, anti-Semitic, amusing, coldhearted, ruthless, a beautiful femme fatale with impeccable taste in house furnishings, linen, shoes, and gowns. Her great love during those years was a good-looking, Bertie-Woosterish man-about-town named Norman Richards, heir to the Vita Bread fortune, by whom she had a daughter, Jonquil. When he neglected to marry her, she changed her name to his by deed poll and allowed everyone to believe a marriage had taken place.

Around the beginning of the 1960s, Joanna, as she was then calling herself, suffered a disastrous physical change; she contracted an ailment that caused excess fluid retention. Floating angrily around London in tentlike garments, a tragic and bloated figure, she spent most of her time warning off Norman's potential girlfriends, often arriving unannounced at his dates and glaring across the room with withering scorn. During this period, she lost most of his money in an ill-conceived real estate venture, but continued to live as though she were rich, buying anything she wanted regardless of whether she had the money.

After Norman's death, Joanna had a short-lived marriage to a man named Phipps. Besieged by creditors at the end of the marriage, she fled to Malta, where the living was cheap, and spent her declining years working on her autobiography and entertaining visitors with smoked salmon and large glasses of gin.

The one person who may be still alive at the time of this writing is Kent's lover in Moscow, Tatiana Alexandrovna Ilovaiskaya. Tanya, who switched her sexual favors to Vice Consul Donald Nichols immediately after Kent left Moscow, is said to have married an American naval doctor sometime during the ambassadorship of Averell Harriman, in 1943 or 1944, and to have returned with her husband to the United States. It is believed that Nichols died in the early 1980s, but that Tanya is living in retirement in Florida. Unfortunately, all our efforts to trace her have proved fruitless; perhaps it is fitting that she remains a beautiful mystery.

Tyler Kent was admitted to the Sid Peterson Memorial Hospital, Kerrville, on November 11, 1988, suffering from carcinoma of the colon. He died there nine days later, on November 20, aged seventy-seven years and eight months.

Appendices

The Churchill-Roosevelt Messages

The fifteen messages between Churchill and Roosevelt before Kent's arrest were printed for the first time in Professor Warren Kimball's *Churchill and Roosevelt: The Complete Correspondence, 1939–45* (Princeton University Press, 1985), though eleven of them had been included in *Roosevelt and Churchill: Their Secret Wartime Correspondence*, edited by Francis Loewenheim, Harold D. Langley, and Manfred Jonas, published in 1975. However, they are printed below for the first time in complete form, including secret notations made by the recipients. The six signals found in Kent's possession are marked.

1. Letter from Roosevelt to Churchill (Delivered by courier)

PRIVATE   September 11, 1939

My dear Churchill:—

It is because you and I occupied similar positions in the World War that I want you to know how glad I am that you are back again in the Admiralty. Your problems are, I realize, complicated by new factors but the essential is not very different. What I want you and the Prime Minister to know is that I shall at all times welcome it if you will keep me in touch personally with anything you want to know about. You can always send sealed letters through your pouch or my pouch.

I am glad you did the Marlboro [sic] volumes before this thing started—and I much enjoyed reading them.

With my sincere regards,
Faithfully yours,
FRANKLIN D. ROOSEVELT

The Right Honorable
Winston Churchill, P.C., C.N.,
First Lord of the Admiralty,
London,
England.

2. Telegram from Churchill to Roosevelt

JR
A portion of this telegram must be closely paraphrased before being communicated to anyone. (br)

> From
> London
> Dated October 5, 1939
> Rec'd 1 P.M.

Secretary of State,
Washington.
RUSH
1939, October 5, 4 P.M.
STRICTLY PERSONAL AND MOST SECRET FOR THE PRESIDENT AND THE SECRETARY.
Churchill sent for me this morning and following our talk sent me the following communication:

"My dear Ambassador, the enclosures cover our conversation this morning. Yours sincerely, Winston S. Churchill."

I am sending memorandum enclosed with Churchill's note.

The following from Naval Person:

We quite understand natural desire of United States to keep belligerents out of their waters. We like the idea of a wide limit of say 300 miles within which no submarines of any belligerent country should act. If America requests all belligerents to comply, we should immediately declare that we would respect your wishes. General questions of international law would of course remain unprejudiced. More difficulty arises about surface ships, because if a raider operates from or takes refuge in the American zone, we should have to be protected or allowed to protect ourselves. We have mentioned several other instances to Mr. Kennedy. We do not mind how far south the prohibited zone goes, provided that it is effectively maintained. We should have great difficulty in accepting a zone which was only policed by some weak neutral. But of course if the American Navy takes care of it, that is all right.

Thirdly, we are still not sure whether raider off Brazil is SCHEER or HIPPER, but widespread movements are being made by us to meet either case. The more American ships cruising along the South American coast the better, as you, sir, would no doubt hear what they saw or did not see. Raider might then find American waters rather crowded, or may anyhow prefer to go on to sort of trade route, where we are preparing.

We wish to help you in every way in keeping the war out of Americas.
(END SECTION ONE)   KENNEDY
RR:CSB

Section Two
JR
A portion of this telegram must be closely paraphrased before being communicated to anyone. (br)

FROM
London
Dated October 5, 1939
Rec'd 1:59 P.M.

Secretary of State,
Washington.
1939, October 5, (Section Two).
Following is note from Admiral Phillips who was present at the conversation with Churchill.
(GRAY) "My dear Ambassador: In accordance with our conversation this morning, I enclose a short note on points which may arise concerning the Panama Conference proposal for a zone round the United States and South America. Yours sincerely, T. S. V. Phillips." (END GRAY)
Following is memorandum enclosed with Admiral Phillips' note.
(GRAY) "While the proposal in general is welcomed, the following points will need attention.
(1) From the point of view of international law, it would obviously be necessary to make it clear that British assent to the proposal was not any precedent and did not imply a recognition of a *right* on the part of a neutral to exclude belligerents from operating anywhere on the high seas (i.e., outside the three mile limit).
(2) It would naturally be necessary for belligerent forces to have free access to their own or allied territory and territorial waters within the zone.
(3) It would be a fundamental part of the scheme that it should be effective, i.e., not only that enemy action against territory, forests, or shipping should be prevented, but also that the use of the area as a sanctuary is clearly very important because, unless such action were prevented, it would clearly facilitate greatly the operations of enemy raiders in areas outside the zone.
(4) The extent of the zone to be finally accepted would presumably be linked up with the possibilities of effective enforcement.
(5) The conversion of belligerent merchant ships into warships in ports within the zone would presumably be prevented.
(6) It would naturally be necessary that a belligerent should retain the right to continue pursuit of the forces of his enemy into that area, because otherwise the existence of the zone might frequently enable a raider to escape destruction and subsequently emerge from the zone to recommence raiding in some other area.
(7) We should, of course, hope to obtain any information concerning the movements of enemy forces within the area since otherwise the operation of the scheme would greatly reduce the possibilities of obtaining such information for ourselves.

(8) The question of enemy warships is also of some importance because the number now interred in various American ports might presumably, under the safety given by the scheme, resume trading on the American continent. Such trading would presumably in any case not be allowed unless the Germans themselves had accepted the scheme and respected it." (END MESSAGE)
CSB   KENNEDY

3. Telegram from Churchill to Roosevelt

EDA
This telegram must be closely paraphrased before being communicated to anyone (C & A)

LONDON
Dated October 16, 1939
Received 5:53 P.M.

Secretary of State
Washington
2061, October 16, 10 P.M.
STRICTLY SECRET AND PERSONAL FOR THE PRESIDENT
The following from Naval Person.
"It is very odd that SCHEER should have made no other prizes since September 30. As I told you we are taking some pains in looking for him. He may be anywhere by now. We have been hitting the U-boats hard with our new apparatus and on Friday 13th four including two of the largest and latest were destroyed. Sinking of ROYAL OAK was a remarkable episode of which I will write you more fully. It in no way affects the naval balance. Our accounts of Hitler's oil position make us feel he is up against time limits. This means that either he will make vehement attacks on us for which we are prepared or that he is being held back by counsellors who see the red light. (?) we propose to see what happens feeling fairly confident that all will be well. We should be quite ready to tell you about our asdic methods whenever you feel they would be of use to the United States Navy and are sure the secret will go no further. They certainly are very remarkable in results and enable two destroyers to do the work that could not have been done by ten last time. We have not been at all impressed by the accuracy of the German air bombing of our warships. They seem to have no effective bomb sights. I have not written as promised because this and my former cable give all my news."
RR:DDM   KENNEDY

4. Telegram from Churchill to Roosevelt
(A copy of this signal was found in Tyler Kent's possession.)

HSM

GRAY
From London
Dated December 25, 1939
Rec'd 9:55 P.M.

Secretary of State
Washington
RUSH
2720 December 25, noon.
STRICTLY SECRET AND PERSONAL FOR THE PRESIDENT FROM NAVAL PERSON:
"We have always conformed to undertaking not to use British submarines inside your zone and I am very sorry there seems to be trouble about recent incidents. We cannot always refrain from stopping enemy ships outside international three-mile limit when these may well be supply ships for U-boats or surface raiders, but instructions have been given only to arrest or fire upon when out of sight of American shores. As a result of action off Plate whole South Atlantic is now clear and may perhaps continue clear of warlike operations. This must be a blessing to South American Republics whose trade was hampered by activities of raider and whose ports were used for his supply ships and information centers. In fact we have rescued all this vast area from war disturbances. Earnestly hope this will be valued by South American States who may likely for long periods enjoy in practice not only three hundred but three thousand miles limit. Laws of war gave raider right capture, or sink after providing for crews, all trade with us in South Atlantic. No protest was made about this although it injured Argentine commercial interests. Why then should complaints be made of our action in ridding area of this raider in strict accordance with same international laws from which we had been suffering? Trust matter can be allowed to die down and see no other reason why any trouble should occur unless another raider is sent which is unlikely after fate of first. South American States should see in Plate action their deliverance perhaps indefinitely from all animosity. Much of world duty is being thrown on Admiralty. Hope burden will not be made too heavy for us to bear. Even a single raider loose in North Atlantic requires employment half our battle fleet to give sure protection. Now unlimited magnetic mining campaign adds to strain upon flotillas and small craft. We are at very full extension till the new war-time construction of anti-submarine craft begins to flow from May onwards. If we should break under load South American Republics would soon have worse worries than the sound of one day's distant seaward cannonade. And you also, Sir, in quite a short time would have more direct cares. I ask that full consideration should be given to strain upon us at this crucial period and best construction put upon action indispensable to end war shortly in right way.

"In case you may be interested in details of recent action am sending various reports by first air mail. Damage to EXETER from eleven-inch guns was most severe and ship must be largely rebuilt. Marvel is she stood up to it so well.

"Magnetic mines very deadly weapon on account of possibility of varying sensitiveness of discharge, but we think we have got hold of its tail though we do not want them to know this.

"Generally speaking think war will soon begin now. Permit me to send you, Sir, all the compliments of the season."

HPD   JOHNSON

5. Letter from Churchill to Roosevelt (Delivered by courier)

Admiralty
Whitehall
7 January, 1940

My dear Mr. President,
    In pursuance of the promise I made you in the telegram I sent on Christmas Day, I now enclose a précis of the reports we have so far received about the Naval action off Montevideo.
Yours sincerely,
WINSTON CHURCHILL

The President of the United States.

[Salutations handwritten. Date and time of receipt in Washington not known. A copy of the précis can be found in Kimball, pp. 30–32.]

6. Telegram from Churchill to Roosevelt
(A copy of this signal was found in Tyler Kent's possession, also a photographic plate negative made from it by photographer Eugene Smirnoff for Anna Wolkoff.)

HSM

GRAY
From London
Dated January 29, 1940
Rec'd 1:20 P.M.

Secretary of State,
Washington.
265, January 29, 7 P.M.
PERSONAL AND SECRET FOR THE PRESIDENT FROM NAVAL PERSON
"I gave orders last night that no American ship should, in any circumstances, be diverted into the combat zone round the British Islands declared by you. I trust this will be satisfactory."
PEG   JOHNSON

[The original message had penciled notation "Sent to the President at 4.05 P.M."]

7. Telegram from Churchill to Roosevelt
(A copy of this signal was found in Tyler Kent's possession.)

JR

GRAY
From London
Dated January 30, 1940
Rec'd 8:30 A.M.

Secretary of State,
Washington.
URGENT
267 January 30, 1 P.M.
PERSONAL AND SECRET FOR THE PRESIDENT FROM NAVAL PERSON
"I trust that the information I gave you last night about the orders sent to British ships will not be made known until measures have been concerted which will remove appearance of discrimination. It has been pointed out to me that my signal to fleet can only be maintained if measures are taken to ensure in advance of their departure that United States ships carry no objectional [sic] cargo. Moreover, in exceptional cases it may be necessary to divert United States ships if we have definite ground for suspicion against them. It

would be most helpful if some arrangement could be reached with Lothian on these lines and meanwhile all publicity avoided."

WSC:HPD   JOHNSON

[Original signal had penciled notation "Sent to the President at 12:20 P.M."]

8. Letter from Roosevelt to Churchill

February 1, 1940

My dear Churchill

Ever so many thanks for that tremendously interesting account of the extraordinarily well-fought action of your three cruisers. I am inclined to think that when we know more about the facts, it will turn out that the damage to the GRAF SPEE was greater than reported.

At the time of dictating this, I think our conversations in regard to search and detention of American ships is working out satisfactorily—but I would not be frank unless I told you that there has been much public criticism here. The general feeling is that the net benefit to your people and to France is hardly worth the definite annoyance caused to us. That is always found to be so in a nation which is 3000 miles away from the fact of war.

I wish much that I could talk things over with you in person—but I am always grateful to you for keeping me in touch, as you do.

Always sincerely,

FRANKLIN D. ROOSEVELT

Right Honorable Winston Churchill,
The Admiralty,
White Hall [sic],
London, England.

[The salutation "My dear Churchill" was penciled in.]

9. Telegram from Churchill to Roosevelt

(A copy of this signal was found in Tyler Kent's possession, also a photographic negative plate made by Eugene Smirnoff for Anna Wolkoff.)

GRAY
From London
Dated February 28, 1940
Rec'd 3 P.M.

Secretary of State,
Washington.
RUSH 490, February 28, 8 P.M.
STRICTLY PERSONAL AND CONFIDENTIAL FOR THE PRESIDENT FROM NAVAL PERSON

"Very many thanks for your most kind letter of February 1. Since on January 29 I gave orders to the fleet not to bring any American ships into the zone you have drawn around our shores, many of the other departments had become much concerned about the efficiency of the blockade and the difficulties of discriminating between various countries. The neutrals are all on them and they are all on me. Nevertheless, the order still stands and no American ship has been brought by the Navy into the danger zone. But you can imagine my embarrassment when Moore McCormack Line actually advertises in Norway that they do not have to worry about navicerts or Kirkwall, and when all the Scandinavian countries complain of discrimination in American favour. I wonder if there is any way in which the Moore McCormack Line could be persuaded, in addition to accepting navicerts as a general rule, not to carry mails for Scandinavia until the arrangements we are trying to make at St. John, New Brunswick, or elsewhere, are ready. All our experience shows that the examination of mails is essential to efficient control as only in this way can we get the evidence of evasion. I do hope that I may be helped to hold the position I have adopted by the American shipping lines availing themselves of the great convenience of navicerts which was [sic] an American invention and thus enable American trade to proceed without hindrance.

It is matter of great pleasure to me to keep you informed about naval matters, although alas I cannot have the honour of a talk with you in person."
HPD   JOHNSON

[The first page of this signal bears the penciled notation, "Copy taken to (unreadable name) at White House by (unreadable name) for the President who arrived at 6 P.M."]

10. Letter from Roosevelt to Churchill

March 5, 1940

AMERICAN EMBASSY
LONDON
SECRET AND CONFIDENTIAL
Your 490, February 28, 8 P.M.
Please convey the following message to the Naval Person from the President:
QUOTE Upon my return to Washington, I received your message. I deeply appreciate your efforts. I am having the situation thoroughly studied and will communicate with you further as soon as possible. END QUOTE

ROOSEVELT

[Signed in pencil.]

11. Letter from Churchill to Roosevelt

May 7, 1940

My dear Mr. President,
In view of the interest you displayed in the Battle of the River Plate, I thought you would like to see an advance copy of the official account of the Battle which we shall shortly be publishing.

Yours sincerely,
WINSTON CHURCHILL

The President of the United States.

[Delivered by courier. Salutation handwritten.]

12. Telegram from Churchill to Roosevelt

GRAY
London
Dated May 15, 1940
Rec'd 12:55 P.M.

Secretary of State,
Washington.
RUSH
1216, May 15, 6 P.M.
SECRET. STRICTLY PERSONAL AND CONFIDENTIAL FOR THE PRESIDENT
MOST SECRET AND PERSONAL. TELEGRAM. PRESIDENT ROOSEVELT FROM FORMER NAVAL PERSON.
"Although I have changed my office, I am sure you would not wish me to discontinue our intimate, private correspondence. As you are no doubt

aware, the scene has darkened swiftly. The enemy have a marked preponderance in the air, and their new technique is making a deep impression upon the French. I think myself the battle on land has only just begun, and I should like to see tanks engaged. Up to the present, Hitler is working with specialized units in tanks and air. The small countries are simply smashed up, one by one, like matchwood. We must expect, though it is not yet certain, that Mussolini will hurry in to share the loot of civilization. We expect to be attacked here ourselves, both from the air and by parachute and air-borne troops in the near future, and are getting ready for them. If necessary we shall continue the war alone and we are not afraid of that. But I trust you realize, Mr. President, that the voice and force of the United States may count for nothing if they are withheld too long. You may have a completely subjugated Nazified Europe established with astonishing swiftness, and the weight may be more than we can bear. All I ask now is that you should proclaim nonbelligerency, which would mean that you would help us with everything short of actually engaging armed forces. Immediate needs are: first of all, the loan of forty or fifty of your older destroyers to bridge the gap between what we have now and the large new construction we put in hand at the beginning of the war. This time next year we shall have plenty. But if in the interval Italy comes in against us with another one hundred submarines, we may be strained to breaking point. Secondly, we want several hundred of the latest types of aircraft, of which you are now getting delivery. These can be repaid by those now being constructed in the United States for us. Thirdly, anti-aircraft equipment and ammunition, of which again there will be plenty next year, if we are alive to see it. Fourthly, the fact that our ore supply is being compromised from Sweden, from North Africa, and perhaps from northern Spain, makes it necessary to purchase steel in the United States. This also applies to other materials. We shall go on paying dollars for as long as we can, but I should like to feel reasonably sure that when we can pay no more you will give us the stuff all the same. Fifthly, we have many reports of possible German parachute or air borne descents into Ireland. The visit of a United States squadron to Irish ports, which might well [apparent omission] prolonged, would be invaluable. Sixthly, I am looking to you to keep that Japanese dog quiet in the Pacific, using Singapore in any way convenient. The details of the material which we have in mind will be communicated to you separately.

"With all good wishes and respect."

RR   KENNEDY

[First page of signal carries handwritten note FILE SECRET.]

13. Telegram from Roosevelt to Churchill
(A copy of this signal, Roosevelt's first telegram to Churchill, was found in
Tyler Kent's possession.)

GRAY
May 16, 1940
1 p.m.

No Distribution
AMERICAN EMBASSY
LONDON
872
URGENT, FOR THE AMBASSADOR.
Your 1216, May 15, 6 P.M.
Please transmit the following message from the President to the former naval
person:
QUOTE I have just received your message and I am sure it is unnecessary for
me to say that I am most happy to continue our private correspondence as we
have in the past.

I am, of course, giving every possible consideration to the suggestions
made in your message. I shall take up your specific proposals one by one.

First, with regard to the possible loan of forty or fifty of our older destroyers. As you know a step of that kind could not be taken except with the
specific authorization of the Congress and I am not certain that it would be
wise for that suggestion to be made to the Congress at this moment. Furthermore, it seems to me doubtful, from the standpoint of our own defense
requirements, which must inevitably be linked with the defense requirements
of this hemisphere and with our obligations in the Pacific, whether we could
dispose even temporarily of these destroyers. Furthermore, even if we could
take the step you suggest, it would be at least six or seven weeks at a minimum, as I see it, before these vessels could undertake active service under the
British flag.

Second. We are now doing everything within our power to make it possible
for the Allied Governments to obtain the latest types of aircraft in the United
States.

Third, if Mr. Purvis may receive immediate instructions to discuss the
question of anti-aircraft equipment and ammunition with the appropriate
authorities here in Washington, the most favorable consideration will be
given to the request made in the light of our own defense needs and requirements.

Fourth. Mr. Purvis has already taken up with the appropriate authorities
here the purchase of steel in the United States and I understand that satisfactory arrangements have been made.

Fifth. I shall give further consideration to your suggestion with regard to
the visit of the United States Squadron to Irish ports.

Sixth. As you know, the American fleet is now concentrated at Hawaii
where it will remain at least for the time being.

I shall communicate with you again as soon as I feel able to make a final decision with regard to some of the other matters dealt with in your message and I hope you will feel free to communicate with me in this way at any time.

The best of luck to you. UNQUOTE

FRANKLIN ROOSEVELT
HULL

14. Telegram from Churchill to Roosevelt

JT

GRAY
LONDON
Dated May 18, 1940
Rec'd 1:14 P.M.

Secretary of State,
Washington
RUSH
1267, May 18, 6 P.M.
Your 872, May 16 and my 1243, May 17, noon.
SECRET AND PERSONAL FOR THE PRESIDENT FROM FORMER NAVAL PERSON.
"Many thanks for your message for which I am grateful. I do not need to tell you about the gravity of what has happened. We are determined to persevere to the very end whatever the result of the great battle raging in France may be. We must expect in any case to be attacked here on the Dutch model before very long and we hope to give a good account of ourselves. But if American assistance is to play any part it must be available soon."
CSB   KENNEDY

15. Telegram from Churchill to Roosevelt
(This was the final telegram to Roosevelt from Churchill encoded by Tyler Kent on his midnight-to-8:00 A.M. shift. A penciled copy was found in his pocket when he was arrested.)

Copy: KDH
GRAY
From London
Dated May 20, 1940
Rec'd 8.40 A.M.

Secretary of State,
Washington.
1271, May 20, 1 P.M.
SECRET AND PERSONAL FOR THE PRESIDENT FROM FORMER NAVAL PERSON:
"Lothian has reported his conversation with you. I understand your difficulties but I am very sorry about the destroyers. If they were here in six weeks they would play an invaluable part. The battle in France is full of danger to both sides. Though we have taken heavy toll of enemy in the air and are clawing down two or three to one of their planes, they still have a formidable numerical superiority. Our most vital need is therefore the delivery at the earliest possible date of the largest possible number of Curtiss P-40 fighters now in course of delivery to your army.

"With regard to the closing part of your talk with Lothian, our intention is whatever happens to fight on to the end in this Island and, provided we can get the help for which we ask, we hope to run them very close to the air battle in view of individual superiority. Members of the present administration would likely go down during this process should it result adversely, but in no conceivable circumstances will we consent to surrender. If members of the present administration were finished and others came in to parlay amid the ruins, you must not be blind to the fact that the sole remaining bargaining counter with Germany would be the fleet, and if this country was left by the United States to its fate no one would have the right to blame those responsible if they made the best terms they could for the surviving inhabitants. Excuse me, Mr. President, for putting this nightmare bluntly. Evidently I could not answer for my successors who in utter despair and helplessness might well have to accommodate themselves to the German will. However, there is happily no need at present to dwell upon such ideas. Once more thanking you for your good will."
HPD   KENNEDY

Telephone conversation

In addition to letters and cables, the records show one direct telephone conversation between Churchill and Roosevelt during the time Tyler Kent was stealing messages from the London embassy. Although Roosevelt liked to use the telephone, Churchill was never happy with it: at that time, even scrambler phones were not secure. The conversation took place on Thursday, October 5, 1939, the same day that Churchill had sent his first telegram to the president, in response to Roosevelt's message of September 11.

Shortly after his 5:00 P.M. lunch on a tray in his second-floor study in the White House, Roosevelt was handed a decoded message from the assistant naval attaché in Berlin. The officer reported that he had been informed by Grand Admiral Erich Raeder that the British had planted a bomb aboard the S.S. *Iroquois,* which had left Cork the previous day. Raeder had implied that this was a plot by Churchill to blame the Germans for the resulting explosion, with the aim of dragging the United States into the war. (The Germans had made similar accusations against the first lord of the Admiralty over the sinking of the *Lusitania* in the First World War, and the *Athenia* in September 1939, both of which had in fact been sunk by German U-boats.)

After consulting briefly with his advisers, Roosevelt personally rang through to London, where Churchill was dining at his flat in Morpeth Mansions, Westminster, with the third sea lord, Rear Admiral Bruce Fraser, and the director of naval construction, Sir Stanley Goodall, to discuss the shipbuilding program. Roosevelt's call came through, redirected from the admiralty, at about 10:00 P.M., toward the end of dinner. In 1954, Fraser recalled the scene when the butler entered the dining room to tell Churchill he was wanted on the telephone:

> "Who is it?"
> "I don't know, sir," said the butler.
> "Well, say I can't attend to it now."
> "I think you ought to come, sir," said the butler, and Churchill got up rather testily. Then we heard his replies, "Yes, sir . . . No, sir" . . .
> The first lord said: "Admiral, I think you must now excuse me. This is very important and I must go and see the Prime Minister at once."

During the conversation, Churchill made notes of what he had said to Roosevelt:

> *Iroquois* is probably a thousand miles West of Ireland. Presume you could not meet her before 50th meridian. There remains about a thousand miles in which outrage might be committed. U-boat danger inconceivable in these broad waters. Only method can be time bomb planted at Queenstown. We think this not impossible.
> Am convinced full exposure of all facts known to United States Government, including sources of information, especially if official, only way of frustrating plot. Action seems urgent. Presume you have warned *Iroquois* to search ship.

Churchill discussed the message with Chamberlain at once, and with the War Cabinet next morning, telling the ministers that "the Germans no doubt hoped to claim credit for the friendly gesture of having warned the Americans and so enabled them to save the crew." But the crew searched the ship from stem to stern and found no bomb. The ship reached port without any further incident.

The Stolen Documents:
Herschel V. Johnson's Summary

LIST OF FOLDERS —packed in carton and sent to State Department, DC/RM attention Mr. Calkin

Chamberlain
Churchill
Halifax
Hore-Belisha
American and European Affairs
Films
Jews
Miscellaneous
Oil
Policy
War—G.B.
To be Filed
Treasury
Unfiled
Balkan States
Belgium
Czechoslovakia
Far East
Finland
France
Germany
Hungary
Ireland
Italy
Poland
Rumania
Russia
Spain
Sweden
Turkey

Bonds
  and duplicates

ENVELOPES

Documents found in *light brown portmanteau—sent in it to State Dept.*

Torn-up telegrams*
Confirmation copies of Telegrams Received from the Department, July 1939
Copies of Telegrams "For the Ambassador's File" November 1939
Folder marked "Telegrams January 1–31, 1938"
Unmarked Folder Telegrams to and from Department, February 1938
Flimsies of miscellaneous Telegrams
Unmarked manila envelope–miscellaneous telegrams from April 22 to October 31, 1939
Folder marked "Telegrams from Department—June 1939"
Folder marked "Telegrams from Department—July 1939"
Folder marked "Telegrams to Misc.—July 1939"
Folder marked "Telegrams from Misc.—Aug. 1939"
Six packets Incoming Telegrams Nos 1–540 Jan.–July 1939
Key to Abbreviations†
Draft of Telegram November 2 by Mr. Ferris and notes on Cotton and Rubber†

* This item on the memorandum is annotated by hand: "destroyed, apparently—not found—D. Jaques."
† These items are annotated by hand: "?do not find—D. Jaques."

Analysis
of the Stolen Documents

AFTER THE WAR, during the great anticommunist drives of the 1950s, MI5 in London and the CIA in Washington re-examined the Tyler Kent affair in an effort to determine whether he had supplied the KGB with secrets during his time in London. While there was no hard evidence that he had done so, analysis of his activities and contacts created sufficient doubt to cause the two organizations to reclassify him as a Soviet agent.

One of the factors involved in reaching that decision was this study by a CIA officer of the sources of the documents he had stolen, and their potential value to Nazi Germany on the one hand and the Soviet Union on the other.

Sources of Messages Stolen by Kent

ORIGIN	1938	JAN–AUG 1939	SEPT 1, 1939– MAY 10, 1940	MAY 10–20, 1940	TOTAL
London	161	963	208	131	1463
Berlin	60	24	22		106
Paris	26	1	5		32
The Hague		1	5		6
Genoa			2		2
Brussels	2	1	2		5
Bucharest	5	1	2		8
Ankara		22	2		24
Warsaw	9	56	1		66
Belgrade	10		1		11
Moscow	5		1		6
Budapest	1		1		2
Rome	47	47	1	1	96
Prague	61				61
Vienna	21				21
Helsinki		4	1		5
Stockholm			1		1
Havana			1		1
Berne			1		1

Singapore			1		1
Oslo			1		1
Manila			1		1
Lagos			1		1
Sophia		1			1
Athens		1			1
Tirana		1			1
San Sebastian		1			1
Dublin	2				2
Barcelona	1				1
Hong Kong	1				1
	412	1124	261	132	1929

2–13 Mar '38   Bukharin, Yagoda, Rykov trials in Moscow
11 Mar '38   Austria entered by German troops
30 Sep '38   Munich Pact
15 Mar '39   German troops enter Czecho
28 Mar '39   Spanish Civil War ends
30 Nov '39   USSR wars with Finland
14 Dec '39   USSR expelled from League of Nations for unprovoked aggression against Finland and Poland
24 Aug '39   German-Soviet Non-aggression Pact
1 Sep '39   War with Brit. Ger. troops into Poland
17 Sep '39   Soviet troops into Poland
5 Oct '39   TGK arrives London
8 Oct '39   TGK meets with Matthias
12 Mar '40   Russ-Finn war ends
15 Jun '40   Sovs occupy Lithuania
28 June '40   Rumania cedes to Soviet Union
28 Sep '39   Sov/Germ Friendship and Boundary Pact
10 May '40   German attack on France
21 Jul '40   Baltic States ask admission to the USSR
27 Sep '39   J. H. King was arrested

TGK's target list in terms of accumulated documents

1. London/Washington
2. Berlin
3. Rome
4. Warsaw
5. Prague
6. Paris

   Cede 1. as obvious first priority particularly in light of cryptanalytic bonanza. Also for British sitreps given to U.S. U.S. intentions to intervene/give clandestine support.

2. Berlin's interest in Berlin would be technical (crypto) in nature. The record shows that in '40 the Germans were advanced in reading U.S. communications. Waste of an asset.

3. Germans had no need for info on Italians. German estimate of Italy as an ally—very low. Could have interest in Italians doing a unilateral with the British though highly improbable at this time since Germans were winning. Waste of an asset.

4. Can see high interest in Warsaw, particularly French-British intentions. Interest would go to zero once Poland secured. Only 1 message in re Poland was plucked after 1 Sep '39. This would have been a valid target except that TGK didn't arrive London until 6 weeks after the 1 Sep '39 attack. Pointless for the Germans to be interested in allied point of view on an event which was absolute triumph for Germans. Waste of an asset.

5. Prior to 15 Mar '39, Prague would have been a hot German target, but, like Poland, it was a success which happened more than 6 months prior to TGK's arrival in London. Pointless.

6. Paris was hot property until late May. In terms of opportunity, collection of docs was meager. A German controlled asset would have taken an obvious focus on Franco-British efforts and US intentions and assurances.

Moscow is tied for 10th place, along with The Hague. Hard to imagine anyone working for and believing in the Nazis would have neglected the Soviet Union.

So much for Germans.

1. Moscow imputes deceptive practices to everyone, despite ample coverage of the British government from within. Hit Washington/London traffic hard! Some obvious crypto advantage in acquiring large volume of true reading cables in all systems. Pick off Liddell-Hoover messages because they relate to Soviet agents, RDF equipment, and in '40, lots of info on deportees to Canada and Australia. Soviets believe British will double-cross Soviets in the long run—watch for indications.

2. Soviets need broadest possible reporting from Germany and Japan. Japan collection mainly in Japan and China. Since British are at war, we can assume that the U.S. has picked up part of the burden on their behalf. London is an ideal site for collection.

3. Italians are weak link in Axis. Although Italian CP has been repressed, action in Italy is much easier than through or in Germany.

4. Once Germany split Poland with the Soviets, the Soviets are somewhat blinded in the west. Also Soviets would want pre–1 Sep '39 coverage to analyse Allied temperament, resolve, points of difference, French-British problems and the role of the U.S.

5. Czechoslovakia impressed Soviets. They would have high interest in the U.S.–British reaction.

6. Strong Soviet controlled resources in France (which we, British–U.S., consistently underestimated throughout the war) were of interest. Disciplined assets could and were ultimately brought under Soviet direction. France had always loomed large as a sympathetic if ineffectual friend.

Sources

A. ARCHIVAL MATERIAL

National Archives, Washington, D.C., Diplomatic Branch: Decimal file 123,
Kent, Tyler G.; Decimal file 123, Offie, Carmel; Decimal file 123, Antheil,
Henry W.; Record group 84, London Station file.

Department of Justice, Washington, D.C., Federal Bureau of Investigation,
Freedom of Information and Privacy Act: Tyler G. Kent reports for years
1941, 1945, 1946, 1950, 1951, 1956, 1961, 1963; Report on Offie, Carmel;
Report on Antheil, Henry W.

Public Record Office, Kew, London: Foreign Office files numbers F0371/
22827, 24248, 24251, 25189, 25248, 38510, 38545, 38704, 44539, 44628;
F0372/4016, 4017; Naturalization records, Wolkoffs and Danischewskys;
Home Office files numbers H0144/20710, 21995, 22454, W14517; Cabinet Papers, CAB65/7, 75/7, 115/83; Prime Minister's Papers, PREM/4/
17/1.

B. PUBLISHED GOVERNMENT DOCUMENTS

Documents on the Events Proceding [sic] *the Outbreak of the War,* German Foreign
Office, Berlin (German) 1939, New York City (English) 1940.

Documents on German Foreign Policy, Series D, Vols. IX, X, Washington, U.S.
Department of State; London, HMSO.

Peace and War 1931–41—United States Foreign Policy, Washington, 1943.

C. TYLER KENT PAPERS

A collection of eight filing cabinet drawers of Kent's own papers, plus approximately 200 selected volumes from his library, supplied to the authors
by Mrs. Clara Kent in February 1989.

1. Basic documents

Birth certificate; Baptismal certificate; Death certificate; Selective Service
(draft) registration card; Social Security card number 264–80–8629; U.S.
passport number K491207, issued April 4, 1969; U.S. passport number
E824495, issued April 10, 1974.

2. Correspondence

Kent's files in the authors' possession contain more than 1000 letters. Those files pertinent to this book are as follows: Tyler Kent to his mother, Ann Kent, 1941–1945; Irene Danischewsky to Ann Kent, 1941–1945; Tyler Kent–Richard Whalen, 1964; Tyler Kent–John Toland, 1978–1982; Tyler Kent–Dr. Harry Elmer Barnes, 1960s; Tyler Kent–Ray Bearse, 1987–1988.

3. Kent versus Miami Herald, St. Petersburg Times and Ambassador Joseph P. Kennedy

Depositions from: David S. Arthurs, publisher *Palatka Daily News* (75 pp.); George H. Beebee, managing editor, *Miami Herald* (29 pp.); David Kraslow, Washington correspondent, Knight Newspapers (47 pp.); John T. McMullen, director, Knight Newspapers, Washington, D.C. (11 pp.); Laurence Leslie Thompson, columnist and reporter, *Miami Herald* (24 pp.); Stephen Trumbull, reporter, *Miami Herald* (114 pp.); Charles E. Ward, news editor, *Miami Herald* (9 pp.); Nathan Perlmutter, director, Anti Defamation League of B'nai B'rith (32 pp.). Kent's personal file containing all lawsuit data save above depositions, plus miscellaneous papers concerning the lawsuit.

4. Kent's unpublished and partially completed memoirs on his U.K. arrest and trial

5. Kent's personal photograph file

Over 200 prints and negatives.

D. INTERVIEWS AND CORRESPONDENCE

Rupert Allason, MP, Michael Bloch, Raymond Carter, John Costello, Patricia Craig, Robert T. Crowley, Monja Danischewsky, Ambassador Elbridge Durbrow, Professor M. R. D. Foot, Professor Richard Griffiths, Robert Grosjean, A. Dana Hodgson, Jr., Ambassador George Frost Kennan, Ambassador Joseph P. Kennedy (Paris, 1949), Tyler Gatewood Kent, Mrs. Clara Kent, Professor Warren Kimball, Louis Lyons, Arthur Moore, Malcolm Muggeridge, Carl and Shelley Mydans, Alexander Poliakoff, Dr. Henry Sanford

In addition, John Costello allowed the authors to quote from two telephone interviews he had with Irene Danischewsky in 1982, for his book *Ten Days That Saved The West*.

Bibliography

ADLER, SELIG. *The Isolationist Impulse: Its 20th-Century Reaction.* London: Abelard-Schuman, 1957.

ALSOP, JOSEPH. *FDR: The Life and Times of Franklin D. Roosevelt.* London: Thames and Hudson, 1982.

ANDREW, CHRISTOPHER. *Secret Service: The Making of the British Intelligence Community.* London: Sceptre, 1986.

BARNES, Dr. HARRY ELMER (ed. and contrib.). *Perpetual War for Perpetual Peace.* Caldwell, Ohio: Caxton Printers, 1953 (privately published).

BERLE, ADOLF A. *Navigating the Rapids, 1918–1971.* New York: Harcourt, Brace, and Jovanovich, 1973.

BESCHLOSS, MICHAEL. *Kennedy and Roosevelt, An Uneasy Alliance.* New York: W. W. Norton, 1980.

BIRKENHEAD, the Earl of. *Halifax.* Boston: Houghton Mifflin, 1966.

BOHLEN, CHARLES E. *Witness to History, 1929–1969.* New York: W. W. Norton, 1973.

BROGAN, HUGH. *Longman History of the United States of America.* London: Longman, 1985.

BROWN, ANTHONY CAVE, and MACDONALD, CHARLES. *On a Field of Red.* New York: G. P. Putnam, 1981.

BULLITT, WILLIAM C. *The Bullitt Mission to Russia.* New York: Ben Huebsch, 1919.

BURNS, JAMES McGREGOR. *Roosevelt: The Lion and the Fox.* New York: Harcourt, Brace, and Jovanovich, 1969.

———. *Roosevelt: Soldier of Freedom.* New York: Harcourt, Brace, and Jovanovich, 1970.

CARLSON, JOHN ROY. *The Plotters.* New York: E. P. Dutton, 1946.

CHURCHILL, Sir WINSTON. *The Second World War. Vol. 1: The Gathering Storm, Vol. 2: Their Finest Hour.* London: Cassell, 1948, 1949.

———. *Great War Speeches.* London: Corgi, 1957.

COLE, J. A. *Lord Haw-Haw, The Full Story of William Joyce.* London: Faber and Faber, 1987.

COLE, WAYNE. *America First: The Battle Against Intervention, 1940–1941.* Madison: University of Wisconsin Press, 1953.

COLVILLE, JOHN. *The Fringes of Power, Downing Street Diaries, 1939–1955.* London: Hodder and Stoughton, 1985.

COSTELLO, JOHN. *The Mask of Treachery.* New York: William Morrow, 1988.

CRAIG, GORDON A., and GILBERT, FELIX. *The Diplomats 1919–1939. Vol. II: The Thirties.* Princeton: Princeton University Press, 1953.

DALLEK, ROBERT. *Franklin D. Roosevelt and American Foreign Policy, 1932–1945.* New York: Oxford University Press, 1979.

DAVIES, JOSEPH E. *Mission to Moscow.* New York: Simon and Schuster, 1941.

DIMBLEBY, DAVID, and REYNOLDS, DAVID. *An Ocean Apart, The Relationship Between Britain and America in the Twentieth Century.* London: BBC Books/Hodder and Stoughton, 1988.

DODD, WILLIAM, Jr., and DODD, MARTHA. *Ambassador Dodd's Diary, 1935–1938.* New York: Harcourt Brace, 1941.

DURANTY, WALTER. *I Write As I Please.* New York: Halcyon House, 1932.

EGGLESTON, GEORGE T. *Roosevelt, Churchill and the World War Two Opposition: A Revisionist Autobiography.* Old Greenwich, Conn.: Devin-Adair, 1979.

FARAGO, LADISLAS. *The Game of the Foxes.* New York: David McKay, 1971.

FEIS, HERBERT. *The Road to Pearl Harbor.* Princeton: Princeton University Press, 1950.

FISH, HAMILTON, Jr. *FDR: The Other Side of the Coin.* Torrance, Cal.: Institute of Historical Review, 1976.

FLEMING, PETER. *Operation Sea Lion.* New York: Simon and Schuster, 1957.

GILBERT, MARTIN. *Finest Hour, Winston S. Churchill, 1939–1941.* London: William Heinemann, 1983.

GOODWIN, DORIS KEARNS. *The Fitzgeralds and the Kennedys.* New York: Saint Martin's Press (paperback), 1987.

GORALSKI, ROBERT. *World War II Almanac: 1931–1945, A Political and Military Record.* London: Hamish Hamilton, 1981.

GUNTHER, JOHN. *Roosevelt in Retrospect: A Profile in History.* New York: Harper, 1950.

HEMPSTEAD, SMITH. *An Illustrated History of St. Albans School.* Privately printed, 1981.

HENDERSON, LOY W. *A Question of Trust: Origins of US Soviet Diplomatic Relations.* Stanford: Hoover Institute Press, Stanford University, 1986.

HENDERSON, Sir NEVILE. *Failure of a Mission: Berlin 1937–1939.* London: Hodder and Stoughton, 1940.

HERWARTH, HANS VON, with STARR, S. FREDERICK. *Against Two Evils.* London: Collins, 1981.

HIGHAM, CHARLES. *Trading with the Enemy.* New York: Delacorte Press, 1983.

HINSLEY, F. H., and SIMKINS, C. A. G. *British Intelligence in the Second World War. Vol. 4: Security and Counter Intelligence.* London: Her Majesty's Stationery Office, 1990.

HULL, CORDELL. *Memoirs, Vol. I.* New York: Macmillan, 1948.

HYDE, H. MONTGOMERY. *The Quiet Canadian.* London: Hamish Hamilton, 1964.

ICKES, HAROLD L. *The Secret Diary of Harold Ickes. Vol. III, The Lowering Clouds.* New York: Simon and Schuster, 1955.

ISAACSON, WALTER, and THOMAS, EVAN. *The Wisemen: Six Friends and the World They Made: Acheson, Bohlen, Harriman, Kennan, Lovett and McCloy.* New York: Simon and Schuster, 1986.

JOWITT, the Earl. *Some Were Spies.* London: Hodder and Stoughton, 1954.

KAHN, DAVID. *The Codebreakers.* New York: Macmillan, 1967.

KENNAN, GEORGE FROST. *Memoirs, 1925–1950.* Boston: Atlantic–Little, Brown, 1967.

———. *Memoirs, 1950–1967.* Boston: Atlantic–Little, Brown, 1972.

KIMBALL, WARREN F. (ed.). *Churchill and Roosevelt: The Complete Correspondence, 1939–1945.* Princeton: Princeton University Press, 1985.

KIRK, LYDIA (Mrs. ALAN). *Postmarked Moscow.* New York: Charles Scribner and Sons, 1952.

KNIGHTLEY, PHILLIP. *The Second Oldest Profession: Spies and Spying in the Twentieth Century.* London: André Deutsch, 1986.

LANGER, WILLIAM L., and GLEASON, EVERETT. *The Challenge to Isolation, 1937–40.* New York: Harper, 1952.

———. *The Undeclared War, 1940–41.* New York: Harper, 1953.

LASH, JOSEPH. *Churchill and Roosevelt 1939–41.* New York: G. P. Putnam, 1976.

LOCHNER, LOUIS P. *The Goebbels Diaries.* New York: Doubleday, 1948.

LOEWENHEIM, FRANCIS, LANGLEY, HAROLD, D., JONAS, MANFRED (eds). *Roosevelt and Churchill, Their Secret Wartime Correspondence.* London: Barrie and Jenkins, 1975.

MACLEAN, FITZROY. *Eastern Approaches.* London: Jonathan Cape, 1949 (reissued 1974).

MASTERS, ANTHONY. *The Man Who Was M: The Life of Maxwell Knight.* Oxford: Basil Blackwell, 1984.

———. *Literary Agents.* Oxford: Basil Blackwell, 1987.

MERCER, DERRICK (editor-in-chief). *Chronicle of the 20th Century.* London: Longman, 1988.

MILLER, JOAN. *One Girl's War.* Dingle, Co. Kerry, Eire: Brandon, 1986.

MORGAN, TED. *FDR: A Biography.* London: Grafton Books, 1985.

MUGGERIDGE, MALCOLM. *Chronicles of Wasted Time. Vol. 2: The Infernal Grove.* London: Fontana, 1975.

MURROW, EDWARD R. (ed. Elmer Davis). *This Is London.* New York: Simon and Schuster, 1941.

NICOLSON, Sir HAROLD. *Diaries and Letters 1930–1939* and *Diaries and Letters 1939–1945.* New York: Atheneum, 1967.

PAYNE, ROBERT. *Life and Death of Adolf Hitler.* New York: Praeger, 1973.

PRANGE, GORDON. *Pearl Harbor: The Verdict of History.* New York: McGraw-Hill, 1986.

PINCHER, CHAPMAN. *Traitors: The Anatomy of Treason.* London: Sidgwick and Jackson, 1987.

READ, ANTHONY, and FISHER, DAVID. *Colonel Z: The Secret Life of a Master of Spies.* London: Hodder and Stoughton, 1984.

———. *The Deadly Embrace: Hitler, Stalin and the Nazi-Soviet Pact, 1939–1941.* London: Michael Joseph, 1988.

———. *Kristallnacht, Unleashing the Holocaust.* London: Michael Joseph, 1989.

ROOSEVELT, JAMES. *My Parents.* Chicago: Playboy Press, 1976.

ROSENMAN, Judge SAMUEL. *Working With Roosevelt.* New York: Harper, 1952.

ROSS, WALTER. *The Last Hero: Charles A. Lindbergh.* New York: Harper and Row, 1967.

SCHLESINGER, ARTHUR M., Jr. *The Age of Roosevelt. Vol. III: The Politics of Upheaval.* Boston: Houghton Mifflin, 1960.

SEYMOUR, CHARLES. *The Intimate Papers of Colonel House.* Boston and New York: Houghton Mifflin, 1926.

SHEPHARDSON, WHITNEY H., and SCROGGS, WILLIAM O. *The United States in World Affairs, 1939.* New York: Harper and Brothers, 1940.

SHERWOOD, ROBERT. *Roosevelt and Hopkins: An Intimate History.* New York: Harper and Brothers, 1948.

SHIRER, WILLIAM L. *Berlin Diary: The Journal of a Foreign Correspondent 1934–1941.* New York: Knopf, 1941.

———. *Rise and Fall of the Third Reich.* New York: Simon and Schuster, 1959.

———. *The Collapse of the Third Republic: An Inquiry into the Fall of France in 1940.* New York: Simon and Schuster, 1969.

SINCLAIR, ANDREW. *The Red and the Blue: Cambridge, Treason and Intelligence.* Boston: Little, Brown, 1986.

SINGER, KURT. *Spies and Traitors of World War Two.* London: Prentice-Hall, 1945.

SMITH, RICHARD HARRIS. *OSS: The Secret History of America's First Central Intelligence Agency.* Berkeley and Los Angeles: University of California Press, 1972.

SMITH, Lieutenant General WALTER BEDELL. *Moscow Mission 1946–49.* London: Heinemann, 1950.

SORENSEN, THEODORE C. *Kennedy.* London: Hodder and Stoughton, 1965.

STETTINIUS, EDWARD. *Lend Lease: Weapon for Victory.* New York: Macmillan, 1944.

STEVENS, Vice Admiral LESLIE. *Russian Assignment.* Boston: Little, Brown, 1953.

STIMSON, HENRY L., and BUNDY, McGEORGE. *On Active Service in Peace and War.* New York: Harper and Brothers, 1948.

STROUT, CUSHING. *The American Image of the Old World.* New York: Harper and Row, 1963.

TOLLEY, Rear Admiral KEMP. *Caviar and Commissars.* Annapolis: U.S. Navy Press, 1983.

WEST, NIGEL. *MI5: British Security Service Operations 1909–1945.* London: The Bodley Head, 1981.

———. *A Thread of Deceit: Espionage Myths of World War II.* New York: Stein and Day, 1985.

WEST, WILLIAM JOHN. *Truth Betrayed.* London: Duckworth, 1987.

WHALEN, RICHARD J. *The Founding Father.* New York: New American Library, 1964.

WILTZ, JOHN E. *In Search of Peace: The Senate Munitions Inquiry, 1934–1936.* Baton Rouge: Louisiana State University Press, 1963.

PAMPHLETS

SMITH, The Reverend GERALD L. K. *The Strange Case of Tyler Kent.* New York: The Cross and the Flag, 1944.

SNOW, JOHN HOWLAND. *The Case of Tyler Kent.* New York and Chicago: Domestic and Foreign Affairs Press, 1946 (still available through the Institute for Historical Review, Torrance, California).

WITHERS, MARY CLOYD KENT. *Word Sketches of Some of Her Relatives.* Wyneheville, Va.: Lewis Jones, printer, 1951.

NEWSPAPERS

For specific references see chapter notes.

LONDON
The Times
The *Sunday Times*
The *Daily Telegraph*
The *Sunday Express*

UNITED STATES
The *New York Times*
The *New York Herald Tribune*
The *New York Journal American*
The *New York Daily News*
PM
The *Washington Post*
The *Washington Times-Herald*
The *Washington Daily News*
The *Chicago Tribune*
The *Miami Herald*
The *St. Petersburg Times*
The *Palatka* (Florida) *Daily News*
The *Putnam County Sun*

ARTICLES

CARLSON, JOHN ROY. "The Case of Tyler Kent," *This Month,* August 1946.

DZWONCHYK, WAYNE M. "Questions Still Linger Over the Arrest of an American Embassy Staffer by British Counter Intelligence," *World War II,* November 1987.

IRVING, DAVID (attributed to). "The Many Motives of a Misguided Cypher Clerk," *Focal Point,* London, November 23, 1981.

KENT, TYLER. "The Roosevelt Legacy and the Kent Case," *Journal of Historical Review,* Vol. 4, No. 2, Summer 1983 (a printed version of Kent's speech to the 1982 annual meeting of the Institute for Historical Review).

KIMBALL, WARREN F., and BARTLETT, BRUCE. "Churchill and Roosevelt; The Personal Equation," *Prologue,* Vol. 6, Fall 1981.

LEUTZE, JAMES. "The Secret of the Churchill-Roosevelt Correspondence," *Journal of Contemporary History,* Vol. 10, No. III, July 1975.

PEAKE, HAYDEN B. "The 'Putative' Spy," *Foreign Intelligence Literary Scene*, March–April 1987, and May–June 1987.

"Was 'M' a Soviet Mole?" *World War II Investigator*, London, April 1988, unsigned.

WHALEN, RICHARD J. "The Strange Case of Tyler Kent," *The Diplomat*, Washington, D.C., Vol. XVII, No. 186, November 1965.

MISCELLANEOUS

Kent School Yearbooks, 1925 and 1926

Notes

Detailed information concerning the books referred to in shortened form in
these notes will be found in the bibliography. The following abbreviations
are used to identify documents and records consulted:

CAB   British Cabinet Papers, in Public Record Office, Kew, London
DF   Decimal File, in DoS records
DFGP   Documents on German Foreign Policy, Series D
DoS   U.S. Department of State
FDRL   Franklin Delano Roosevelt Library, Hyde Park, N.Y.
FO   British Foreign Office files in Public Record Office
FRUS   Foreign Relations of the United States, Diplomatic Papers
HO   British Home Office files in Public Record Office
NA   U.S. National Archives, Washington, D.C.
OTT   Official Trial Transcript of Kent's trial
PREM   Prime Minister's Papers, in Public Record Office
TGK Papers Kent's files, records, and unpublished memoirs, in the posses-
           sion of the authors
USFP   *Peace and War, U.S. Foreign Policy 1931–39.* Collected docu-
           ments published by Department of State.

PROLOGUE

page 1   "swept like a sharp scythe . . ." : Churchill, *Speeches,* p. 18 (June 4,
    1940).
page 1   "a monstrous tyranny . . ." : Ibid., p. 12 (May 13, 1940).
page 1   "Here's a telegram for those bloody Yankees . . ." : Colville, p.
    126.
pages 1 and 2   Churchill's and Roosevelt's telegrams: FDRL
page 3   At 11:20 that same morning: Gowen's report, NA DoS Decimal File
    123, Kent, Tyler/5–3040.
page 5   1929 documents: CIA analysis (see Appendix 2)
page 5   Description of red book: authors' personal observation.

ONE: *High Hopes*

page 7   Kent: TGK papers; Kent's DF123. Family background: Withers, pp. 30–31.

pages 8–9   Kent's schooling: Various FBI reports; Kent School Yearbook, 1925, 1926; St. Albans History; interviews and correspondence with John Davies and Robert Ober, Kent Alumni Office.

page 9   Kent at Princeton: interviews and correspondence with Raymond Carter, Arthur Moody, and others.

page 10   Kent heard that an opportunity: Various FBI reports; interview with Kent, May 5, 1988.

page 11   "an effervescent personality . . ." : Bohlen, p. 15.

pages 11–12   Bullitt in Paris and Russia: *Who's Who in America;* DoS Biographical Register; Bullitt, pp. 4–5; Henderson, pp. 220–223; Steffens, pp. 790–802.

page 12   "very much the aristocrat" : Steffens, pp. 793–794.

page 12   Bullitt and peace terms: Bullitt, pp. 36–37

page 13   Bullitt's resignation: Bullitt, pp. 96–97.

page 14   "inexperienced and greatly excited" : Kennan, p. 134.

page 14   Roosevelt speech: Rosenman, pp. 90–91.

page 14   Roosevelt and Duranty: Duranty, pp. 320–321.

page 15   DoS suspicion: Hull, vol. 1, pp. 298–299.

page 15   Pressures on Dos and White House: Kennan, p. 85; Bohlen, pp. 39–41.

pages 15–16   Roosevelt's conditions: Henderson, pp. 244–257; Bohlen, p. 32.

pages 16–17   Kennan in Moscow: Kennan, p. 59.

pages 16–17   Thayer's activities: Henderson, p. 279.

page 17   Stalin's concessions to Bullitt: Henderson, pp. 265–267.

pages 18–19   Biographies of Foreign Service officers: DoS Biographical Register; Henderson, pp. 300–310; Bohlen, pp. 16–18.

pages 19–20   Kent's application and acceptance: interview with Kent; Kent's DF123; TGK Papers.

page 20   Scene on board the S.S. *Washington:* interview with Kent.

page 21   List of personnel: Henderson, p. 272.

page 21   Soon after sailing: Ibid.

page 22   Among the other passengers: Henderson to Robert T. Crowley.

page 23   Arrival and stay in Berlin: Henderson, pp. 274–275.

page 23   First sight and smell of Russia: Bohlen, p. 13.

page 23   Arrival in Moscow: Henderson, p. 278.

page 23   Description of Spaso House: interview with Ambassador Durbrow; Bohlen, pp. 14–15; Kirk, pp. 26–27; Stevens, pp. 13–14.

page 24   Bullitt's reception in Moscow: Bohlen, p. 14.

page 25   Bullitt's letter to Moore: FDRL.

page 26   Description of Mokhovaya building: interview with Ambassador Durbrow; FBI Special Agent Beck's report to Hoover/FDR, in FDRL.

page 27 "I'm his Russian language teacher" : Bohlen, p. 20. (N.B.: Bohlen misspells Odien as O'Dean.)

TWO: *Moscow: Lost Illusions*
page 29 Bullitt's letter to Moore: FDRL.
page 30 Initial contacts with Russians: DF124.61/232, report by Walter Thurston.
page 31 "a dreary, scrubby-looking group . . ." : Bohlen, p. 20.
page 31 Dacha and "mutual admiration society" : Bohlen, pp. 67–69; MacLean, p. 80; Herwarth, p. 73; Read and Fisher, *Deadly Embrace*, p. 90.
page 31 FBI agent's report: FDRL.
page 32 Bullitt's letter to Moore: FDRL, Bullitt file.
page 32 Wiley's letter to Moore: FDRL.
page 33 Wiley's cable to Moore: NA, Moscow Station File, Records Group 84.
page 33 Bullitt's letter to Moore: FDRL, Bullitt file.
pages 34–35 Description of Tatiana Ilovaiskaya: interview with Kent; Kent's address file in DF123.
page 35 NKVD surveillance: Henderson, pp. 292–293.
page 36 Thurston's report: DF124.61/232.
page 36 Nichols as Tanya's lover: FBI agent's report, FDRL.
pages 37–38 Bullitt's note on Soviet failings: FDRL, Bullitt to Moore, April 25, 1935.
page 37 "I believe that we should employ this occasion . . ." : Ibid.
page 38 "the most serious consequences" : Henderson, pp. 356–365.
page 38 "We must never send a spy" : Bohlen, p. 34.
page 39 Withdrawal of Marines: Henderson, pp. 316–317.
page 39 Departure of Lt. White: Ibid., pp. 352–353.
page 39 Bullitt's disillusionment: Bohlen, p. 34.
page 41 Kent's biannual leave: Kent's DF123.

THREE: *Beavers and Bolos*
pages 42–43 Security situation in Moscow embassy: FBI Special Agent Beck's report, FDRL.
pages 45–46 Ambassador Davies's relationship with staff: Kennan, pp. 82–83; Bohlen, pp. 44–45.
page 45 Davies's naïveté: Bohlen, pp. 52, 56–57.
page 46 Grosjean's experiences: interview with Grosjean.
pages 46–47 NKVD blackmail of Barrett: Henderson, pp. 390–391; interview with Robert T. Crowley.
page 47 "A few of the men . . ." : FBI Special Agent Beck's report, FDRL.
page 47 FBI Special Agent Beck's report, FDRL; interview with Kirk.
page 48 Carmel Offie: Henderson, p. 391; DF123, Offie, Carmel; interview with Robert T. Crowley.
pages 48–49 Kent's smuggling activities, and "Dearest Pucia" letter: Kent's DF123/5-3040.

page 51   Kent's efforts to become a Foreign Service officer: Kent's DF123/ 40.

page 52   Henry Antheil: DF123, Antheil, Henry/43.

page 53   Grummon's requests to Washington: Kent's DF123/46 and 47.

pages 53–54   Herwarth passing information: Herwarth, pp. 145–167, also interview; Bohlen, pp. 69–85.

page 54   Antheil's death: *New York Times*, June 16, 1940; Read and Fisher, *Deadly Embrace*, p. 466.

page 54   Evidence of Antheil's treachery: FBI report, File No. 65–63587.

page 55   "What chance transfer to Department?" : Kent's DF123/49½.

page 55   "Your 13 September" : Kent's DF123/50½.

page 55   Kent's assignment approved: Kent's DF123/50.

page 55   Automobile accident: Kent's DF123/51, 54, 55.

pages 56–57   Kent's departure and journey: Kent's DF123/51; TGK Papers.

pages 57–58   Contents of Kent's briefcase: Kent's DF123/166.

FOUR: *The Bore War*

page 59   Kent reported for duty: Kent's DF123/57.

page 59   Stalin and the Baltic states: Read and Fisher, *Deadly Embrace*, pp. 363–366, 381.

pages 60–61   Churchill's message to Roosevelt: FDRL/Map Room.

pages 61–62   Carl and Shelley Mydans recollections: letter to Bearse, January 25, 1990.

page 63   "The British prosecutors at Nuremberg . . ." : TGK Papers.

page 64   Kent's meeting with Matthias: Kent's DF123/57; interviews with Robert T. Crowley.

pages 65–66   Kennedy biographical information: Whalen; Goodwin; Beschloss.

page 67   "Joe, take your pants down" : Roosevelt.

page 68   "One of the most important problems . . ." : F0371/24251.

page 69   "You are a man of courage" : JPK Papers, John Kennedy Memorial Library.

page 69   Kennedy's arrival in London: Goodwin, pp. 595–596.

page 71   "Well, Rose, this is a helluva long ways . . ." : Whalen, p. 205.

page 71   "If Joseph Patrick Kennedy ever gets to be president . . ." : *Life*, April 11, 1938.

page 72   Kennedy's speeches: DF123, JPK; *New York Times*, October 21, 1938.

pages 73–74   Kristallnacht details: Read and Fisher, *Kristallnacht*, pp. 73–74.

page 74   Kennedy conversation with Dirksen: DGFP.

page 75   "He [Kennedy] cheerfully entered into the conversation . . ." : Harold Ickes, diary mss., Library of Congress.

page 75   Kennedy's meeting with Wohlthat: Higham, pp. 168–170.

page 76   "Dine with Kenneth Clark . . ." : Nicolson, p. 401.

page 76   Reports flooding into Foreign Office: F0371/24251.

page 77   Kennedy's triple-priority telegram: FDRL.

page 78   Roosevelt's reply: Ibid.

page 78   Embassy description: Grosvenor Estates archives; DoS Historical Section; Goodwin, pp. 594–595.

page 78   Embassy staff details: DoS Historical Section, London personnel October 1, 1939.

page 81   U.S. coding systems: Kahn, pp. 488–501.

page 81   Kent's recollections on codes, etc: TGK Papers.

page 82   "One of the ways in which this was done . . ." : interview with Kent.

pages 82–83   Armand Labis details: Robert T. Crowley to authors, interviews and correspondence.

FIVE: *"The Best Caviar in All London"*

page 86   Kent's contacts in the press world: TGK Papers.

page 86   Mrs. Straker: Ibid.

page 87   London's White Russian community: *Sunday Express*, November 10, 1940; Jowitt, p. 43; Miller, pp. 22–26.

page 88   "wore a monocle . . ." : interview with Dr. Henry Sanford.

page 88   Gabriel Wolkoff's appeal: Jowitt, p. 68.

page 88   Anna Wolkoff's visit to Czechoslovakia: Ibid., pp. 65–66.

page 89   "She took herself and her causes . . ." : Miller, p. 24.

page 90   Car and weekend trips: TGK Papers.

page 90   Kent's meeting with Irene Danischewsky: Irene Danischewsky interview with John Costello; Monja Danischewsky interview with Read.

page 90   Danischewsky business: F0371/3347–8; London Business Directory; Home Office naturalization records.

page 91   Dinner with Maringliano and Riddell: OTT; TGK Papers; NA 800 DoS London Embassy; Confidential Station File, RG84/F79009–1411.

pages 95–96   Ramsay details: Eton College Register, Part VII; *Who Was Who 1951–1960; Who Was Who, British Members of Parliament 1919–1945*, p. 293; Major General R. C. Keightley, Commandant, Royal Military Academy, Sandhurst; Ramsay, 1931 and 1935 Parliamentary election brochures; Conservative Party Research Department; Jowitt, pp. 44–50; numerous newspaper accounts, including *New York Times* lawsuits; Ramsay's book, *The Nameless War.*

page 92   "You believe, do you not . . ." : Jowitt, pp. 44–45.

page 95   Right Club list of members: Read, personal observation.

page 95   Anna's flat: Miller, p. 24.

page 96   "Naturally, we closed down . . ." : West, *MI5*, p. 128.

pages 96–97   Ramsay's poem: Professor R. Griffiths

page 97   Sticky-back campaign: Miller, p. 26; Jowitt, pp. 66–67; OTT.

page 97   "Walk on dark side of road . . ." : Jowitt, p. 67.

page 98   "New Year's Resolution" : Jowitt, p. 46; OTT.

page 98   Wolkoff and Ramsay visiting Kent's flat: OTT; London Station File, RG84/F790009–1373.

page 99   Two documents in particular: OTT; Jowitt, p. 47.

page 99   *City of Flint* incident: Read and Fisher, *Deadly Embrace*, pp. 427–429.

page 100   *Mooremacsun* incident: FRUS, 1940, p. 10.

page 100   Hull-Lothian meeting: Hull, pp. 748–749.

page 101   "I would not be frank . . ." : FDRL, Map Room.

pages 101–02   Churchill's response: Ibid.

page 103   "I was quite surprised . . ." : Interview with Kent.

page 103   Kent's messages to and from Kirk: London Station File, RG84/ F790009–1325.

SIX: *Knight's Black Agents*

pages 105–06   NKVD influence on White Russians: Robert T. Crowley, interviews and correspondence.

page 108   Sir Claude Dansey and General Marshall-Cornwall: Read and Fisher, *Colonel Z.*

pages 109–10   Vernon Kell details: Andrew, pp. 101–102; Masters, *The Man Who Was M,* pp. 15–16; West, *MI5,* pp. 34–38.

pages 111–12   Max Knight details: Masters, Ibid.; Miller, pp. 16–19; West, Ibid.; p. 45; Andrew, pp. 474, 521–523.

pages 112–13   Liddell details: West, Ibid., pp. 42–44; Andrew, pp. 513, 643; Costello, p. 107.

page 115   Olga Gray details: Miller, pp. 18–19; Andrew pp. 520–524; West, Ibid., pp. 66–71; Masters, *The Man Who Was M,* pp. 29–54.

pages 115–16   MI5 section B5(b): West, Ibid., p. 45; Andrew, pp. 521–523; Miller, pp. 17–18; Masters, Ibid., pp. 78–80.

page 118   Joan Miller details: Miller, pp. 7–19.

SEVEN: *M and the Mata Hari of Dolphin Square*

page 120   "I was ready to agree to anything . . ." : Miller, p. 16.

page 121   "She completely dominated Max" : Masters, *The Man Who Was M,* p. 117.

pages 121–22   Knight's teaching of Joan Miller: Miller, pp. 49–50.

page 123   Joan Miller's introduction to Right Club: Ibid., pp. 22–28.

page 126   Helene de Munck and letter to Joyce: Ibid., pp. 34–35.

page 127   Contents of letter: Jowitt, pp. 71–72.

page 127   GCCS intercepts: West, p. 125.

page 128   Barzini: Farago, p. 341.

page 129   Liddell's letter to Johnson: London Station File RG82/0.02.

page 130   "[I]t could not possibly . . ." : Ibid.

page 130   The British informant: Ibid.

page 131   Thomsen's cable to Berlin: DGFP, 1940, vol. IX, p. 73.

page 131   "blond Viking" : Farago, p. 473.

page 131   Dugan's details: Ibid.

pages 132–33   May 23 signal: DGFP, Vol. IX, pp. 417–418.

pages 133–34   MI5 report on Anna Wolkoff and Kent: London Station File, RG84/F790009–1373.

EIGHT: *A Fool or a Rogue*

page 137 "Can you see one of my assistants . . ." : Johnson Report to Hull, May 28, 1940, in Kent's DF 123/5–3040, and duplicated to London Station File RG84/F790009.

page 140 "melted away . . ." : Colville, p. 135.

page 140 "His spirit is indomitable . . ." : Ibid., p. 136.

page 141 "We must expect . . ." : Churchill, *Speeches*, p. 16.

page 142 Churchill's telegram: FDRL, Map Room.

page 143 Schoenfeld's actions: Schoenfeld's report, May 20, 1940, in Kent's DF123, as above.

pages 145–46 Len Deighton's experience: Masters, *Literary Agents*, p. 257.

page 146 Events of May 20: Gowen's report, and official verbatim transcript of interrogation, in DF123, as above.

page 148 "Send the traitorous bastard in!" : Kennedy to Bearse, Hôtel George V, Paris, April 1949.

NINE: *A Terrible Blow*

page 160 Kennedy's signal: London Station File RG84.

page 161 Long was in a foul mood: Long's diary, Manuscript Division, Library of Congress, p. 99.

page 162 May 20 signals: Kent's DF123/71, 72, 73; also London Station File RG84.

pages 163–64 "I copied very few signals . . ." : Interview with Kent.

page 164 "They are a complete history . . ." : Long's diary, p. 134.

page 165 Beginning on June 4: Ibid., pp. 113–114.

page 165 "I have come to the conclusion . . ." : Ibid., pp. 102–103.

page 165 "huge iron gates . . ." : TGK Papers.

page 166 What Knight was most interested in: TGK Papers; Kent's DF123/ 75; London Station File RG84.

page 167 ". . . we could not telegraph the Embassy . . ." : Long's diary, p. 114.

page 167 Messages to and from Madrid: Kent's DF123/84, 85.

pages 168–69 Anderson's paper to Cabinet: CAB75/7, War Cabinet No. 128 of 1940.

page 169 "I will agree to whatever . . ." : Churchill Papers 20/13 (quoted in Gilbert, p. 378).

page 169 This suggestion: CAB65/7. War Cabinet No. 133 of 1940.

page 169 a total of 1373: West, *MI5*, p. 128.

page 169 Admiral Wolkoff's internment: HO144/W14517/47/48.

page 169 Deportation order: original document in TGK Papers.

page 169 Kent was delighted: Interview with Kent.

page 170 Knight's resumed interrogation of Kent: Kent's DF123; NA DoS 123 File.

pages 170–71 Kent's statement: London Station File, RG84/F790009/- 1411.

page 171 Knight's report to Johnson: Kent's DF123; NA DoS 123 File.

page 173   "I thought Roosevelt's policy . . ." : TGK Papers; interview with
    Kent.
page 173   Welles May 22 cable: Kent's DF123; NA DoS 123 File.
page 173   Kennedy's report to Hull: Ibid.
page 174   Home Office statements: Ibid.; *Chicago Tribune*, June 2, 1940.
page 174   Mrs Kent's cable, Johnson's signal: Kent's DF123/88, 89, 90.
page 175   Mrs Kent's interview with Long: Long's diary, pp. 116–117.
page 175   Hull cable to Kennedy: Kent's DF123; NA DoS 123.
page 175   "As prisons go . . ." : TGK Papers.
page 175   "As the officer from the War Office . . ." : Kent's DF123.
pages 176–77   "Papers dealing with a serious leakage . . ." : Ibid.

TEN: *We Must Protect the Chief*
page 179   "We must take immediate action . . ." : Long's diary, p. 134.
page 179   "No doubt the Germans will publish . . ." : Ibid.
page 180   Roosevelt's appointments: FDRL.
page 181   "It ain't worth a pitcher . . ." : Hull, p. 398.
page 182   7.7 percent: Brogan, p. 574.
page 182   "to bring her powerful material aid . . ." : Churchill, *Speeches*, p.
    50.
pages 182–83   Churchill's appeal for destroyers: FDRL, Map Room.
page 186   "It is almost a truism . . ." : quoted in Wiltz, p. 15.
page 186   "Of the hell broth . . ." : quoted in Strout, p. 205.
page 188   Roosevelt's "fireside chat" : USFP, *Peace and War*, pp. 483–486;
    Dallek, p. 199.
page 188   President invokes the Neutrality Act: Shephardson, p. 51.
page 188   President calls special session: USFP, *Peace and War*, pp. 69–70.
page 190   Lindbergh details: Cole, p. 91.
pages 190–91   Coughlin details: Schlesinger, pp. 16–28.
page 191   "I have to be like the captain . . ." : Fairbanks, in BBC interview
    with David Dimbleby.
page 191   America First details: Cole, p. 91 et seq., Dimbleby, p. 129.
page 192   German legation report: DGFP, Vol. X, 1940, No. 301.
page 193   "The English translation . . ." : Ibid., No. 39.
page 194   On Thursday, August 1: TGK Papers.
page 195   "Lawyers point out . . ." : Kent's DF123.
page 197   "Sock 'em to Hell!" : Dimbleby, p. 127.
page 197   "The air raid is still on . . ." : Murrow, p. 167.
page 197   "I was delighted to see . . ." : Kennedy's DF123.
page 198   "To be fair to Kennedy . . ." : quoted in Goodwin, p. 695.
pages 200–01   "Donovan believes . . ." : CAB115/83; Hyde, Ch. 2; An-
    drew, p. 651.

ELEVEN: *Rex versus Tyler Kent*
All details of Kent's trial itself are taken from the Official Trial Transcript.
    Unless otherwise noted, details of Anna Wolkoff's trial are taken from
    Lord Jowitt's book, *Some Were Spies*. Other references as follows:

page 202 "Kent was driven . . ." : TGK Papers.

page 203 "a strange, remote, barely human figure . . ." : Muggeridge, p. 116.

pages 203–04 Jowitt, p. 50.

page 205 "I became quite absorbed . . ." : Muggeridge, p. 116.

page 209 "one of those intensely gentlemanly Americans . . ." Ibid.

page 216 "At one point . . ." : Ibid., pp. 116–117.

page 220 "The spectators did not find . . ." : *Daily Express*, November 7, 1940.

page 221 *New York Herald Tribune* report: *New York Herald Tribune*, November 8, 1940.

pages 221–22 Kennedy's return to USA and radio speech: Kennedy's DF123; Goodwin, pp. 707–716; Whalen, pp. 330–348.

pages 222–23 Kennedy's Boston interview: Ibid.; Lyons, personally to Bearse.

page 223 John McCutcheon cartoon: *Chicago Tribune*, November 11, 1940.

page 224 "It is all to the good . . ." : *News Chronicle*, December 6, 1940.

page 224 "You have said things . . ." : *Daily Mail*, November 29, 1940.

page 224 Kennedy's Hollywood meeting: *Washington Times-Herald*, November 24, 1940; FO371/24251.

pages 224–25 "I never want to see that son of a bitch . . ." : Lash, p. 287.

TWELVE: *This Unspeakable Blackguard*

page 226 Kent's appeal: London Station File RG84/F790009–1269; F)371/T/603/1603/373, T/13427/93/373.

page 226 Kent chose to conduct his own case: TGK Papers.

page 227 Christabel Nicholson trial and internment: *Washington Times-Herald*, June 25, 1945.

pages 227–28 Particulars against Ramsay: HO144/21995, 22454.

page 228 Committee on Parliamentary Privilege: *The Times*, August 14, 1940.

page 229 "At my request . . ." : *New York Times*, August 24, 1940.

page 231 "the most unsordid act . . ." : Churchill, *The Second World War*, Vol. II, p. 503.

page 231 "It is not fitting . . ." : PREM/4/17/1.

page 231 "certain things were done . . ." : Churchill, *The Second World War*, Vol. I, p. 506.

page 232 *New York Times* request for trial transcript: Kent's DF123/133.

page 232 "under Section 16 . . ." : Ibid., 149.

pages 232–33 Details of libel trial: Ibid. (number illegible); Johnson's report to Hull, August 27, 1941.

page 233 Ramsay's statement: TGK Papers.

pages 234–35 Proceedings in Parliament: *Hansard*, September 26, 1944, Cols. 41–42.

page 236 ". . . These messages, together with others . . ." : FDRL.

pages 236–237 Ann Kent's campaign: FO371/38704.

page 239 Irene Danischewsky's visits to Kent: TGK Papers.

page 239   Alexander Danischewsky's service with Chindits: Monja Danischewsky to Read.

page 239   Irene Danischewsky correspondence with Ann Kent: FO371/
38704.

page 240   "If I were in Tyler's position . . ." : Ibid.

page 241   "The fact that I always linked Tyler . . ." : Ibid.

page 241   Owen's connection with Lehman family: Snow; *New York Times;
New York Herald Tribune.*

THIRTEEN: *The Myths Exploded*

page 245   "I have been told . . ." : Hansard, June 16, 1944.

pages 245–46   Proceedings in Senate: *Congressional Record,* June 19, 1944.

page 248   "My Appeal for Fairness" : TGK Papers.

page 249   "Tyler Kent is in a British prison . . ." : FO371/38704.

page 249   Lord Halifax report: Ibid.

page 251   Kent's attempt to sue Kennedy: F0371/38704, 44628.

page 252   *Chicago Tribune,* October 16, 1944; FO371/38704.

page 252   Kent's attempt to sue U.S. government: FO371/44628.

pages 253–54   "My friendship with the great man . . ." : Churchill, *Speeches,*
pp. 341–342.

page 256   "I went up to my father's bedroom . . ." : Randolph Churchill,
quoted in Gilbert, p. 358.

page 256   "should be able to satisfy Congress . . ." : FDRL.

FOURTEEN: *Going Home*

page 259   Kent's sentence remitted: FO371/44628.

page 260   Kent registered for draft: Kent's DF123.

page 260   Kent's request to be sent to Argentina: FO371/44628.

page 260   Kent's demand for first-class passage: Ibid.

page 260   Choice of ship: Ibid.

page 260   Request for transcript of trial: Ibid.

page 261   Voyage and arrival in NY: TGK Papers.

page 262   Kent's contract with Consolidated Features: TGK Papers.

page 262   Kent's correspondence with Byrnes: Ibid.

pages 263–64   Kent's marriage and subsequent life: Ibid.; interviews with
Kent and Clara Hyatt Kent.

page 271   Kent trailer: personal observation by Bearse.

pages 271–72   Anna Wolkoff's later life and death: Masters, *The Man Who
Was M,* p. 106; interview with Patricia Craig.

page 272   Knight details: Masters, *The Man Who Was M,* pp. 196–198.

pages 272–73   Joan Miller details: Interview with Patricia Craig.

Acknowledgments

WE ARE INDEBTED to many individuals and institutions, without whose help this book would not have been possible. A full list of those who provided information through interviews, telephone conversations, and correspondence appears elsewhere, but we must record our grateful thanks here to those who were especially helpful to us in our researches.

We owe our largest debt to Robert T. Crowley, of Washington, D.C., who shared with us his vast knowledge of the Tyler Kent case, accumulated during his many years of service with the Central Intelligence Agency. He steered us in several directions where we were able to pursue our investigations most fruitfully. Robert and his wife, Emily, also provided Ray Bearse with sumptuous repasts and a comfortable bed during his Washington forays, for which he is truly grateful.

Our special thanks are also due to Mrs. Clara Kent, Tyler Kent's widow, for her hospitality and for sharing with us her memories of forty-two years with him. She gave us unrestricted access to Kent's personal records and presented us with two filing cabinets of his papers, plus a selection of whatever books we cared to choose from his extensive library, which filled substantial gaps in our knowledge.

We were fortunate in locating three distinguished people who knew Kent during his five years in Moscow. They are Ambassador George Frost Kennan, now with the Institute for Advanced Studies, Princeton; Ambassador Elbridge Durbrow, of Walnut Creek, California; and Robert Grosjean, of Brussels and New Canaan, Connecticut. We thank them all for sharing their memories with us.

Arthur Moore, of Philadelphia, secretary of Princeton's class of 1933, kindly invited Bearse to meet several of Kent's Princeton classmates.

Warren Kimball of Rutgers, the pre-eminent authority on the Roosevelt-Churchill correspondence, provided guidance and was responsible for putting us in touch with Robert Crowley.

Carl and Shelley Mydans shared their wartime experiences as a *Life* photographer-reporter team with their old friend and colleague, Ray Bearse.

In Great Britain, we had interesting and fruitful discussions with many individuals, including Professor M. R. D. Foot, who gave us valuable advice and an introduction to Patricia Craig, ghost writer of the late Joan Miller's autobiography; Dr. Henry Sanford, who provided information on London's White Russian community during the Second World War, as did Alexander Poliakoff, who also gave us an introduction to Monja Danischewsky, brother-in-law of the late Irene Danischewsky; the late Malcolm Muggeridge, probably the last survivor of the 1940 trials of Kent and Wolkoff; Professor Richard Griffiths, who shared some of his knowledge of the British profascist fifth column and gave Anthony Read access to the Right Club's records; Rupert Allason, MP, who gave helpful advice on MI5 and provided useful documents; James Rusbridger, who provided useful documents and introductions; and Michael Bloch, who not only shared his extensive knowledge of the period but also found and made a present to Read of a rare copy of Lord Jowitt's book, which contains vital accounts of the trials.

We are indebted to John Costello, for permission to quote from his two telephone interviews with the late Irene Danischewsky for his book *Ten Days That Saved The West*.

As always with any work of this nature, the authors depended on the help of many librarians, archivists, and other custodians of historical documents, who responded with interest and dedication to the demands we made on them. The Washington staff of Senator Patrick Leahy of Vermont provided copies of the *Congressional Record* covering the great debate of June 19, 1944. Travis Westley, of the Periodical Section of the Library of Congress, supplied copies of Washington, New York, and Chicago newspapers. Luana Bradley, of the Associated Press library, New York, supplied a copy of Ambassador Kennedy's historic interview of September 4, 1944. Paul Donovan, of the Periodical Section of the Vermont State Library, Montpelier, supplied photocopies of the *New York Times* on the Ramsay libel case. Janet Bacon and Stewart Granger supplied copies of *Hansard* containing all references to Captain Ramsay, Tyler Kent, and the Roosevelt-Churchill correspondence.

Director William Emerson, Robert Parks, and Raymond Teichman, of the Franklin D. Roosevelt Library, Hyde Park, New York, provided us with much material of which we were unaware. This included the correspondence between Ambassador Bullitt and John Wiley and Assistant Secretary of State Judge R. Walton Moore. They also provided copies of the Roosevelt-Churchill correspondence between September 11, 1939, and May 20, 1940, which included marginal data not found in any published version of the letters. They supplied the highly illuminating report from FBI Special Agent Louis Beck to J. Edgar Hoover on security in the Moscow embassy, and all information that indicated Roosevelt's knowledge of the Kent affair.

Milton C. Gustafsson and William J. Walsh, Diplomatic History Section of the National Archives, Washington, D.C., supplied decimal files 123 on Tyler Kent, Henry W. Antheil, and Carmel Offie, a total of more than two thousand pages. Emil P. Moshella, chief of the Freedom of Information–Privacy Acts Section, Records Management Division, Federal Bureau of Investigation, Department of Justice, provided several hundred usable pages of FBI reports on Tyler Kent, Henry W. Antheil, and Carmel Offie.

Judith Ann Schiff, Sterling Library, Yale University, provided from the Charles B. Parsons Collection a microfilm of Kent's official trial transcript and dozens of letters between Ann Kent and various congressmen and right-wing sympathizers. Robert Ober of the Kent School alumni office, Diane Finklestein of the St. Albans School office, and Rick Ryan of the Princeton alumni records office, provided material on Kent's student days. The staff of the New York office of the Anti Defamation League of B'nai B'rith sent us a large amount of material concerning

Kent's anti-Semitic activities. Andrew Barnes, editor of the *St. Petersburg Times,* provided data on Kent's lawsuit.

We are grateful to the librarians and staff of the Egbert Starr Memorial Library, Middlebury College, Middlebury, Vermont; the Bixby Library, Vergennes, Vermont; the Brandon Free Public Library, Brandon, Vermont; and, in England, the Berkshire Public Libraries, Maidenhead and Slough; and the London Library.

Also in England, we received fine cooperation from Major General R. C. Keightley, commandant, Royal Military Academy, Sandhurst; Colonel R. A. Whitman, commanding officer, the Coldstream Guards; R. Head, chief librarian, Eton College; Dr. Meryl R. Foster, assistant keeper, Search Department, the Public Record Office, Kew; Dr. S. Street, archivist, Conservative Party archives, the Bodleian Library, Oxford University; organization department, Conservative Central Office, London; the House of Commons library; R. W. Mason, information officer, Meteorological Office, London; M. Feldon, *The Times,* and K. Beard, chief librarian, Express Newspapers Ltd.

Bearse notes his obligations to his friends and booksellers Dan Halpin, of Cloak and Dagger Books, Bedford, New Hampshire, for securing more than two hundred books on espionage (not all of them involving Tyler Kent!) and to Lawrence Washington of Otter Creek Books, East Middlebury, Vermont.

Our editor, Nan A. Talese, deserves great credit for her perception and patience. We are also grateful to Jesse Cohen, Gail R. Buchiccio, and Randall Pollock for numerous invaluable services during the preparation of this book, and to Frances Apt for her magisterial copy editing. Our agent, Julian Bach, discovering our separate interests in Tyler Kent, brought us together for a happy collaboration, for which we thank him. Julian has not only fulfilled his role as literary agent with his customary skill, but has also graciously and kindly assisted us with much indispensable help along the way.

Finally, but by no means least, we must separately record our thanks and appreciation to Virginia McLoughlin and Rosemary Read, for moral support, stimulating conversation, fine food and companionship, and perhaps above all their tolerance during the years this book has been in gestation.

RAY BEARSE
Brandon, Vermont, U.S.

ANTHONY READ
Taplow, Buckinghamshire, U.K.

Index